CHASING DEAN

SURFING AMERICA'S HURRICANE STATES

INTERSTATE

95

EVACUATION ROUTE

NORTH

TOM ANDERSON

summersdale

CHASING DEAN

Summersdale Publishers Ltd
46 West Street
Chichester
West Sussex
PO19 1RP
UK

www.summersdale.com

Printed and bound in Great Britain

ISBN: 978-1-84024-741-1

Substantial discounts on bulk quantities of Summersdale books
are available to corporations, professional associations and other
organisations. For details telephone Summersdale Publishers on
(+44-1243-771107), fax (+44-1243-786300) or email (nicky@
summersdale.com).

For my sister Mara Ruth Anderson
(1976–2008)

CONTENTS

PART ONE

Hurricane Me..11

A Tale of Two Summers..13

PART TWO

1. Tropical Storm Chantal....................................21
2. Making Landfall...39
3. Hurricane Who?...58
4. The Gulf of Mexico..60
5. Hurricane Katrina...85
6. Off-track..110

PART THREE

7. Tropical Depression Four.................................114
8. Hurricane Flossie..138
9. Hurricane Isabel...157
10. Named...168
11. Tropical Storm Dean.....................................178
12. Tropical Storm Erin.....................................186
13. Sandy Hook..210
14. NYC..220
15. Ocean Avenue: The Swell Builds.........................248

PART FOUR

16. Hurricane Dean..280
17. The Right Coast...312
18. Extra-tropical Transition..............................342

ACKNOWLEDGEMENTS................................350

Like an unseen dial, feedback is operating in all living creatures. It makes sure that, wherever possible, their internal environments remain stable and sound. But this feedback is not only present within single organisms. The 'Gaia' theory has suggested it may in fact be at work in the planet's biosphere as a whole — adjusting to change and safeguarding the right conditions for life.

HURRICANE TRAJECTORIES IN THE AMERICAS

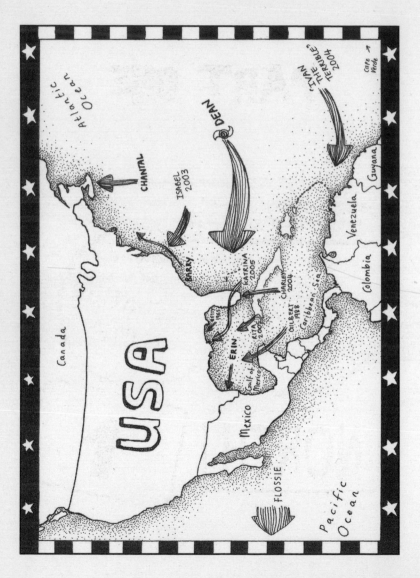

PART ONE

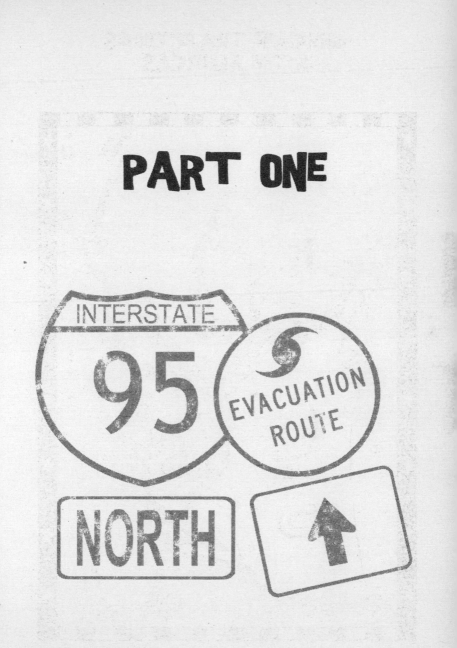

HURRICANE ME

I was fortunate to meet up with Dean one last time the day he died. In fact, he'd been dead for some time prior to that, but his generosity was so far-reaching nobody actually noticed.

Our rendezvous took place at the end of Ocean Avenue and Pearl Street in Maine, just south of the city of Portland – on and around Higgins Beach. The morning was deathly calm, except for the pleasant waist-high waves crackling over a mid-tide sandbar. The water was deep blue and harshly cold. Higgins beachfront lay postcard-still, devoid of the summer bustle that had pushed it to near bursting point just weeks earlier.

Dean had got there some time before me. Someone said he'd made it into town three days ago, but hadn't impressed people as much as he had elsewhere in New England. As a result his passing wasn't being mourned with quite the same sense of loss as further south along Interstate 95, where he had been considered a kind of saviour to some.

I tried to deny it, to kid myself into thinking he could survive just a little longer, but I knew the thing to do was just accept what had happened. The problem was that now, with Marc gone, my bank empty of funds and Dean dead I was, for the first time on this continent, totally alone. The ride was over, and there was nothing that could be done about it.

But at least I had been able to meet Dean at his best. I'd seen his good side. Others had not, and they were the people I should have really felt for.

Because Dean, for all his virtues, had been much crueller than he had been kind. And some were glad that he, and Erin like him, were both dead.

I had never cared for Erin, but Dean was different – the least I can do is explain what he had meant to me...

A TALE OF TWO SUMMERS

Vale of Glamorgan coastline; Atlantic Ocean. Pressure: Record-breakingly high.
Tuesday 18 July, 2006; two months prior to the start of El Niño.
Heavy air, no sign of thunder clouds.

It's not often you can feel completely crushed by heat in South Wales, but that July ruthless sunshine was blazing through the sticky atmosphere and the air was so thick you couldn't even hide in the shade.

I was staring lethargically at the shoreline from the car park at Llantwit Major beach. The sea was feeling it too. A mass of water, the volume of which we mere mortals cannot even begin to comprehend, was completely motionless. Even the mighty Atlantic was unable to muster the energy to move in these conditions.

Behind me, a dog tried to resist going for a walk over the chevron-fold cliffs, and an elderly couple sat eating lunch in the front seats of their car (the heat even forcing Mr to take the drastic action of undoing a shirt button). This was South Wales's Vale of Glamorgan as seldom seen. A July heatwave, an unusual weather system bringing overland winds from the sweltering mid-summer European mainland – the same system that was causing fires in the Algarve, and placing *pompiers* in the pine forests of southern France on twenty-four-hour call at a time of year when all they wanted to do was sit on the beach. An entire continent had ground to a halt.

Meanwhile, thousands of miles away, in anonymous waters just east of the Caribbean Sea, the second phase of this weather pattern was soon to begin. The stillness, the weight of air on water, the pounding sun and atmospherically retained heat were all building up, until the ocean could take no more, hitting back and restoring the meteorological status quo. Tropical Storm Beryl was, quite literally, warming up. From this stillness would soon come a natural force capable of generating more energy in a few hours than that stored by all the nuclear weapons in the belligerent northern hemisphere combined.

She would, in the course of the following three months, be followed by Chris, Debby, Ernesto, Florence, Gordon, Helene and Isaac – an unusually short but violent season, ending two storms short of 'K'.

For now, Beryl's payload was still over a week away. She had yet to spin up towards New York, sending an unexpected blip across to the frustratingly calm summer seas. In the meantime, all we could do was wait, and sweat. And wish we lived on Cape Cod, where some of the best waves in recent surfing history were shortly to find their way ashore.

Lost for ways to spend the rest of this sub-tropical day, I turned back to my ageing Nissan Micra, fired the engine up with a burst of blue smoke, plenty of acceleration and clutching, cursed the car's lack of air-conditioning and began to drive home. Maybe there was something in that Cape Cod thought?

For several seasons I had been monitoring hurricanes as a surfer, seeing them in a different light to those who didn't ride waves for a hobby. I knew about the havoc they could wreak on tin-roofed Central American towns, but it was hard for me and my fellow surfers to attach ourselves emotionally to these horror stories. For most of us, Atlantic hurricanes meant one thing: surf.

This was typical of how I viewed most of the world's significant goings-on. Since moving to Porthcawl as a kid, surfing had basically run my life. It had governed the jobs I did and the people I knew, as well as the places I went, of course. Between surf trips, I usually worked on *ideas* for surf trips – from the monotony of whatever job was currently letting me save the necessary money. Even after getting my lucky breaks with writing, it was still common to find me 'hobbling' in some manner for extra cash to get away on another wave-finding mission – a quick winter hop to Morocco, a summer sojourn in France or a red-eyed drive up to Scotland if the weather charts suddenly demanded it.

I'd been aware for a while now that pretty much the best place on earth to be a surfer during hurricane season was the Eastern Seaboard of the United States, as it got almost all the swell from these tropical storms. With my mother living in Toronto, only a day and a half's drive from the US coast, it was a place well within my reach. Could I find an excuse to take a more long-term leave from Wales for the promise of North America's luring line-ups?

These Atlantic hurricane storms usually moved into the Gulf of Mexico, the Caribbean or to the Atlantic near Florida, and we in Porthcawl would get no surf from them. Once or twice a year, perhaps, their trajectory would veer north towards the Azores, and that would be the time to start waxing your board. But the thought of chasing these storms to whichever locale was the best placed along a vast coastline was something I couldn't help but feel drawn to – something that just wasn't possible in Europe. I wasn't sure if I knew any surfers who'd been to New York; the neon billboards of Times Square weren't the sort of vistas you dreamed of if you'd given your life to riding waves.

Eventually, summer began to give way and further changes occurred in the northern hemisphere's weather that, again, nobody had been able to predict. All of a sudden, the small part of the Atlantic that we in

South Wales relied upon for waves was calmer than usual. September and October went by without any serious autumn swells and then, in a few days, we had gone from one of the warmest summers on record to a soaking wet winter. The straw yellows of the mid-August grass soon disappeared as rainfalls ran into early frosts. Schools were closing due to snow and central heating bills reached for the dark, grey clouds.

At that time, as in past years, US storm chasing remained just an idea. I hadn't yet realised that it was only the first of two exceptionally odd years of wind and waves.

Porthcawl, South Wales. Pressure: 1006 mb.
Thursday 20 July, 2007. One summer later. El Niño season
confirmed. Still wet as ever. Fifth consecutive day of rain
– northern England and Midlands underwater.

The following summer, alas, was nothing like its predecessor. Any hopes that those warm seasons were going to become the norm faded away as we moved into a spring that was grim and depressing. Not merely a return to the usual UK routine of drab holiday seasons, this was something else altogether.

As June washed into July, the British people had grown so used to the patter of raindrops battering windowpanes that the few dry spells were barely noticed. The media, of course, continued to be obsessed with the story:

'Record-breaking rains at Wimbledon.'
'A tale of two summers.'
'Storm surges more likely from now on.'
'Bitter North "left to drown" by government...'

This July was characterised by floods. The North of England was deluged first, before the Midlands were almost washed away.

In a gloomy living room, flitting between the apocalyptic news scenes and a live webcast of pro surfers scoring gorgeous South Seas perfection, all sorts of useless meteorological statistics swirled around my head like a growing mist. Among them was the fact that my wetsuit had been soaking for a fortnight but had only been used twice. It was sodden with rainwater. Not only were there no storms in the East Atlantic to produce waves, but anything that did trickle ashore was being ravaged by nasty sea breezes and local squalls. All the while, the rest of the world seemed abundant with great surf.

'Let's be honest,' declaimed one of Radio Four's stiff voices. 'We haven't really been too concerned with climate change as long as it gave us warm summers, but this year the Great British public are having a nasty scare.'

On the other side of the all-governing Atlantic, summer on the US East Coast had got off to yet another fantastic start. *Surfer* magazine was doing an online feature on North Carolina's Outer Banks, a thin strip of land that had been given an early season gift in the form of Tropical Storm Barry, another disturbance tauntingly out of range for British surfers. But my attention was no longer on the European forecasts...

'It's hard to predict the exact nature of this year's hurricane season,' claimed a weatherman on CNN, 'but most American experts are still expecting above average activity in the Atlantic this year. There is a one-in-three chance of a storm equal to, or more powerful than, Hurricane Katrina. We advise all East Coasters and Gulf Coasters to be extra cautious this year. Know your evacuation route. Know where to get gas in an emergency, and keep watching the weather reports.'

'Know where to get gas in emergencies for sure,' I thought, 'but know where to get surf wax too!'

The afternoon I booked the flight was the wettest I'd ever seen Porthcawl. After listening to three continuous hours of water rapping on my windows, I logged on to the Internet to see if there were waves, and on confirming that there weren't, looked at some flight quotes to Toronto. I knew my mother kept an old car in her driveway and hardly ever needed it.

On one of the sites, there was an open-ended ticket going for a drop-down price.

Engulfed in July Welsh gloom, I took a deep breath. This was it. I entered my credit card details, pressed 'BOOK FLIGHT' and then did not allow myself to press anything else until it was too late to cancel.

I was going to the hurricane continent, and would soon be within striking distance of what American surfers called the 'Right Coast' – due both to its fortunate placement for tropical storm surf and the fact it faced east on most maps.

Of course, I didn't realise back then that, with these actions, I'd already made firm arrangements to meet up with Dean. I thought that aimless and soul-cleansing wandering lay ahead but, looking back, there really wasn't much free will in it at all. My path was already set. But as I knew nothing of it at the time, it didn't make much difference.

Feeling pleased with myself, I then picked up the phone and made a call to the University of Wales's Physics Department.

'Oh yes, hello. I wonder if I could be put through to Marc Rhys please?' I asked.

'*Dr* Marc Rhys. Yes, I'll put you through to his extension now...'

But would Marc buy the idea? Of course he would. He had to.

PART TWO

THE SOUTHERN STATES

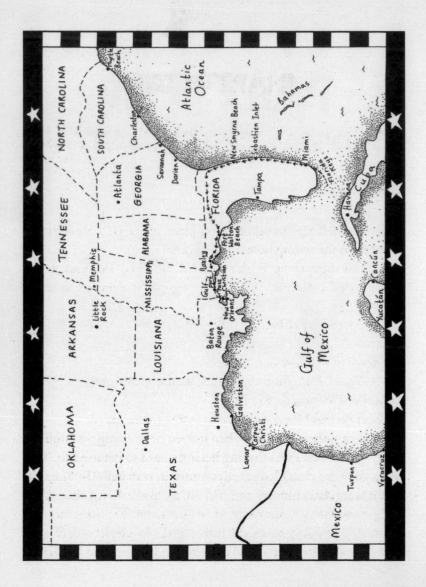

CHAPTER ONE

TROPICAL STORM CHANTAL

'What the hell are you doing in a place like this? I thought I'd called in to the wrong hotel for a minute!'

'Ah, I'm moving up in the world these days, see, matey. Just getting what I deserve, that's all. D'you want someone to bring you a cocktail?'

'Will I have to pay for it?'

'You will!'

'Then I won't have one.'

'Tight arse! All right then, I'll put it on my tab.'

'Really? Can you do that?'

'Can I do that? I can do bloody anything these days!'

Marc, or rather 'Dr Rhys', had indeed been rising through the ranks of late, and I was finding it a little hard to get used to. This was a guy who chuckled at toilet humour, watched *The Simpsons* as if it were daily prayers and had once travelled on a shoestring budget that would put most of us to shame. Yet someone had deemed it sensible to award him a PhD in physics. And now here he was, arranging for us to meet at The Standard in Miami.

Not the kind of haunt I'd usually expect for a rendezvous with Marc.

'While you're at it then, Marc, someone just drove my car away...'

'Valet parking, Tom, that's what they, sorry, *we*, call it. You uncultured swine, you!' He lay back in his chair and stretched, grinning at me through a face full of beach-freckles – the kind that only surf and sun can give you. He rubbed his hair, originally a strawberry colour but now salt-bleached and messy, lifted away a pair of sunnies to show his green eyes, and winked.

'Er, right, valet,' I said, raising my eyebrows, and folding my arms. I had a couple of inches on Marc, and stared down my nose at him, dismissively. 'Doesn't matter what you and your new friends call it. He said it was going to be forty dollars. Money – you know, the thing I don't really tend to have much of? Any chance of putting that on the tab too?'

'I'll think about it. Your car's gonna look wicked next to some of the nonsense I've seen those boys driving around in since I got here though – but then I don't suppose you give a shit...'

Before you learn any more about Marc Rhys, let me tell you about The Standard. Tasteful, plush and indulgent: this was not something of a habit for me (and Marc for that matter). The Standard was what you got when you put Miami's heritage of wealth and high living in the hands of good architects and interior designers.

This was, apparently, the old 'Lido Spa Hotel', given one heck of a facelift. The Lido Spa had become a symbol of Miami's golden days, until its clientele retired permanently to Florida condominiums and the place ran out of momentum. That was when a guy called Andre Balazs stepped in and bought it up, creating a chain of luxury hotels. The first Standard in Los Angeles had quickly become a hangout for the rich and famous, and now the sister hotel here in Miami was attracting a pretty exclusive scene too (Dr Marc Rhys for one).

The management of the new Standard had consulted all kinds of minimalist architects and designers, adding touches of Scandinavia ('fucking IKEA generation,' moaned Marc) with Roman indulgence and excess. The place was all about luxurious materials, soft sofas, tranquil space, rocking chairs and water features. Cold plunge baths and hot fountains bordered an infinity pool that appeared to run straight into Biscayne Bay behind. Upstairs, Miami residents who could afford it attended the gym and unwound in heated marble seats and peppermint-scented saunas.

Somehow, while the rest of Florida was being crushed by a heat so oppressive it made you fear for your life, the garden of The Standard remained serene and comfortable. Diligent staff waited to refresh your towel, move your parasol or bring you a drink, and stepped forward with raised eyebrows any time you made eye contact: 'Me? Do you need something, sir?'

Around us, despite being moments away from a fairly busy street, Miami's vast lagoons were the dominant setting. Pillared mansions and custom dwellings surrounded the bays, each boasting a different architectural style: Art Deco, Venetian, Bourgeois French, Rococo. And the millionaire yachts that sat moored to the shoreline lawns and landscaped gardens were just as varied. Some had gone for size, others design. Occasionally, a jet ski cruised past the hotel's quayside, its rider pausing to chat to one of the guests – the only motor sounds despite the fact that in the hazy distance you could see two major bridges, both teeming with freeway traffic. Fringed by thick, symmetrical palm trees, and decorated simply with a handful of mild colours complementing the sound of running water, The Standard was as much life in a bubble as Americans had yet managed to create.

'Classic – the food here is so good I almost don't want to eat it,' Marc explained. 'This guy brought me some kind of spinach thing yesterday and I thought fuck it – I'm just gonna sit and look at that for a minute. Like a bloody work of modern art it was, son. Tasted crap though, I think... not really being educated in what to expect from that kind of cuisine. Crossed my mind to complain – just coz I could. Imagine that: Excuse me sir, this jus de whateveryoucallit is not quite balanced to my taste – could you take it back so the chef may feed his cat with it? I didn't though, coz I'm not that much of a tosser.'

'You sure about that?'

'About what? Shut up. Mind you, I do make them call me Dr Rhys.'

Although he didn't look it at the moment, slouching back in just a pair of boardshorts and wraparound sunnies, Marc was here 'on work'. In other words, he was attending a conference.

'Attending and bloody presenting a paper, I'll have you know.'

Sorry – he was appearing at a conference. With hair like his and a slender frame pushing out at the shoulders, he would always be a surfer to me, but this was what my old school friend now did with his summers. He'd tried countless times to explain his research interest, but it was so wordy nobody ever managed to remember it (and those who could didn't care). It was something to do with electricity and computers: a popular combination these days. So popular, in fact, that a company that made things out of electricity and computers, among other ingredients, had agreed to fly him to Miami as a special 'guest speaker', and somehow or other this was where he'd been put up.

I'm sure the cost was nothing to them, but I couldn't help grinning. Here was a guy who, for all his recent accolades, certainly still would have been willing to stay just about anywhere. Even a Motel 6 with a free shower cap would have been upmarket to him, regardless of whether or not he could afford more.

'And, as you told me to, I haven't got a flight back yet, although they've agreed to pay for it wherever I do eventually decide to go from. Got some important research to do, see, haven't we?'

'Good work,' I told him. We had a storm to chase.

Tropical Storm Chantal had begun as a non-tropical weather system just north of Bermuda. What I didn't really know at the time was that all evidence suggested Chantal was going to move north and be of little use to any surfers south of the Carolinas. But getting things wrong was the best way to learn (where was the adventure in knowing it all before going?), and Marc had needed rescuing anyway – from conferences, from academia and from The Standard.

This first and mightily unsuccessful chase had begun when I hit the US National Hurricane Center's website back at my mother's in Toronto. This was the message I read:

```
FOR THE NORTH ATLANTIC - CARIBBEAN SEA AND
THE GULF OF MEXICO - AN AREA OF DISTURBED
WEATHER HAS FORMED ABOUT 100 MILES EAST OF
THE CENTRAL BAHAMAS IN ASSOCIATION WITH A WEAK
LOW PRESSURE SYSTEM. THERE IS SOME POTENTIAL
FOR DEVELOPMENT AS THE SYSTEM MOVES WESTWARD
OVER THE NEXT DAY OR TWO.
```

That had been enough for me to start making plans. I had been in Canada for over two weeks, waiting for the Atlantic to show signs of disturbance and staring longingly at the clapped-out Ford Escort Estate in the driveway, which was ready and waiting for the right conditions to make the trip.

In Miami, Marc must have been checking the charts almost as often as me because he phoned within half an hour of this information going online.

At first I suggested he made his way to Toronto, and that we both set out for New England together. But he didn't like this idea:

'Nah, statistically it's always the Gulf that plays up first. We would need to be south rather than north, if this storm doesn't develop. We could catch a quick wave down there before we hit the Outer Banks. How's that for a plan?'

'Do I have a choice?' I asked.

'Do any of us? Now get off the phone and start tuning your mum to lend you that feckin' car!'

My mother loved Marc, which made her all the more willing to help out. He was a good influence on me, apparently. He hadn't been on the scene trying to persuade me to skive off school and surf during my GCSE and A Level revision time all those years ago (as his grades later showed), and she had never forgotten this. Now he was a 'Dr' too, even better. She was unconcerned by my claims that he could one day design weapons to wipe out half the universe if he wanted.

I began thinking of names for the car that would become my home for the immediate future. One name stood out above the others: 'The Betty Ford'. She was as keen for this journey as anyone, and was the perfect car for a long road trip. I am as much a motor lover as the next person and my passion is for old bangers. I'd fallen in love with this 1987, white, 1.2 litre Ford Escort Estate at first sight. What clinched it for me was when my mum's husband Dave showed me how to keep the boot open by clamping a mole wrench against the failing pneumatic hinges ('Your mother never had need to use the trunk,' he explained). The door edges had rust patches like nicotine stains and were partly held together by duct tape. Driving Betty Ford was a hoot; she would misfire from time to time and make a hypnotic squealing sound whenever she turned right at speed. She needed gentle coaxing over long distances.

'You'll also have fun with the Ontario licence plates,' my stepfather warned in jest. 'People will think you're Canadian, and it'll make them even madder when they can't pass you on the interstates. It'll be kind of like driving through England with Welsh plates.'

'Is that a good thing?' I asked.

'I'd say so,' he replied.

He went on to tell me about how each state had a slogan that would usually be displayed on car licence plates, and how Florida's was 'The Sunshine State' – before adding, 'Although you probably want it to be "The Hurricane State" right now?'

That was something I hadn't really thought about until now – was it actually right of me to wish for these storms? Marc thought it fine because they either were or weren't going to happen regardless of what we hoped for. He didn't follow any kind of karmic beliefs: God, Gaia, or anything else. To him, it was all bollocks.

'If a cracker does come along and harm anyone, we can relax as it won't be our fault anyway,' he stated. 'We're emitting virtually no CO_2 in your mum's wagon.'

'What about our flights?' I asked.

'What about them?' he replied.

'They'll create CO_2?'

'Ah – I carbon offset when I fly,' Marc replied, confidently. 'On expenses, of course. But I'll sleep at night.'

'Probably because you're staying in a posh hotel.'

'Too bloody right. And also on expenses!'

As I loaded up my surfing gear and whatever else could help me live on the road for a summer, Marc called again. In just a few hours the situation had already grown in urgency:

THE AREA OF LOW PRESSURE THAT PASSED TO THE WEST OF BERMUDA EARLIER TODAY HAS BEEN

MAINTAINING CONSISTENT DEEP CONVECTION. THE
LOW-LEVEL CIRCULATION CENTER - EXPOSED FOR
MUCH OF THE DAY - HAS MADE A COUPLE OF FORAYS
UNDERNEATH THE CONVECTION - AND IS WELL-ENOUGH
INVOLVED TO CONSIDER THE SYSTEM A TROPICAL
DEPRESSION. WITH ANOTHER TWELVE HOURS OR SO
OVER WARM WATERS - THE CYCLONE WILL HAVE AN
OPPORTUNITY TO REACH STORM STRENGTH AS IT
ACCELERATES WESTWARD.

Storm strength westerly winds were expected, and in only twelve hours or so. I needed to find some stay-awake tablets if I was going to cross the States in time to catch this one.

'Nah, you'll be fine,' Marc insisted. 'Just leave now, and go across into New York State. I've even done your route for you. Go down to Georgia and then into Florida. Easy. It's only twenty-odd hours. This storm hasn't even been named yet. Just leave all your handguns behind, hope immigration don't query any dodgy stamps in your passport – and you'll be in Yankland by dark.'

Marc was one of those guys who'll tell you whatever suits him. This storm could be setting up to deliver perfect surf to the shores of Lake Ontario – a few miles from my mother's doorstep – and he'd still be telling me to head to Miami so that he could grab a lift. But, from my point of view, the perks to having him on your side were enormous. Once he was in the car with you, you could be assured that, as he always made the right call for himself, he would duly be making the right call for you too. Before going into his current field, Marc had spent some time creating and running computer programs that modelled and simulated water movement and storm developments. He knew more about this stuff than anyone.

The idea for this trip had indeed been Marc's to begin with; the US hurricane season, a surf dash up the Right Coast – he first mentioned it when we were both fifteen. But it had always been my job to keep it alive.

Marc and I started surfing at the same time – around the ages of twelve and thirteen. We, along with a group of about five schoolmates, quickly became obsessed. How we became so enthusiastic so quickly beats me completely, because when you grow up in Wales surfing is a sport that has a lot more to do with commitment than it does pleasure. My memories of our teenage years often involve getting up at the crack of dawn to beat the Bristol Channel winds, only to find they'd foreseen our insolence and had begun to blow strong and early. Wind in Wales does as it pleases – irrespective of what the weather man says.

In winter, when the last remnants of the Atlantic hurricane season would drift overland, followed by the December to January storms, we'd don five millimetres of oppressive neoprene and head to Coney to go surfing. The beach's best, and most elusive, asset was a wave that rebounded off the sea wall at Porthcawl's Eastern Promenade. It would stumble back over itself and pitch forward with enough juice to form a barrel, or tube. The same sea wall that caused the wave to break would also protect it from the worst of the wind – making a man-made surfing haven. This spot was known as The Wedge – a dead-of-winter phenomenon that the tourists never saw.

'Wedge conditions' would be characterised by storm surges bashing against the nearby pier and exploding high into the grey skies, spray blowing over into the harbour to soak anyone stupid enough to be standing there – before pounding the already lethal Ferris wheel with corrosive salt air. As far as we knew, The Wedge had no equal.

That was until Marc bought a surfing video that showed a wave breaking exactly like it – except this time the backdrop was a sunlit jetty full of tanned fishermen, and the surfers were wearing shorts instead of full-body wetsuits.

'Where is that?' I asked him.

'It's in Florida. My dad says we drove right past it when we went there on holiday last summer, but we didn't go to the beach.'

'That wave is near Disney World?'

'Yeah, it is. It's in a place called Cocoa Beach. It's Kelly Slater's local wave.'

Kelly Slater, the most successful competitive surfer at the time, had just won his first world title. In later years much would be made of the fact that someone from Florida had been able to beat rivals from Australia, Hawaii, California, Brazil and South Africa.

As it happened, the wave was just south of Cocoa Beach, in a place called Sebastian Inlet. This would be the last remembered instance of Marc getting any geographical, scientific or historical fact even slightly out. The years that followed took us on very different journeys. While I flicked elastic bands across the biology class, he listened. While I doodled imaginary point breaks on my maths book, he worked through extension activities. Over time, he studied his way to becoming one of the youngest experts his field had ever seen. He was a proper prodigy; someone who would probably take a place in history (even if the history of *Computational Geoscience and Markov Chain Theoretics* only mattered to a few hyper-nerds anyway). Yours truly, meanwhile, studied surfing – wherever in the world that required me to go. The circuitous academic prospects were something I could live with in return for the travel, although it would have been nice to have someone else agree to meet my expenses, instead of raising them myself on the minimum wage.

Throughout the best part of a decade in which Marc and I had seen little of each other, we'd always kept in touch enough to promise that this particular trip would be done together.

Which is why he had been the first person I called after booking that flight to North America. Once he told me about his Miami plans we both knew that the long-awaited trip was finally going to happen.

'D'you know much about the predictions for this season?' I asked.

'Well, put it this way, this year there's a one-in-three chance of a hurricane as powerful as Katrina, and experts are predicting a way above average storm season. Look at Tropical Storm Barry; the Outer Banks have had swell already. So my official verdict is that it's gonna pump – probably.'

He had been glued to the same websites and CNN weather bulletins as me. The conference had given Marc an excuse to fly to the East Coast, but the thought of him beating me to Florida somehow seemed a bit cheeky. Not long later though, to make up for it, I beat Marc to the warm-water wedge at Sebastian Inlet, en route to meeting him in Miami.

'Just a hop from Toronto,' Marc had advised. 'A hop' wasn't really the term I'd use for three days of non-stop driving.

By the time I'd reached West Virginia, it was clear my choice of transport was going to require tender care if it was to successfully roll around the grand US Interstate System for a summer. It wasn't my fault the Betty Ford and I had to stop at Sebastian – the car needed to cool down.

He can't be aggrieved about that, I told myself as I walked from the parking lot and across the sun-baked boardwalks to get my feet wet for the first time on the Right Coast. Besides, Marc had always agreed with me that old bangers were an essential part of a classic road trip.

'You've got to give it a name as early as possible,' he had told me. 'Cars always run forever once you christen them.'

'Is that a scientific fact?'

'If you want it to be, son. I'll even smash a bottle of champers against its side if you like.' He'd be pleased to know I'd followed his advice.

As I sat in the balmy waters of Sebastian Inlet, the precarious relationship between pleasure and the earth's wrath again came to the front of my mind.

Sebastian Inlet was a place where all forms of enjoyment derived from nature. In the lee of the pier surfers craved storms, while at the end of it fishermen waited patiently in blissful sunshine. Behind us was a state park – an oasis of unspoilt greenery parallel to the seafront. The surf spot was a picture of tranquillity, apart from the occasional jet-skiers who revved in and out of the waterway to the south of the break.

Behind the line-up a group of manatees floated, sometimes sticking their heads out of the water to size up the human activity.

The surf was very, very small – but the way the wave ran off the jetty meant that it still had enough power to push you along nicely. Sebastian Inlet was a dreamy place to surf. Waves, waist-high or less, would reel across the shore break, folding over themselves exactly like The Wedge did at home. This meant you were always riding from a bigger section of wave to a smaller one – like a ramp of water – and it made surfing your best a simple task. With less of a wall to climb back up, you often had more speed than you knew what to do with. Between sets I'd sit, feeling the sunlight on my back, hearing the water swirl around me, amidst the smell of sunscreen and algae from the boulder jetty. This was a world away from my own wedge – the turd-coloured slosh of freezing water that had inspired me to come here all those years before.

About once every quarter of an hour a bigger set of waves would come through, sending the surfers scrambling after a good take-off position. I thought about how far away the rains of South Wales were. Most of my friends at home were still grumbling under layers of cloud cover, lamenting the worst summer they could recall, while I was sitting in the delicious waters of the Sunshine State.

Most of the other surfers here were kids, as school was still out for another week or so. Having grown up in Wales and therefore well accustomed to tiny surf, I was able to get a few good ones, staying in the water most of the morning. By the time the afternoon winds came up, I had already forgotten the arduous nature of the drive down – and was thinking about how to put the best possible gloss on this story for when I met Marc in Miami later that day: *Yes, I did stop for a quick surf mate... Sebastian... yeah, it was lovely...*

That would be exactly how he'd expect to meet me anyway: picking sand out of my ears and fresh from a day's surfing. It was the impression I wanted to give. If it was going to be possible to make Marc forget himself before he reported for lecturing duties later in the autumn, then I'd need to lead by example.

The Betty Ford was also grateful for the rest. A bridge swooped over the car park at the inlet, and other surfers were lining up their vehicles so that the peak of the afternoon sun would be shielded by this flyover. There had still been a few of those spaces when I first arrived, and that shade was now welcome. Post-surf, I opened the boot, secured it with the mole wrench and sat against the rear bumper, taking in my surroundings.

The sun was so powerful now that it took only seconds to start sweating when out of the shade, and the air was thickening quickly – humidity building all the time. Parked on either side of the Betty Ford were some monstrous trucks: a Ford F-350 on one side and Chevrolet Suburban on the other (don't be fooled by the name – this thing looked more appropriate for 'Operation Desert Storm' than suburbia).

Changes in landscape and culture had been hard to spot on the interstate – three days of monotonous roads were a blur – but now it was clear I was in a new land. The rains of home, and then the mellow Toronto summer had slipped into the sweltering August atmosphere of the southern states – likely to result in thunder come the afternoon. Vehicles, meanwhile, had doubled or even tripled in size. New accents caught my ear, as the precise 'o' sounds of Ontario speak were long behind, replaced by twangy Florida drawl.

Sebastian Inlet was calm; the car park was almost full, yet virtually empty of human life. Everyone was either in the water or on the sand. I didn't fancy leaving for Miami in any hurry, so I lay back and tried to think of nothing.

'Wow – you've come a long damn way from Ontario,' a woman in her fifties said, walking past.

'Yeah, I suppose.'

'Are you a Canadian?'

'No – I'm from Wales.'

'Oh, OK. What are you doing here? Surfing?'

'Yeah.'

'Oh, it's very good here for surfing, this beach is home to Kelly Slater. He's very famous.'

'I know.'

Something I must offer as an almost universal compliment to Americans is that they are unbelievably friendly. This woman had no reason to talk to me at all but, seeing my licence plates were from out of state, she couldn't resist. And it's not as if out-of-state plates were rare in Florida either.

'So how are you liking Florida? Bit warmer than England huh!' If I have a universal complaint though, it is this misunderstanding.

Wales is some place in England if you're American, and that won't change in a hurry.

'Yes, much warmer.'

'And you've been having rain over there this year too, haven't you?' she added. 'I've been watching the news on BBC and CNN. The Weather Channel doesn't cover the European stories enough though; they only worry about American weather and American people, but I do still look at it, mind. Only at this time of year, though – just for the storm updates.'

I wondered if it was rude of me to just sit here with my stiff upper lip and not offer back any conversation in return. Here was a chance, though.

'Really? There's a Weather Channel?'

'Sure – Americans are crazy about weather. It's the only thing we're afraid of!'

I laughed. 'Is there any news on that new storm – the one near Bermuda?'

'Oh, yeah. It got named yesterday. "Chantal". Looks like it's gonna miss us for once though. I think the north is gonna get this one...'

'It went north?'

'Yeah.'

'That's not good for surfing,' I offered. That was the woman's turn to laugh.

'Oh, you care about the surfing? I hear that a lot here. I'm sorry to say, but I don't worry about your surfing. I just want to be sure my house isn't going to blow away!' Although dead serious, she said it with a smile, and a gentle chuckle. A Brit would have sounded frosty saying something like this, for sure.

'Have you ever had to evacuate?' I carried on.

'I haven't – some people have though. They worried a bit during Charlie – and Katrina of course. Most people don't realise that

Katrina hit Florida first, but I stayed here. My husband even went out once during that storm.'

All around these southern beaches of Florida I'd noticed repeated signs showing the official evacuation routes. Were they that necessary?

'Yes, the evacuation routes. We always joke that they were put there to help tourists find their way back to Interstate 95! No one else really uses them. Not until storms are only a few miles off – and then it's always too late. Anyway, I must go. My name's Jan, it was a pleasure to meet you.'

With that Jan offered a handshake and boarded the Suburban parked next to me.

'Oh, one last thing,' I asked. 'D'you know how long it'll take me to get to Miami from here?'

'Miami? About five hours? Yeah, let me think. Yeah, it's about five hours.'

My heart sank.

'Thanks.'

However, at the next gas station I asked the cashier, and this figure had been significantly reduced.

'About two and a half hours.'

'Thank you.'

This is another quirk of the American public: ask them to estimate a long distance and nobody will know the answer. But ask them how far the post office or the next gas station is and they will all answer correctly, and often with incredible precision – sometimes to the nearest hundred yards, or even closer.

The checkout assistant at this gas station looked to have estimated Miami about right, I was relieved to learn, as my own map tallied the same journey time. I picked up a copy of *RoomSaver* for the Florida area, and a BP-sponsored 'storm preparedness' pamphlet. Better safe than sorry, I thought.

Full of gas, surfed and well-rested, the Betty Ford and her occupant began the final leg of their journey towards Dr Rhys and The Standard.

When we arrived in Miami, as Jan had told me, it was to the news that Chantal was going to be a dud – in Florida at least.

Tropical Storm Chantal had swung north and was soon expected to undergo 'extra-tropical transition', winding down and sending swell only to New England and, to my exasperation, western Europe.

I would later learn from a phone call to Mum and Dave that it had still given a good wallop to the Avalon Peninsula of Newfoundland, causing flooding, knocking a bridge out and generally hitting some buildings and infrastructure around. In fact, Chantal's damage bill eventually approached CDN$6 million. This storm went on to make fairly major news there, but the last I ever heard of Chantal beyond chatting to my mother was when Marc went online to decode the official stance from the National Hurricane Center.

'There's going to be no swell from it, and they have stopped issuing advisories,' he confirmed. 'We're going to have to wait for the next one. Gutted, eh?'

I looked over his shoulder at the final advisory issued by the trackers of Tropical Storm Chantal. In the idiosyncratic prose there was no feeling, no art. Hurricane forecasting, I was beginning to realise, was pure science – Marc's domain for sure. There I was just assuming that if I wanted a swell to meet me in Florida, one would simply come. But that wasn't how it worked. If the ocean had other ideas, then all you could do was accept it and wait for the next one – and in the case of the National Hurricane Center, commentate on the facts and facts alone:

SATELLITE IMAGES AND QUIKSCAT DATA INDICATE THAT TROPICAL DEPRESSION THREE BECAME A

TROPICAL STORM YESTERDAY WITH ESTIMATED MAXIMUM WINDS OF 50 MPH - 81 KM/HR WITH HIGHER GUSTS. CHANTAL IS LOCATED ABOUT 330 MILES - 530 KM - SOUTH OF HALIFAX NOVA SCOTIA AND IS MOVING RAPIDLY TOWARD THE NORTHEAST NEAR 23 MPH - 37 KM/HR. CHANTAL IS NOT A THREAT TO THE UNITED STATES.

CHAPTER TWO

MAKING LANDFALL

'Did you know, son, that there are meant to be two cities in America that are at least as unprepared for a hurricane strike as New Orleans was in 2005?'

Marc asked me this as we sat in The Standard's restaurant, eating a meal and enjoying the view over the waterway shortly before dusk.

'I didn't. Let me guess... Well, Miami has to be one, coz that's probably what made you think of it...'

'Correct.'

'And as for the other... Well, Orlando's quite far from the coast and hurricanes don't last long over land, do they?'

'They do not,' Marc confirmed.

'OK then, I'll go for Miami and Tampa.'

'And you'd be wrong.' This was Marc's favourite phrase.

'OK, I give up.'

'Right – well you got Miami; that's one. The other city in the US that would be in deepest shit if it took a direct hit from anything

Category three or up... would be the Big Apple – New York City! Manhattan's below bloody sea level in places, did you know?'

You learned something new every day with Dr Rhys around.

'Yep, New York would be done for if a Cat three hit it – but that's not going to happen for a while, because hurricanes need warm water to survive, and north of Chesapeake Bay the Atlantic gets much colder. They rarely have the legs to get up there. But in the future it might change. If El Niño can move the Humboldt Current – the one by Chile – then it's not inconceivable that at some point in the not-too-distant future the Gulf Stream and others could move too. If that happened, Hurricane Alley might send storms New York's way more often. At the moment we'd be talking something like a three-hundred-year storm to hit it dead-on though. So they're due one, mind.'

'Three hundred years?'

'Aye, as in it only happens every three hundred years. Katrina was a one-hundred-year storm – so it won't come again in our lifetimes, unless the poor old residents of the Big Easy get desperately unlucky. Miami Beach is much more likely...'

Looking around, it seemed hard to imagine scenes here in Miami like those from Hurricane Katrina's ravaging of New Orleans. As city tours go, driving straight into the city's South Beach district and parking up at The Standard couldn't have been the most thorough, but I'd seen enough to know this was an area where displaying your wealth seemed at least as important as enjoying it. It was a place that didn't have any spare time to entertain a hurricane strike.

Across Biscayne Bay, the silent traffic was still streaming over bridges, now a steady flow of headlights and tail lights, and to our left, beyond the man-made Venetian Causeway, sat the central skyscrapers of the city's financial district. One by one, as dusk drew further upon us, the buildings began lighting up. By night the Miami skyline was a new sight – and in a way just as beautiful as its daytime seascape of palm trees and yachts.

'Did you know that once in a blue moon they get steaming surf in South Beach too?' Marc continued. 'Just behind us, over there!' he pointed over my head, towards the city and its Atlantic-facing beaches. 'If the hurricanes pass close enough on their way into the Gulf. When that happens, it's cack yourself time for anyone in Mexico, Texas or Louisiana.'

Marc was spinning facts like a juggler tonight. Weather and geography were passions of his long before he sold his soul to 'computers and electricity'.

'They call South Beach 'Scarface Beach' – and I bet you can't tell me why...' he went on.

'Because of Al Pacino in *Scarface*?' I offered.

'Er, no,' Marc replied, grinning. 'It's coz of Al Capone. He used to be called "Scarface", and this was where he hung out during his best years. Although, that said, some would probably call his time at Alcatraz his best years... Excuse me – can I get another glass of wine please?'

This was a new world to me – The Standard, its codes of conduct and expensive food – and I wasn't really sure what to make of it. In some ways it felt a little wrong; too decadent. There were some astonishingly loud voices on the table opposite us, as a birthday party of yuppie twenty-somethings congregated after a day at work, each dressed in clothes I'd be scared to wear for fear of spilling something on them. Meanwhile, on another table a lone man in his forties was talking quietly on a cellphone, while allowing a hundred dollars worth of food to go cold. He, unlike the youngsters, was dressed in a logo-free grey vest, and a pair of poorly chosen swimming trunks. If I had to guess, I'd say the latter was the wealthier.

Dr Marc didn't need to try as hard as me to feel at home, perhaps because he cared less about fitting in anyway.

'This place is a blast, isn't it?' he said, swigging another glass of pricey white wine.

These kinds of places usually made me want to swear loudly, do push-ups in public, break, steal or throw something. My needs were so much simpler than this place, and I felt resentful of those whose desires had paved the way for this 'lifestyle of more'. Keeping decorum among pretentious people was normally something I felt obliged *not* to do. But there were aspects to The Standard that anyone, regardless of their moral or social compass, could easily find themselves liking. On my way down to Florida my diet had been chosen entirely from gas stations and roadside franchises. I'd eaten breakfast at McDonalds and Denny's, snacked on vacuum-packed sweet bread sandwiches of fake turkey and plastic cheese – and during the evenings logged a visit to both KFC and Pizza Hut. Here, though, on the verge of getting the shakes from too much junk food, the fresh flavours of the farmer's market vegetables served to me were out of this world. The wine Marc ordered also seemed to add to the healthy feel.

'Good wine does that see, son,' he explained. 'If you've been eating crap for a while – like you often do...'

In front of me lay a range of appetisers: cashew nuts, asparagus, artichokes, crunchy chunks of pungent garlic and cured hams, all lightly drizzled with the finest extra virgin olive oil. By the time I'd eaten a main course (of swordfish wrapped in proscuitto), I felt stable again and strong enough to begin making further plans. As we were still in August, Marc explained to me that the Gulf Coast would be the most likely place to 'flare up next'.

Hurricanes came from two main zones; the best storms for surf would originate somewhere off the western coast of Africa. From here they would be able to gather power as they moved over warm water close to the tropics. If a storm did this with any strength, then good waves would be sent to Florida, the Carolinas and further north. Given the distances involved, these coasts could then receive very cleanly lined-up, organised swells as waves marched relentlessly to shore from over a thousand miles out to sea. However, that was only likely as we approached September.

In the early part of the hurricane season – well, in fact throughout the season – the more active area was always the Caribbean and the Gulf of Mexico. But these storms were much harder to predict, and often had violent tempers.

Storms of this magnitude form, and more importantly gain power, when they are over warm water. In the Gulf there exists an area of very, very warm water called the Loop Current. To give you an example of this current's potential for storm fuelling, one need look no further than the mother of all recent storms, Hurricane Katrina. Katrina formed in the Atlantic, and actually made landfall in Florida first – with nowhere near the level of damage it would go on to cause. The storm then lost its power as it crossed the peninsula – only to begin spinning again over the waters of the Gulf. At that point, it was a pain in the arse – an inconvenience to people who didn't fancy boarding up their windows just in case, or putting a tarpaulin over the car – but not a major threat.

Cue the Loop Current.

Once Katrina found the Loop Current, she hit Category 5 in no time – forming one of the most devastating natural disasters ever to hit the US. Her storm surge famously all but washed New Orleans away.

'It's going to be really interesting to see how the city's coping now,' said Marc, browsing a dessert menu. He was full, but planned to order one anyway. 'Aye, nasty situation that,' he continued. 'Imagine getting your house and half your friends just washed out of your life, live on television – coz that's pretty much what happened. If we end up over there, we owe it to them to spend as much money as we can.'

He signed our bill – to be passed on to the company that had invited him to the States. Meanwhile, we agreed to move towards the Gulf in the morning. Even if the next tropical storm was a while off, we could still always drop by New Orleans.

'Right.' Marc stood up. 'There's a couch in my room so you might as well crash there – probably more comfy than your bed at home anyway. And if you can kip in a car – ya low life – then you can kip anywhere!'

This was rich coming from him. I knew in the weeks to follow he would be sleeping in cars, tents – anywhere we could find. Once someone else was no longer paying, Dr Marc was far more masterful than me at pinching pennies – his determination to live frugally was legendary in our circle of friends.

It was more comfy than my bed at home, though – he was right; a wide, nothing-coloured couch, soft enough for even the lightest of sleepers. Luxury had its benefits.

'So far it's only been used for my luggage,' he said, dismissively.

With a light head from the wine, and a weird aroma of menthol air-con filling the wastefully spacious room, sleep was going to come quickly.

'I've got one more presentation to give at eight tomorrow,' Marc explained, 'which will be done by half nine – and then we can hit the road.'

After another look at the latest advisories, I thought, before pulling one of the four spare cushions over my ears to drown out the noise of the fan. It had been a long day. Sebastian Inlet, Miami, and hours of driving in humidity and then heavy talking had wiped me out.

Although we were both hoping longer days would soon follow.

Once Marc had left for his final conference, I went to breakfast. There was Wi-Fi throughout The Standard, so I was able to munch on French pastries and Nicaraguan coffee while tapping into the latest news from the Atlantic using one of the three laptops Marc had in his possession. This time the message from the National Hurricane Center was simple – and not promising:

```
TROPICAL CYCLONE FORMATION IS NOT EXPECTED
WITHIN THE NEXT 24 HRS.
```

Ah, cold, hard facts. How could Marc deal in such a currency? I mean – there had to be more to the story than that. There must be a wind blowing somewhere, or perhaps a rainstorm with potential to cause big drops in pressure. This was the season now – something had to be out there.

I flipped through the various pages of the extensive website – it was easy to get lost among the archives and predictions. After a while I learned that both the Gulf and African coast of the Atlantic had already reached the temperatures at which tropical cyclones could form – so it really was imminent. A recent press release also confirmed that an 'above average' storm season was still predicted. I remembered Marc telling me that the Atlantic 'going to sleep' was often a precursor to intense storm activity.

Here's hoping, I thought, before wondering if that wasn't just a little selfish of me.

So Marc knew how to roughly track the storm movements. But my area of research strength – acquired through years of staring at surf mags, videos and listening to on-the-road gossip – lay in which parts of the East Coast were the best known for good waves. At this point my information would be of greater use, as it looked as if we were now essentially looking for the most exposed beach within driving range that day. 'A swell magnet', as surfers would call it: somewhere that could guarantee you some kind of breaking wave on most days.

Because of the need to run year-round surf contests, lessons and holidays, you could assume that somewhere with a famous name would usually be a 'swell magnet'. In the Carolinas that would be Cape Hatteras or Wrightsville Beach – places which basically had a good 'fetch' area, and deep water immediately behind the shoreline. Here in Florida our best bet would be New Smyrna Beach – about four-plus hours north. Could the Betty Ford be persuaded?

Marc returned dressed in a light, cream-coloured suit. I was powerless not to burst out laughing at the sight of him. Something about him didn't seem right in a suit. His scruffy hair with matted, salt-blonde fringe pushed up out of his eyes didn't go with the slick outfit he had hoped would allow him to look like he fitted in here.

He didn't have the time to defend his choice of clothes though, rushing to check out immediately, ordering a porter to collect his things and requesting that the car be brought over from the valet parking lot.

'I want to be gone before anyone from that conference comes over here to try and meet up,' he explained to either me or the receptionist – whoever was listening.

It felt like getting a beloved dog back from the kennels, seeing the car chug up to the doors of The Standard at the hands of an immaculately dressed *chasseur*.

'That's a fine automobile you've got there, sir,' the boy said as he handed me the keys. Behind his immaculate uniform and polite front I detected a cheap attempt at sarcasm – an area of expertise in which I'd always assumed Americans to be famously hit-and-miss.

'Glad you think so,' I replied in a flattered tone, as if oblivious to the dig. He looked a little confused.

The back end was almost full with our surfboards and bags, so the rear seats had to be folded down. One part of the car was already like a walk-in wardrobe for my clothes, while Marc had three laptops – all in one mother bag – and two boards. The rest of his things were stored in a shabby backpack – complete with roll mat and a few pots and pans. Suited and booted ten minutes ago and now looking like he was ready to hike through India or Cambodia.

'Got a map?' he asked.

'I have.'

'Right, let's get out of this godforsaken heck-hole.' Marc's turns of phrase often recalled the hours of *Blackadder*, *Bottom* and *Red Dwarf* we'd watched during flat spells when younger. It always made me laugh, although I was worried some of our in-jokes were nearing their use-by date – Marc reckoned most of his students had no idea what he was on about when making such references.

It didn't take long after leaving The Standard to be lost in a four-lane freeway. No palm trees, no ocean breeze, no evidence of where you were other than the appalling heat pouring through the windows – and the roadside adverts:

Aggressive legal representation: A. E. Popenheimer Personal Injury Claims. Call 834.211.4129.

Your world is wireless – AT&T is wireless.

Bud Light is flipping cold.

Club Pink Pussycat Late Night Revue: Open till 5 a.m.!

The last one was my favourite so far, passing us on the left as the freeway rose into a bridge just on the outskirts of Miami Beach.

It made me think of Michelle Pfeiffer with that eighties barnet, and Al Pacino diving under a table to avoid the suited machine gunner, while the rest of Miami's underworld danced the evening away to hideous electronica.

As the Betty Ford bore north, her rattling engine began to gain momentum, every ten seconds or so going into a little humming noise. One thing she did have was a stereo, while Marc had an MP3 player which could connect to it through the tape deck. His first choice of music was Metallica, and he wouldn't listen to any of my appeals.

'Why do you still listen to "mullet music"?' I demanded.

'Coz it's *the shit*!'

Marc loved this kind of metal – and I knew why. It was because of all the layers of technical know-how required to replicate it. Metallica used classical chord sequences and played super-tight riffs and solos. When we were younger I used to try to make him listen to surf punk, but all he'd ever do was tut and dismiss it saying, 'that's crap – I could play it easily', as if that was all that mattered. To me, the mood was what made music. To him, though, it was about the science, even then.

'Stop off soon to buy some beef jerky and the classic American road trip is under way,' he shouted over the din made by aching pistons and even more pained electric guitars.

Fort Lauderdale passed by quickly, and the freeway dropped to two lanes, flanked by long areas of grassland and intermittent roadside settlements of food chains, gas stations and motels.

'Look – Vero Beach and *Lake Wales*!' Marc shouted as we passed one sign. He was too late with the camera, and cursed accordingly.

Meanwhile a lorry was crawling along to our right, its cargo of planks tipping dangerously; ready to fall on any car that tried to overtake. A hand-painted warning on its rear read, 'OVERSIZEL OAD'. I got around that one by dropping off two-hundred yards, and then accelerating to our top speed of around seventy miles an hour – which was enough to catapult us past the hazard and on to the safety of two free lanes again.

We made it to New Smyrna Beach after lunching at a Quiznos just north of Cocoa Beach. It was the hottest part of the afternoon, and Marc had grown restless in the last hour after learning we could have stopped off to watch a rocket launch at Cape Canaveral.

'Space Shuttle Endeavour!' he yelled. 'Wouldn't that be awesome?'

I wasn't too fussed on the idea – the 'space race' had always seemed a bit unnecessary to me.

'There are no waves on the moon,' I told him. 'So why worry about going there?'

'Shut up! Mars *pumped* back in the day, from what I've heard,' said Marc. 'And loads of other planets might have had oceans once. Best thing we ever did, getting into space.'

'Who's "we"?' I asked.

Ahead of us was a bridge. Most of Florida's eastern coastline is made up of thin fingers of land, beyond lagoons of water. A series of urbanised sandbanks, if you like. New Smyrna Beach was no different. A small town located on the mainland, and a bridge over to the beaches. The elevated flyover gave you a pretty neat view of the ocean ahead to our east, and what looked like an inlet, or harbour entrance, to the north.

We stayed on the main road until it ran out at the edge of the Atlantic Ocean. This was Flagler Avenue – and the surf was dire. Knee-high wind-slop washing over a stretch of disorganised sandbars, which were filled to the brim with sunburnt tourists.

'Great – we're in the fuckin' Costa del Sol!' Marc groaned.

I walked to the edge of the parking lot and stepped onto the sand. I had to get my feet wet. The ocean was the same temperature as the air – offering no refuge from heat, heat and more heat.

I looked north and south. No sign of waves that would be of any interest to a surfer.

'Gutted,' I mumbled to Marc.

'Well,' he suggested, 'it is high tide. You never know, in an hour or two it could do something, especially if the sea breeze dies when the land cools off.'

Back by the car I noticed a truck with New Jersey plates and a surfboard in the back. Its driver was sitting in the front seat.

'Excuse me,' I asked him, 'how were the waves here earlier?'

'I didn't see it, man, but there should be some later,' he replied.

'Really?'

'Yeah, but check out the inlet – north of here. There'll be no swell here, this is a family beach.'

I thanked him.

'You drive all the way here from Ontario?' he asked.

'Yeah.'

'Unreal – how long did that take ya?'

'Er, three days.'

'Oh, that's not bad, huh? I drove from Jersey and it took me like twenty hours. Come here every year, man – got an apartment in Ponce. Oh well, have a nice day.'

'In what way was that little fact relevant?' Marc asked me, as we squashed ourselves back into the car.

'It wasn't – but I think it's nice the way people tell you about themselves here. I'd have speculated anyway. I mean, Jersey plates in Florida? I was interested to know why he was here.'

'He's on bloody *vacation* isn't he, like everyone else. No story to that. Just shut up and drive.' Marc needed some waves – he knew I'd already surfed yesterday, and it was a source of annoyance. I could tell.

It took us about twenty minutes to find the inlet, and a parking lot that this time was a hive of surfer activity. The vehicles of choice were still incredibly large trucks, but most now bore evidence of surfer owners; board bags rolled up inside the cockpits, along with clothes, or surf stickers on the bumper (often alongside faded slogans like 'Support our troops' and 'Four more years!').

We took a ten-minute walk across a wide area of wooden walkways and scrubland – a mini nature reserve – until one of the boardwalks led over to the shoreline. Here there were waves – and fairly good ones too. A boulder jetty to the north was focussing swell on three separate peaks – providing about fifty surfers with a head-high and playful beach break.

We watched the surf for a few minutes, getting our breath back after walking through the heat. People had driven SUVs for miles along the sand to get here – which explained how there were so many in the water.

'I did see a sign back at Flagler Avenue saying you could drive on the beach for ten dollars,' Marc noted. 'Hope they get stuck, the lazy bastards.'

'Let's go get our boards,' I suggested. We were going to return to the surf on foot. Marc didn't fancy driving, and I suppose that even if we had done, it would have been just our luck to get caught in the sand. Not to mention sticking out like a sore thumb amidst all the flash trucks.

'In Europe you'd be strung up for taking a car on the beach,' Marc went on, as we made our way back at a pace that fell somewhere between a brisk walk and a light jog. 'And that's how it should be. Having cars on beaches is just wrong.'

There was a serenity about the little nature reserve behind New Smyrna Inlet that was quite a relief after beginning the day in busy downtown Miami. Just like in Sebastian, once the authorities had decided to make somewhere a reserve or 'state park' they did it in style. Colourful birds perched on wooden posts – preening themselves and twitching – while turtles peered out of holes they had dug in the dunes.

We lifted our boards from the car, covering Marc's valuables with blankets. I locked up and attached the key to the inside pocket of my shorts. Our third time crossing the boardwalks was the easiest; both barefoot, carrying boards under our arms and winds dying down. The sun was easing in intensity, tingeing the sand and sea with pink early evening hues. I felt blessed. Sweet surfing conditions had yet again found me, and immediately all the other good surf sessions I'd had in my life returned to my soul like a constant force. It was a privilege to be sharing such a situation with Marc too. It had been almost a decade since we'd last been on a beach together outside of Porthcawl. Marc's total dedication to his work, and my tendency to go away for months at a time, meant that we only ever surfed together at home – and usually on weekends or public holidays. But now here we were, reunited to share in the excitement of paddling out in a foreign line-up.

The small waves were made easy to ride by the welcoming, warm, cerulean water, and we set about surfing until dark. It felt as if we had literally walked, or paddled, off the edge of the continent and into the ocean, where the surfers' code applied, and you no longer had to worry about traffic rules, finances, work or travel plans.

After half an hour of picking off waves at a relaxed pace, I could hear what sounded like a loudspeaker announcement from a lifeguard tower – although none were in sight. I couldn't make out what was being said, and therefore didn't worry about it. Minutes later, though, the noise came again, but became louder, and this time I saw the source.

Two police trucks were heading up the beach towards us, lights flashing and a voice on a loudspeaker was addressing the surfers: 'For your attention: the beach is now *closing for traffic*. Could the owners of all vehicles please remove them. You have ten minutes to comply...'

Immediately the water began emptying.

As the last of the trucks pulled off, I took a look around. There were eleven people left in the line-up.

The nearest of them, a blonde girl on a blue hybrid shortboard, smiled and said: 'Happens every evening, dude – and they never learn!'

'Why?' I asked.

'I don't know – Floridians love their cars, I guess. Where are you guys from anyway – Australia?'

'No, Wales,' Marc replied – friendly for now, but expecting to take offence imminently (in the form of being called English).

'Oh cool! So what brings you here?'

'Well, my mother lives in Toronto,' I replied. 'So I borrowed her car and drove down. We're hoping for a hurricane.'

'Oh, that's awesome! Well you might get one, you know. It's the time of year. Jeez – what an *awesome* trip you guys are gonna have!'

'Do you get hurricane swells in August?'

'Oh sure, and we're well overdue. September is the best month for hurricanes, though. Everyone keeps saying there's one coming next week, but we've been waiting on next week for a while now. I heard there really was one last week, only it didn't come south enough for us.'

She meant Chantal.

'Do you need storms to move close to get waves here?' I continued.

'Uh, it can help. So long as they stay out at sea! The ones that come close to Miami always send epic waves – and they break to the right then, too.'

A 'right-breaking wave' was one which peeled, on this coast, from south to north, allowing surfers who stood with their left foot forward to face the wave as they rode. It made sense that a storm passing below Florida would send waves which would break in such a direction.

'Really?' I asked 'But you don't like the storms to come ashore though?'

'Well, not *exactly* here!' The smile was still there. 'Although the best swell I can ever remember was Hurricane Charley and that went pretty much directly over us.'

I looked at Marc.

'It's possible,' he muttered. 'Odd direction to send surf, as it went across Cuba on the way in – but I can see how the eastern side of that storm could have sent some very powerful waves up here – especially as it changed track. Interesting, very interesting.'

'Er, yeah.' The girl beamed back at him. She had no reply to that. Nor did I.

A few more waves were on the horizon, so this became a good point to cut off the conversation as we paddled after them and back into our own individual worlds for a little while longer. Almost three-quarters of an hour of daylight remained, which was spent racing along the buzzing, sand bottom, warm water peaks – a plentiful supply for the handful of surfers left. With so few others in the water you could spread out, find your own space and have any wave you wanted.

Back in the car park after dark, as we dried and packed up again ready to drive on, Marc returned to the subject of Hurricane Charley.

'You know, Charley was, I think, the worst hurricane to hit Florida since Andrew something like a decade before,' he explained, as we turned back off the coastal road and onto the bridge that lead out of town. 'I didn't think they'd get waves so close to its eye. Normally it would have been impossible to walk in a straight line – let alone carry a surfboard down the beach and paddle out. To be honest, I'm surprised surfers are talking about it like that – as if it had been a good one for waves. It was a Category four, and a really naughty one too. The famous thing about Charley was that it changed direction. Everyone predicted it would hit Tampa, but then it swung and slammed Orlando instead – so it must have been pretty windy here.'

'Did people die?' I asked.

'In Cuba, yeah – but not here that I know of.'

Without thinking, I'd run us up onto I-95 again, northbound.

'Hang on,' said Marc. 'Sod doing more driving today. Bed is where to go now, I reckon. Let's find a motel – I'll see if I can swing one on the faculty card.'

At the Palm Coast junction, a few miles on, there were several places to stay that were visible from the road. The moment he mentioned stopping, I had also suddenly become consumed by tiredness, albeit of a blissful post-surf variety.

'The nearest one,' said Marc, scouring the roadside buildings. 'I hate choice. Here you go, what's this? Hampton Inn? Perfect.'

Especially since they had Internet access.

Marc went online immediately. Emails from work, emails from his hosts in Miami (presumably asking where he was) and research papers to read – but for him there was only one site that needed to be checked urgently.

As I looked for a vending machine to get a drink, I heard him call, 'The Gulf!'

'What?'

'The Gulf. Yep. That's where we're going next all right. We have to. It's not a dead cert, but just in case. We need to get up early tomorrow and drive.'

'Let me see,' I said.

He leaned out of the way.

A TROPICAL WAVE ABOUT 270 MILES NORTH-EAST OF
TUXPAN MEXICO IS GENERATING INTERMITTENT SHOWER

AND THUNDERSTORM ACTIVITY. ENVIRONMENTAL
CONDITIONS MAY BECOME FAVOURABLE FOR FURTHER
DEVELOPMENT OF THIS SYSTEM DURING THE NEXT
24 HRS.

This time we were pretty much in the right place already. Wrong coast maybe, but that could be remedied by tomorrow afternoon.

I went upstairs to the room and began watching the Weather Channel. They were talking about the same system of rain and thunder.

Well, all we can say now is scientists are watching this for further developments. Although at this stage they're not ready to issue any advisories, so stay put for the moment if you live on the Gulf. We see a lot of these kinds of patterns and only around a half make it to full-blown hurricanes. However, given the time of year, the National Hurricane Center is urging caution – so keep tuned to our bulletins to see how this system develops over the next few days. Anyone planning vacations along the Gulf Coast might want to wait on our next reports before making a decision, though.

I presumed this didn't include us.

After that there followed a break, during which I was told about a new pillow that made (all) neck problems go away, as well as a local dentist that could guarantee to make anyone's teeth white – usually without you needing to change your health or dental plan. When we returned from the ads it was to *Extreme Weather Tales* – and a feature programme on Hurricane Charley – clearly a popular one in local lore.

Apparently, a woman had gone into labour during the storm and the doctor had been held up in traffic on his way to the ward because of high wind and lashing rain. The story unfolded in dramatic fashion – although in the end all parties survived and were relieved to be telling the tale from the comfort of their still intact homes. The punch line at the show's end was that the happy couple had considered naming the child Charley – after the deadly weather system in which she was born.

Marc had finished whatever he was doing online in time to catch the end of the programme – and to learn how a hospital window had blown through during the landfall, only forty feet from where the alarmed mother was giving birth.

'That's a hell of a wind,' he remarked, pulling out one of his laptops. 'Smashing a sturdy US hospital window. Bet you a brick might even take a couple of attempts to do that. Anyway, is there any baseball on? Change the channel.'

I threw him the remote.

Moments later he'd found a baseball game.

'Awesome. Got to cram in as much telly as we can before we get to the Deep South and all the channels change to church services. Then we'll have to read, and I do enough of that at work.'

CHAPTER THREE

HURRICANE WHO?

I fell asleep in no time at all, only to wake up again in the middle of the night. It was partly the heat, the rumbling of the air conditioning and the sound of Marc snoring a few metres away. They all played a part, but my active mind was the main culprit. There was too much anticipation in my world right now to just switch off.

Staring at the darkness, I remembered printing off the list of Atlantic hurricane names for the season ahead. I'd given it another look when we were at The Standard too, mainly to draw a big black line through the name 'Chantal'.

Without a storm to put to it a week ago, the word 'Chantal' had kind of clung to the page. It had no character at all. But now I felt as if Chantal's personality was clear: a snobby kind of storm – rude and aloof – didn't give us anything other than a little tease before going up to east Canada and having a bit of a tantrum. When I thought about it, I should have known as much by the name – it seemed better suited to a model or a high-maintenance girlfriend.

I wondered what sorts of moods the next storms would have, but it was impossible to imagine. Parents decided on names for unborn babies as if the child might then start to embody the title given. It didn't work for hurricanes that hadn't even been conceived yet, though. The names held nothing:

Dean
Erin
Felix

These storms could go on to be anything, any*one*.

I rolled over and tried to get comfy again – still no sign of sleep. I wished I'd been named after a storm.

So 'Dean' was the next on the list. Was this little swirl of cloud in the Gulf going to become Dean? Or was he yet to be born elsewhere in this now fertile swathe of ocean?

And what should I want the newborn child to be like, or to do?

Taking a sip of room-temperature water from the bottle next to me, I just wanted the night to be over so we could get on with finding out.

CHAPTER FOUR

THE GULF OF MEXICO

You can often suffer from information overload when you spend too much time with Dr Marc Rhys. I certainly felt sorry for anyone who had to actually listen to him giving a lecture, uninterrupted, back home.

Over breakfast he'd bored me half to death talking about a birdwatching trip he'd been on in the forests of Costa Rica (a total waste, if you ask me, seeing as the country has great surf), before telling me about the wildlife of Guantanamo Bay, and then asking if I'd seen any Cuban people in Miami. I hadn't because, like him, my knowledge of the city had been kind of limited to one very plush hotel, and a few freeways in and out.

'Yeah, pity that,' he said. 'We'll have to go back one day, won't we?'

'Well, you never know. What if one of those South Beach hurricanes turns up?'

He pursed his lips, eyebrows raised. 'Well statistically while it's not impossible those swells are very rare. I'd forget about that idea if I were you.'

'So how are we ever going to go to Miami again then?' I asked, before remembering that Marc could always attend another conference there – although that wasn't to say he would do it any differently next time.

'Did you know they don't stamp your passport in Havana?' he cut in, suddenly. 'So that the Yanks won't know you went to Cuba?'

I did not.

'Well – they don't. Might if you asked though, you know; if your passport was at the end of its term – for your collection. But if we went tomorrow they'd swipe it, but nothing else. You ever had grief for having visas for dodgy countries? Indonesia is probably one that surfers have to answer questions about quite a lot.'

Among the most sought-after destinations for any hard-core surfer, Indonesia was the one place Marc had been to on a proper surf trip – and I knew it was something he wished he had done more of.

As kids, the thrill of waiting for a good day of surfing at home was what kept us keen. But as the world beyond got nearer, we'd both had important decisions to make. Marc used to laugh at my claims that any sort of roof would suffice to live under as long as it meant waking up to good surf the next day. He had what I and the rest of our friends called the 'sensible gene'; he could never leap before looking – or at least not before having a long think.

'What are you going to do about jobs?' he used to ask me. 'You can't live out of a board bag forever, Tom.'

'What d'you mean?' I'd reply. 'If you're surfing regularly then any job is bearable.' That was always the point at which he would frown.

Of course, we were both right in a way. But Marc needed something substantial or meaningful to apply himself to – and while in fairness to him he had tried to work crap jobs and travel, he only lasted one year before going to university inland. After that – as the title 'Dr Rhys' now showed – he never looked back. (Or at least that was the impression he wanted to give.)

During that one year, though, Marc went for it more than anyone. He ignored letters from his credit card company, and advice from family not to spend savings they'd hoped would last 'until something important came along'. First he drove to the Alps, and then over to the west coast of France for spring, before ending his single year of wanderlust with that three-month solo sojourn in Indonesia. It was a trip during which he tried to get a lifetime of adventure out of his system. He slept in the jungles of Lombok in order to surf the rarely breaking Desert Point at first light, got reef rash at Bingin and rode 'chicken buses' to Nias – all the while knowing, it seemed, that by that autumn he'd be sitting in a lecture hall making notes. Driving across the state of Florida now, a sixth sense of some kind was telling me this old part of Marc could still be revived.

In the early days he had, of course, spent some considerable time skint – as all postgrads do. But once a university in London snapped him up on a hefty research wage, travel had again become a possibility for him – only it would never be as he had previously experienced it. His ocean senses had been dulled by inner-city life. He had used time away to engage in activities other than surfing – such as attending conferences or bird-watching.

This all meant he had experienced very few of the complications that made more impromptu travellers into the people they are. He usually journeyed on package tours, and to appointments, conferences or interviews wearing a shirt and tie – with accommodation pre-booked and often with a laptop as carry-on luggage and a little black corporate suitcase checked in hours in advance.

'I've never been given any grief when coming into the States,' he told me in a tone that bordered on wistful, 'even though I've got an Indo stamp.'

The Indo stamp, I thought, proof that he had once tasted that life.

My border crossing earlier in the week had been very different to Marc's experiences of travel. A 'Department of Homeland Security' officer had climbed right into the boot of my car to have a rummage before letting me through.

I began telling Marc about what the guard had said when I explained my reasons for going in to the US. 'To find a hurricane,' as it so ineloquently came out when I was put on the spot.

'You going to New Orleans then?' the officer asked, raising an eyebrow.

'Maybe at some point,' I answered, trying to guess the right blend between casual and rigid. 'It depends whether there's waves in the Gulf.'

'And you've definitely got no guns in the car?' he had asked, while looking through my boards.

'No,' I repeated, knowing not to even joke about this sort of thing with these guys.

'Well,' he'd shrugged, giving me back my passport. 'It's your funeral, buddy. You should be armed when going there. It ain't safe in N'Orleans no more, man. Crime's real bad right now, after the hurricane – people getting mugged, guns, gangs. It's not a nice place.'

A guard sniffing around the boot of my car was fine, but his last words had stuck with me: 'Be really careful if you go to New Orleans. We wouldn't want something bad to happen to you...'

Marc, though, was about to give off an early sign that his intrepid side wasn't yet gone for good – that it was still there somewhere and could be reawakened. To my surprise, he shrugged his shoulders at this mention of New Orleans being dangerous and I asked if he had been serious about trying to go there.

'Everywhere's dangerous, man. Everywhere's dangerous,' he responded.

'What d'you mean by that?' I demanded.

'Exactly what I said – you can get mugged in Cardiff these days. Everywhere's dangerous.'

The guy at border control had mentioned guns though. Mugging I could handle – never carrying much of value anyway. But guns didn't sound like much fun. Again, Marc was unconcerned:

'Well, I want to go there. It's quite easy for somewhere to get a bad reputation. But for me it's all about the attitude you bring. If we go to New Orleans looking to have fun and show respect for our fellow humans, then it'll be fine.'

'Sounds like a karmic argument if ever I heard one.'

'Yeah, whatever.' Marc rolled his eyes. 'And anyway, I want to get myself into shit somewhere on this trip. It might give me an excuse not to go back...'

About ten minutes of silence followed that. Both of us gazed out of the window at rows of semi-tropical trees, as the road undulated slightly in and out of what was, besides the palms, an essentially featureless landscape. Every now and then you could see tracks emerging from the wide ditches of grass and scrub that separated the east and westbound carriageways. These had been made by the tyres of highway patrol cars that were known to hide like lions in the undergrowth, looking for prey to chase. They would have no such luck with the Betty Ford. We were passing Tallahassee now – and would soon be moving into Central Eastern Time. The best chance of waves on the Gulf Coast was the stretch from Panama City to Pensacola – so we'd need to get off I-10 soon and look for Highway 98.

'Have a look at the map, Marc,' I said. 'I think the connecting road is the 231?' Remembering numbers was one skill I thought I did possess.

'I'm gonna text Craig,' he replied. 'Gonna tell him where we are and see if he's got any tips for what to do if we're waiting for waves. He spent a month in the Deep South a few years ago and said it was fuckin' awesome.' Craig was another one of our closest friends from home. He was Marc's neighbour when they were growing up, and now lived his life from one surf trip to the next.

'Make sure you tell him we're scoring perfect waves!' I added.

'Of course. I'll tell him it's pumping here and that we're fed up with constant surf!' Marc began rapping on the keys of his mobile phone.

'And once you're done, look at that map,' I repeated.

'It's the 331,' said Marc, eyes still stuck on his phone keypad. 'And I'll tell you the exit too.'

Getting the most from a long drive in the US is dependent on staying off the interstate highways, as they tend not to reveal much of interest (as would be the case if you drove only on M-roads in Britain). However, when you have a car like the Betty Ford, which is uncomfortable for stop-start driving, and for the distances we hoped to cover, these roads were a godsend. They assured you a smooth, straight route to wherever you were going, and could make long distances seem to disappear in a few simple hours. Congestion was rare on the ones I had driven so far, and the 4x4 drivers were, in general, reasonably accommodating to my old banger with Canadian plates. In fact, it tended to be me doing a lot of the cutting up – something which I was sure could be partly excused by my Ontario plates anyway. ('Fricken Canadians!' I imagined to be the common response from drivers who fell foul of my slow overtaking, or last second junction pull-offs.)

The Florida 331 wasn't much more scenic than the interstate at first, though. It too was lined with trees, the occasional roadside shop (selling either sweets or 'gator meat) and gas station. But once we arrived at the Gulf Coast and bore right, the Panhandle's shore came into view.

A thin, dazzling blue ocean spilled onto beaches so bright you had to squint. White-capped waves ran to the horizon, and the tropical shrubbery swayed gently in the ocean breeze.

'Bollocks – it's windy,' said Marc. We'd both thought it.

Wind at the beach is not a good thing for surfing – and we could see immediately that conditions weren't very clean or organised.

The beaches were thin and in most cases were either public and industrialised with scaffolding, piers and docks, or protected but private. This incensed me immediately. How could you privatise the sea? The gated communities that owned many of the beaches contained holiday homes for the wealthy – occupied by those who I thought probably didn't deserve such a privilege, and were unlikely to use it to its full potential.

'Shit – if I owned a beach,' I began...

'If you owned a fucking beach, you'd be just as much of a bastard as those who own these,' Marc cut in. 'You'd be delighted, and would be certain to ban other surfers from coming onto the sand.'

'Well, I dunno about that...'

'I do.'

'But what is important is that I'd be surfing *all the time*. Imagine some of the waves that must go to waste here when there's a swell running.'

'Well, it's not worth worrying about today,' Marc announced. We had arrived at a stretch of road that afforded a view of the surf. It was less than knee-high and blown out by the afternoon onshore winds. These winds would be far more regular in the Gulf than on the Atlantic as the water temperatures were so much higher.

I was beginning to realise from talking to Marc how simple an equation this was: warm water = wind. This was why the Florida Panhandle's coast had a scraggy look. Sand had been pushed onto the edge of the road so often and the trees all drooped to the right – bent by years of prevailing onshore breezes.

'Next time you have a cup of tea,' Marc explained, 'pause before putting the milk in and watch the way the steam evaporates off the surface of the hot water. You'll notice lots of air currents; the rising vapour will be swirling all over the place. As one patch of warm air rises, more air rushes in to fill the gap. It's a mini wind storm.'

'A storm in a teacup?' I laughed.

'Yeah. It is, actually.'

A tropical cyclone would form, according to my slowly improving understanding, where upper-level winds blew, rising water vapour away from warm sea surfaces. This would cause more air to flow into the area for the process to then repeat itself – leading to higher winds. The earth's own rotation would cause the whole thing to form into a spin cycle. The amount of power generated would depend on how warm the water was. Apparently anything about 26°C or more could lead to a hurricane. Right now, most of the Gulf's milky blue waters were well over 28°C. She was, quite literally, *on heat* – ready to be with child. But would she catch this time? And who would that child be? Dean? Erin? Or neither for now?

We parked up and walked to the edge of the sand where tiny pulses of miniature swell lapped at my toes.

'D'you know, you could ride those waves on a longboard?' I suggested. (A longboard is over 9 feet in length – which gives you the buoyancy to catch very small waves indeed.)

Marc raised his eyebrows. 'I don't reckon you could, and we haven't got one so it's irrelevant.'

'Er, yeah – you're not getting off that lightly. I bet we could hire one.'

'Sod that,' said Marc.

'Come on – it's boiling. How sweet would it be to cool off with a few waves right now?'

'Cool us *down*? That's some of the warmest water on earth. And is there a rule against just going for a swim?'

'What about being able to say you've surfed the Gulf Coast? And when do we ever get to surf in shorts at home?' I couldn't see why Marc was so against the idea.

'I don't care.' He had gone back into his shell.

'What's wrong with you? You know some of the best surfs we've ever had have been just for the novelty of claiming to ride waves somewhere nuts. Remember that time back home when we surfed *east* of Barry Island with Craig? Those waves were utter cack, but you *loved* it.'

This mention of our intrepid buddy Craig again was deliberate. Marc often used to talk about Craig's travelling as if it were a path he wished he had taken himself. I was now talking about a time when in a powerful winter storm, me, Marc, and Craig had surfed a spot that didn't normally exist. An Australian friend of Craig's had visited for the day from London, and had been desperate to 'ride a wave of any kind on Welsh shores'. However, the sea had been deathly tempestuous that day, so we ended up going after a sheltered and secret reef break, miles further up the Bristol Channel than any of us really believed you could surf. The waves weren't anything special that day, but the novelty of changing into wetsuits in a Cardiff suburb, as snowflakes and freezing sleet fell around us, made it a legendary afternoon.

'Come on Marc,' I continued. 'Let's go and rent a longboard. What if there's no more waves tomorrow? We might never come here again.'

'There could be a swell soon though.'

'But what if there's not, eh?'

Marc paused to think. 'Go on then – let's just carry on driving west, and if we see a surf shop we'll go in and ask.'

'That's the spirit!' I congratulated him. 'We'll be riding waves in no time now – you watch. I'm excited already.'

'Oh great,' Marc mumbled as we walked back to the car. 'I can't wait. Oh, Craig's texted back by the way...' He showed me the screen of his mobile phone:

LIARS. PAIR OF YOU. NO SURF ON GULF COAST EVER. KNOW COZ IM WATCHING IT ON WEBCAM. HA HA

'He's bluffing,' I told Marc. 'And anyway, I bet he'd switch places with us if he could.'

'Whatever. Come on, let's get driving.'

We saw a surf shop about five miles up the road, just past 'Gulf Winds Personal Credit: Making dream cars possible as low as 5.4 per cent'.

Inside were three assistants, and no customers. The first, a guy in his early twenties with a large mop of curly, light-brown hair, asked if he could help.

'Yes, we're wondering if it'd be possible to hire surfboards from anywhere round here?'

A second assistant, slightly older with a shaved head piped up. 'Dude, it's so shitty right now.' Not all of the world's surfers shared my enthusiasm; I needed to remember this at times.

'I know, it's not looking too clever. It's just that...' I was struggling for a way to convey why we would even think of surfing in these conditions. 'OK. What it is... Well, we've been driving for a week. Been to the Midwest, working, and we haven't seen waves of any kind since July. We're desperate to ride *anything*, plus we'll never be on the Gulf Coast again. We would just love to claim we've ridden a wave here.'

'Dude, that's awesome!'

Now they sympathised.

Between them, the two shop workers told us to look 'about one and three-quarter miles' up the road for a place called Aqua. Apparently if we asked for Kevin he would rent us a board for the night. But we'd have to be quick; he closed at six.

'We don't want one overnight,' Marc whispered to me. 'I reckon we want to get into Alabama straight after this.'

'Well, let's just see what he says.' I'd decided on this now. It was my mission to ride a wave today.

Inside Aqua Surf Shop, Kevin was sitting behind the counter looking at swell charts. Just like I had done for most of the spring back home. He was thrilled to be able to help.

At first he claimed the only way we could rent a board would be to return it in the morning, as he planned to leave at six on the dot. But I promised fervently to have it back by then, without fail, explaining we only needed to ride one or two waves each.

'You know what? Let me show you what I can do for you guys,' Kevin continued, smiling at us from under a neat moustache. 'I'll lend you this board.' He opened a 10-foot board bag and pulled out an almost brand new epoxy model. 'I could have lent you my stand-up paddleboard, but it's at home. If you guys are in a hurry though, you'll be able to get in a few on this. You'll have a blast.'

It was gone half past five.

'Do you need a credit card or anything to look after? For security.'

'Eh, only if you've got one. I can trust ya though.'

Marc wouldn't stand for such open-hearted courtesy, and handed the faculty card over for safekeeping. 'If we're a minute late,' I added, 'bill us fifty dollars'.

As our rear door had no hinges, we simply wedged the board in the open boot of the Betty Ford. We followed Kevin's directions; a block south, past two gated communities to a public stretch of beach in a place called Miramar. The Betty Ford's slipstream pulled fumes into the car through the rear, but it was only for a short distance so it didn't matter.

Around us were hotels and apartment buildings; tall, clean, modern. Ocean views from every window, and courtyards with palm trees. The main road was ragged, unfinished at the edges and without curbs. Marram grass was pushing through in places – probably intending to carry out its primary function of binding the land in place. It wasn't working, though, as parts of the tar surface were beginning to crack and drift away. It felt like this road had only ever been built to last in the short term. A fragile landscape of drifting dunes combined with a volatile climate made it a pointless exercise to hope for anything more.

I wasn't sure where we could or couldn't park, but since we weren't going to be more than fifteen minutes it was well worth the risk of a ticket. I squeezed the Betty Ford into a space behind a car with Tennessee plates – at least we weren't the only tourists – and stripped down to my shorts.

'I'm going first. This was my idea. You watch the car.'

Before Marc could reply, I was running down the slope of loose rubble used for coastal defence, onto the sand and into the tepid Gulf of Mexico. The longboard paddled like a boat, ploughing through wind-chop. Within seconds I was sitting behind the breaking waves, looking back at the silent mainland that I had left behind. A few swimmers looked interested in what I was doing, and I could see Marc on the beach holding his Welsh flag towel.

Picking a slightly bigger lump of water than the average, I aimed for shore and paddled. I was soon up and riding a wave in the Gulf.

I wasn't travelling fast, but the sensation was of pure delight. The sea, beach and nearby buildings were brightly lit with sunshine, and the water was warm beyond anything I could have imagined. Immediately I could feel my head being cleared of any worries. The fullness of all the surrounding colours fixed my eyes open, and the excitement of surfing again tightened my face – a treatment that the rich and famous might pay thousands to surgically replicate.

Two waves later I was a new person. The road was gone from my memory. I was energised and ready for whatever lay ahead.

My fourth wave led me right up onto the sand, where Marc was eagerly awaiting his turn, grabbing the board off me like a relay baton.

As Marc paddled out, I closed my eyes and felt the sun pouring its energy over me. Comforted by the lapping sounds of the shore break, I couldn't remember what it felt like to be cold, to be staring out of a window at an overcast Welsh spring. For the moment, that was something I never again cared to witness.

Marc was up and riding, his fingers touching the surface as little patches of algae drifted up the face of a small, balmy wave. We had eight minutes left.

It was long enough for me to catch two more waves after Marc came in. The thrill of what we were doing made me paddle fast enough to chase anything down.

Still dripping wet, we jumped straight back into the car and turned north, away from the relief of the coast again and back towards Aqua's shopfront on the US 98.

As promised, the Betty Ford chugged up to the front door in time for Kevin to close up at six.

'Woah – I wasn't expecting you guys to make it,' he grinned. 'I'm stoked you rode a few – sorry you couldn't get anything more here. Maybe in the next few weeks there'll be some action.'

Marc and I both looked at each other. Then I looked back to Kevin.

'Isn't there a bit of a swell due? I saw on the National Hurricane Center's site...'

Kevin cut in. 'You guys know about that site? Man, you're really on the ball. I'm impressed. Nothing major on there last time I was on it, but we can go online and look again now.'

I dusted as much sand off as possible, quickly changed out of my wet shorts, and then followed him into the shop. As we walked to the counter, Marc explained that as hurricanes formed from showers and thunderstorms, they didn't produce much wind until they reached tropical cyclone status – so surf prediction sites that worked off wind speeds could often completely fail to include building hurricanes into their forecasts.

Our excitement was short-lived though. Kevin frowned, tutted a few times and then swung the monitor of his computer to face us on the shop side of the counter. It was the first time I'd seen him look even slightly worried about anything. He would lend five-hundred dollars' worth of surfboard to complete strangers, but when it came to a bad chart... Well that obviously was something to be concerned about.

'That might have been the best of it, guys. It's not looking good.' His tone sounded almost apologetic; as if it was his responsibility to ensure surfers coming through this town got waves whenever possible.

On the monitor was the tropical weather outlook – that page we'd looked at a few times already. Again, a brief message – to the point. And, as Kevin had said, not good news:

```
THE  TROPICAL  WAVE  MOVING  EAST-NORTH-EAST
OF TUXPAN MEXICO HAS DISSIPATED. ELSEWHERE
- TROPICAL CYCLONE FORMATION IS NOT EXPECTED
DURING THE NEXT 48 HRS.
```

It was a stillborn. Or not even that. There was no storm. Our trip to the Gulf had been in vain.

That last statement about no expected activity within forty-eight hours counted for the whole of the Atlantic, so there was little point in hurrying back to the East Coast either.

'Saturday night in Alabama for us then,' Marc grinned.

'Good luck,' Kevin smiled. 'You gotta be patient to get it good round here, anyway. But it's the time of year for it, so don't go too far...'

As he didn't seem in that much of a hurry, I asked whether he had any idea how the storm season may pan out.

'Well, the Caribbean's going *crazy* right now – and it has been since the spring. There's loadsa storms out there, but we're not really getting those big Cape Verde hurricanes yet.'

'Cape Verde?'

'Yeah, the ones that spin off Africa. They're the ones that have the most power. The waters west of Africa haven't really done much this season so far, although I hear they're warm enough to kick up something any time now.'

'How about the Gulf?' I asked.

'Oh, it's warm. I mean, didn't you feel it? It's in the nineties now – but it should get even warmer, man. And I reckon it needs to if we wanna get any local-formed hurricanes.' He gently rubbed his moustache, as if thinking over what he'd just said. This guy wanted to be able to give us some good news – you could see it in his eyes.

'Do you look at the temperature readings online?' Marc asked him.

'Well, yeah, but it's not necessary – we can feel it. We're in there every day – more than the guys from the National Hurricane Center! Most of those dudes have never been in the ocean. They think you're supposed to wear fricken socks under a pair of Reefs, man. I mean, I could have told you 2005 – the Katrina year – was gonna go off way before they started calling it. You know – the year we got like ten full-on storms? Well, that was the warmest water I've ever felt here. Surfers could have given those warnings, for sure. We beat billions of dollars of satellites to it by months. That year we had like three of the most powerful storms in the history of mankind...'

'Katrina, Rita and Wilma,' Marc recited. Hurricane names rose alphabetically as the season went on – although that year was an anomaly in that they ran out of names.

'Yeah – they went beyond the letter Z and started using the Greek alphabet,' Kevin said. 'Surfers were going crazy – but I still felt kinda bad for what happened in New Orleans though.' His smile wavered.

'Why – how was it *your* fault?' Marc queried.

'Well, you know. You do think it – everyone does. Anyone with a drop of humanity in them would. We pray for storms – so when one goes wrong...'

Marc told Kevin that we were heading there next.

'Oh, you'll love it. It's awesome. But you must make sure you take a look at some of the damaged areas. As surfers you have to see what the power of Mother Nature can do. And also it'll show you how bad those storms can be to some people. That's why I'm so reluctant to call a big one a good thing, you know – especially here in the Gulf. Anything that gives us surf has to be a volatile mother of a storm, so they usually run in to somewhere afterwards. There's always a victim.'

'Where will we see the damage?'

'Everywhere, man. It'll start before you get there – check out Biloxi. That place was pretty much flattened.'

Kevin tried to refuse any money for the board rental but Marc insisted, forcing a ten-dollar bill into the guy's hand.

'I liked him,' Dr Rhys mused as we drove away. He was looking at a hand-drawn map we now had for the best route into Alabama. 'He was a real genuine guy. Yeah, a real nice guy.'

There was a northbound road out of Fort Walton Beach back to the interstate, and as we turned onto it I noticed a sign announcing that this area had been voted the tenth best place to live in America – according to *Money* magazine. That kind of stat would put me off a place for sure, but we were leaving anyway.

Marc was texting Craig again. 'I'm telling him we scored fun waves, and that we're off to Alabama for the night.'

I was deflated to learn the system we had tracked two days before at The Standard wasn't going to turn into anything, and also couldn't help but feel a bit of a stone in my throat at the thought of going to New Orleans so soon – and before getting any significant surf. Had I wanted to end up in this situation? Life would certainly have been easier if we had simply scored a throbbing Atlantic hurricane that tracked up the East Coast, making no landfalls and sending sweet waves everywhere from Florida to New York. But then again, in our different ways, Marc and I had never sought out easy lives – so why should this trip be any different?

Alabama, despite actually holding annual state surfing championships, got far fewer waves than the Florida coast we had just left. This was due to a swell-sapping continental shelf that meant any wave approaching the 'God Bless America' state would lose a lot of its power moving over shallow waters. The same shelf was at its narrowest by Fort Walton, the area we'd just surfed – so that was pretty much the focus of any energy present in the Gulf that day. For once, I'd found a community that had to make do with less surf than Wales – although they'd probably keep this in return for not having to wear wetsuits.

Besides 'God Bless America', the state licence plates sometimes bore the slogan 'Stars fell on Alabama'. Both phrases were always accompanied by a small red heart the size of a few thumbprints, in which ran the statement Heart of Dixie. This was a reference to 'Dixieland', the Confederate States' nickname during the Civil War. Alabama was the spiritual home of traditional southern life.

The gas light had come on again, with a short ping sound. I'd taken to calling it the 'dinner bell'. Tonight its timing was perfect.

Alabama seemed a state with a lot more spare room than Florida. Getting gas was still easy – stations were a dime a dozen here in a country that sold fuel for way less than half the price in the UK. But finding anything fresh to eat was a challenge – and one that we wouldn't succeed in rising to tonight.

As darkness fell, both of us were feeling hungry and drained of energy. It was still hot as hell too. Crawling out of the car, my T-shirt was stuck to my back. Dinner was a plastic, refrigerated pasta salad bowl from the gas station we had filled up in (followed by a lime-green banana each), and Marc's vision of a rocking Saturday night out in Alabama was wishful thinking.

We ended up driving into a small town called Loxley – essentially a crossroads, with a few gas stations, a market and post office – again serviced by roads that looked old, neglected, forgotten. A privately run motel by the side of the road, about a mile beyond the settlement, sported a neon sign that flashed 'Vacancy'.

An Indian woman sceptically opened the door, slowly, slightly, with safety chain still connected.

'What?' she demanded, as if wanting a room could be my last purpose for having rung the bell. Through the small gap I could make out a statue of Ganesh on top of a flickering television.

'Do you have any space tonight?'

'How many people?'

'Two?'

The door closed again. I looked back at Marc, still sitting in the car and shrugged my shoulders.

'Wait by there, son,' he whispered.

In the humid night air, standing alone on the gravel by this door painted a glossy blue, I felt vulnerable, blind to everything around me, and with no idea what kind of place this was. All I could see were the Betty Ford's headlights beaming on me, and whether this woman was going to come back was anyone's guess.

After what felt like five minutes she emerged from the backyard, tapping me on the shoulder and making me jump. She was holding a handbag in one hand, and was still dressed in her nightie. (The handbag had to be for a small firearm.)

'Double room, two beds.' In tentative English it sounded like an instruction.

'Sounds perfect,' I offered.

'Where you from? UK?'

'Yes.' I smiled politely.

'OK. I'll give you a good price. Who pays? You or him?'

'Him.'

A little later, as I gave up trying to read in the gloomy light of the room we had been given, Marc offered his opinion on what had happened outside.

'Son, she was scared we might have been a gay couple. There are three churches within view of here – and I'll bet you anything they'd frown on that sort of thing. Don't blame her. Who'd want to take a chance on that?'

He too had given up reading, and was watching the 'UFC Saturday Bout' on ESPN – no-rules cage fighting. It was so far from my scene that I would have probably rather watched a bullfight, or even bear-baiting, but Marc had the remote, and sleep was again close – this time without any imminent storm developments to toss and turn over.

'Shall we go to church tomorrow?' I suggested.

Marc didn't reply. But I knew he could get easily wound up if I wanted to continue. Any charity work or organised morality was just a screen in his opinion; to him the church existed solely to enable the rich and powerful to manipulate those below. Being more into spiritual stuff of all kinds though, I often liked to wind Marc up by deliberately taking opposing views. He was *not* a fan of religion.

He was, therefore, delighted when we resurfaced into the glaring Deep South light the next morning, to note that the chapel car parks were now home to the most concentrated collections of ostentatious SUVs we'd yet seen. Hummers, Chevy Silverados, Suburbans and Avalanches, the Toyota 4Runner, a Ford F-350, the horrid Dodge Ram several times over – and one bearing a hunting shop slogan: 'Grab life by the horns!' Sunday morning here was a day to show off your motor as well as your best church outfit.

'Reckon the "Life Saving Christian Church" would be impressed if we strolled in wearing our boardshorts and parked our wagon next to the pastor's bright red Mustang?' I asked Marc.

Feeling Loxley didn't have a lot to offer us, I diplomatically suggested we continue promptly to New Orleans – after breakfast, of course.

'Bloody right,' Marc nodded.

At the crossroads that defined the centre of Loxley we found a fruit stall from which we bought some nuts, oranges and bananas – enough to eat on the road. Then I filled the car with petrol and washed about 300 dead flies off the windscreen.

As I did this, a couple at the opposite pump were arguing. The woman's white hair was so badly bleached it seemed to be made of wire, while her partner wore a cowboy hat and boots. His T-shirt boasted a picture of a stallion being ridden by a spear-holding warrior. When he yelled, it was through missing teeth.

But before I could point them out to Marc, they were kissing and had driven off in a silver Ford Escort that looked the same age as ours. The front licence plate was from Alabama, but the rear was customised; a cartoon Cupid and an arrow-pierced heart, this time with no mention of 'Dixie', but a simple message instead: *Randy & Brenda* ♥♥♥.

For a moment, I felt like staying in Loxley for a little longer, before sense got the better of me and our own Ford began to make its way west again towards the bayous of the Mississippi Delta.

Now only two hours from the scene of one of the biggest hurricane strikes in recent history, I decided to ask Marc's opinion on something I'd been reading about:

'What do you think of the Gaia theory?'

'The what?'

'Gaia,' I repeated, turning down the Pearl Jam album I'd managed to find in Marc's collection – a welcome let-off from yet more technically tight but infinitely annoying heavy metal.

'Gaia? Never heard of him,' he shot back with a tell-tale smirk.

Marc didn't read the same stuff as me that much. He was more into publications like the enthralling *Computational Geosciences* or *The European Journal of Markov Chains* – in the pages of which he was virtually a celebrity.

Gaia was the idea that conditions on earth were maintained by a feedback system, not unlike that of a living organism. I knew Marc would be suspicious, and would say it was all just pop science (after all, I'd first heard about it on a *Surfer* magazine forum), but I wanted to ask him anyway – for entertainment, if nothing else.

The crux of the Gaia idea was that the natural world worked in unison to preserve the temperatures that kept earth inhabitable. Rather than survival of the fittest, it purported that living things, without knowing it, worked together to stay alive. Plants breathing carbons was a big part of the idea, as were rainforests and glaciers, but apparently hurricanes could fit into it as well.

Marc snorted at my first attempt to explain. It was always hard to talk to him about science, because getting the exact terms was near impossible – and if you didn't, he often wouldn't listen to you at all. Sometimes traits like that made me wonder why I bothered keeping in touch with him, but I believed the Marc of old was still in there somewhere – a person who loved the ocean at least as much as me and would be interested in anything to do with it.

I tried again to explain the idea.

'Well I've never heard of it,' he declared dismissively.

'Yes, but you've never heard of lots of things people your age should know about. Coz all you do is read maths and physics papers – or listen to Metallica.'

'So?'

'So. This is quite a popular idea.'

I tried to explain to him the two bits I'd liked best about it. Firstly the way that, if earth were a single living thing, then its 'immune system' might soon decide humankind was a virus. Either the virus would get killed off by the immune system, or it would win out – in which case both disease and host would expire together.

'Well, it sounds like cod science!' Marc grunted.

'Yeah, but the other bit I found interesting was about hurricanes,' I insisted. 'I mean, they could...'

Marc interjected, '... be the spirit of Gaia trying to throw us off the planet? Cosmic antibodies? Utter cack! Total nonsense! Yeah – so by wiping out hundreds of thousands of people in a natural disaster, Gaia is trying to warn us off damaging the environment? What a load of toss!'

'You think? But we do kind of deserve it, don't you reckon? I mean, isn't it a bit spooky how our lifestyle – you know, use of oil, electricity and all that – has led to the rising temperatures that make these storms thrive? It's pretty simple – we abuse the planet and it punishes us for doing so.'

'It's coincidence, son. That's all – simple as that. Things often are.'

The next theory I tried to explain, to while away yet more interstate monotony, was one Marc knew about already. The world's warm and cool water currents ran along very regular, reliable paths, as part of one huge marine circuit or cycle. And oceanographers were now beginning to think hurricanes helped maintain these currents. The role of water on our planet, besides giving life, was to regulate and stabilise weather by maintaining even temperatures. Hurricanes, it was thought, helped this process by stirring up the points where different currents met – kind of like a cog, or an engine driving a conveyor belt.

'We've known that for yonks,' Marc mumbled.

'But that's really, really interesting,' I insisted. 'Humans cause global warming, making hurricanes more powerful...'

'Possibly making hurricanes more powerful – no one knows for sure.'

'Whatever. And probably leading to stronger storms, which if that bit about currents is true, would eventually make the world's weather stable again. Don't you see how brilliant that is? It's all a cycle – a self-regulating dial. It's like an immune system!'

'If you need to think that to understand it, Tom, I'm not standing in your way,' Marc tutted.

At the Betty Ford's full speed of sixty-five miles an hour, conversation was becoming hard work. The engine was deafening, there was no air conditioning and the windows had to be wound down to prevent us dying of heat exhaustion. Although obviously better than sealing yourself in a sun-baked glass box, this still meant you were getting blasted by sticky, humid air the whole time. After ten minutes without talk, Marc, who was spending a lot of time studying his maps, suggested we get off the interstate again at Biloxi – the place Kevin told us to go if we wanted to see some of the damage caused by Katrina. From here a coastal road would cut through a small part of the state of Mississippi to New Orleans.

'You can see the reality of what you've been talking about then,' he added, before another spell of silence.

Within a few miles the wreckage began. The first I saw was a boat that had been picked up by the storm surge and dropped onto a house on the other side of the highway. It was a casino ship that was meant to stay offshore due to gambling restrictions, but Hurricane Katrina obviously didn't care about state laws. After that, every few hundred yards would reveal properties either flattened or under total reconstruction. You could imagine this place looking no different to Florida's coast at one time, but now it had an eerie atmosphere. And I knew this was only the beginning. Before long the destruction had spread to almost every building in sight. Many were being rebuilt, but occasionally you would see houses and hotels that had been destroyed indefinitely. The road was even cut up in places and the trees alongside often torn out at the roots, appearing snapped or smashed out of shape.

After another hour or so, in which we saw the towns of Gulfport and Pass Christian – both of which had been all but annihilated by Hurricane Katrina – we came to a bridge. Marc had feared that it wouldn't be safe, having been dragged into the sea during the storm, but a few miles earlier a sign had confirmed the Bay St Louis Bridge was now in use again.

'That's some power to knock out an entire bridge,' I commented.

'Aye, and some spirit to rebuild it too,' Marc replied.

Arriving back on land, we saw a sign advertising that both the Louisiana state line and New Orleans were getting considerably closer, and then my attention was drawn to another notice. A Stars and Stripes wrapped around a defiant statement: *We've bridged the Bay*!!!

'Good on them,' Marc cheered, as the marshes of the Mississippi estuary's meeting with the Gulf drew near. 'A stunning feat of construction. So much for Gaia! Think these guys are bothered by that nonsense? No way. Good effort, I say. So what happens next? Is Gaia gonna knock the bugger down again?'

He laughed out loud.

CHAPTER FIVE

HURRICANE KATRINA

It seems a strange, even morbid idea to ascribe human names to hurricanes. A name elevates something from a concept into an entity – gives it life and character. A natural disaster with a name suddenly feels like the work of an out-of-control vandal, a barbaric dictator, terrorist or even serial killer (while the ones that send good waves are remembered as saints by surfers who reaped the rewards). With this in mind, I felt a stone in my throat at the sight of a small spray-painted blue line on the steps to the India House hostel (a tidemark, lest we forget), besides which ran this statement:

Katrina woz ere.

No shit.

New Orleans had, since the storm of storms, become almost more famous for the hammering it took at the hands of merciless Hurricane Katrina than for being the spiritual home of jazz – the jewel of the Deep South.

Here was a place that, while the rest of the region struggled with bitter civil rights injustices, had simply fandangoed on through history – playing no small part in the making of Louis Armstrong, one of the greatest black musicians of all time. A man and a city whose music transcended race, while most of the Deep South around it repeatedly voted as right wing as the US political system would let them. New Orleans remained an island of tolerance and bohemian living.

So why on earth did it deserve to get so savaged by first Katrina, and then Rita, within a few short months?

'Simple, son,' Marc exclaimed. 'It's because there's no such fuckin' thing as karma, Gaia, God or 'owt like it. It was simply a case of where the air and water currents at the time sent it.'

'*It*?'

'Yeah – "it". "The Storm", if you want. The meteorological phenomenon that, for record keeping purposes, analysts decided to categorise as "Hurricane Katrina". And anyway, the extent of the damage was nothing to do with the storm's strength – it had already dropped from Cat five to Cat three when *it* made second landfall here in Louisiana.'

Let me explain to you exactly what this disaster – Hurricane Katrina – had meant to the USA. One August a few years ago, an innocuous bit of tropical rain had developed into a powerful storm, which had tracked across the Atlantic before taking a sudden turn and swinging towards Florida. Tropical Storm Katrina had been born. She was upgraded before hitting Florida to become a low-level hurricane, but kept her worst for the Louisiana and Mississippi coasts.

Once in the Gulf of Mexico (and the Loop Current, as I mentioned before), this hurricane suddenly rose to a devastating Category 5 status – the most powerful storm possible. It was only then that the National Hurricane Center began stating a serious concern that the system could be heading towards New Orleans – a place that had always been living on borrowed time from such a threat. This focal point of festivity and collective goodwill was America's most vulnerable coastal city. Slouching on the final estuaries of the mammoth Mississippi River, most of the city was several feet below sea level, and sinking.

Evacuations began, but with little organisation, and many decided to stay put – not trusting the authorities' take on the situation. (False alarms are a regular occurrence in hurricane forecasting.)

This time the storm *was* worth worrying about though. Because New Orleans lies so low, the US Army Corps of Engineers had built a levee system around the city to protect it from such an event – as hurricanes often bring heavy storm surges. But, live on television, the world quickly learned that the levees were painfully inadequate. Although the surge came from the sea, New Orleans flooded from behind – the inland waterway to its north upwelling and spilling onto the city's suburbs. The canal system and levees channelled unprecedented volumes of water into Lake Pontchartrain, which lay just to the north of the city. Once the lake burst its shores the flood defence system failed, and one of America's greatest communities was deluged with filthy water, submerging houses and killing nearly two thousand inhabitants – mostly from the working class and predominantly black residential zones of the Lower Ninth Ward and St Bernard Parish.

Despite the scale of damage done, the only real help (for almost a week) came from either locals with boats, the regional coastguard or a handful of other near and willing parties. Oscar-winning actor Sean Penn, on seeing the desperate television scenes, arrived in town and spent days pulling sick and injured people out of sinking homes. Meanwhile, President Bush and his Cabinet only ever flew over the wreckage at altitude, and were seen to do very little for a community that they knew wouldn't vote for them come hell or – quite literally – high water.

At the time of our arrival the wounds from this event were still deep. While we had been surfing tiny Gulf Coast waves and making our way over to the Big Easy, I learned that a bridge had just collapsed in one of the northern states, Minnesota. The town of Minneapolis in which this happened did have a significant number of Republican voters, which must have been why several senior party officials were at the scene within a day.

'Fuckin' assholes,' cursed a long-haired man, watching this on the news in the lounge of India House hostel. He was in clothes that may or may not have been pyjamas, and his hoarse voice filtered through a mousy brown goatee and moustache that masked his mouth. He took another spoon of the cereal he was eating and continued his rant, mouth full. 'Six people dead in fuckin' Minnesota and they're on the scene in a few hours. Thousands in New Orleans and the pricks don't get here for a frickin' week!'

Having chosen a dormitory bunk and hidden my valuables under the back seats of the Betty Ford, I sat on a beanbag and drew a few deep breaths, inhaling the atmosphere at India House. Marc paced anxiously by the door though, looking at notices in the foyer. I could tell the relaxed pace of this place perturbed him – Marc always needed to be going somewhere or planning something.

After the report finished, I asked the long-haired guy what he was doing here. He was born in Texas, but moved to New Orleans after finishing school 'very young'. He had surfed on and off, too – whenever the right storms had come along. Post Katrina he, like many others, moved away until recovery and repair had been carried out sufficiently to make the place look 'just a little something like the old New Orleans'. In his case San

Diego, California, had been his temporary home. But despite the consistent waves of Del Mar, La Jolla and Black's Beach, Louisiana had remained in his heart.

'How long have you been back?' I asked.

'Since Mardi Gras.'

'But that's only six months ago,' I said. Mardi Gras took place in February. 'That means you moved away for a couple of years!'

'Yeah, dude. It was a fuckin' slow process, man. No help from anyone. Unless you had insurance you had to rebuild yourself from scratch. And I tell ya, how many people d'ya think had insurance in the fuckin' Lower Ninth Ward and St Bernards? Fuckin' no one, man. You think they got the money to worry about shit like that? Nah, man, the real bastards in all this are FEMA. The fuckin' "Federal Emergency Management Agency" or whatever they're meant to be called. Fricken "Federal Rich Motherfuckers in Industry Preservation Agency" you ask me. Most people here ain't ever gotten a dime from Katrina. And they ain't moved back neither. D'ya fuckin' blame them? Although some never left, and still can't.'

Once the guy finished his cereal, the conversation was also clearly over. But, in hostels, silence never lasts long. A tall guy with unbrushed black hair but a freshly shaven face burst through the front door, clearly delighted about something. He was wearing a shiny grey suit, with a crumpled shirt and tie underneath, and a pair of trainers. In his excitement he almost walked straight into Marc.

'Hey, man, howsit goin'?'

Marc replied, smiling. 'All right, mate. Not bad. How are you?'

'Oh man, I'm fuckin' *great*, dude. Just got me a job, right in the French Quarter, just off Canal Street, managing a hotel. It's awesome. Just had my interview now. They want me to start tomorrow. Man, that's fantastic for me. I'm gonna crack open a beer right now. Tell the people who run this place I'm gonna be staying a while.'

This guy was from Missouri, but had moved here because of the employment promises, which oddly enough had got better since the hurricane.

'People gotta start coming again, man. Gotta help this place get back on its feet. Even if it does take twenty years. Since everyone left, there's plenty of work here for anyone. I mean, you guys could get jobs tomorrow if you wanted.'

Marc looked interested. At first I thought it was a noble attempt to be polite, but later, as we drove the Betty Ford south along the arterial Canal Street, destination the French Quarter and live music, he came back to the subject.

'Don't you ever think it though?' he mused. 'I could go home and hide away in my university offices, or we could both just disappear into some Deep South city and work bars, cruising around living from swell to swell.'

'Swell to swell? In the *Deep South*?' I choked 'They only get waves in a hurricane, and then it's pretty much only Florida and Texas that have decent surf.'

'I suppose,' Marc lamented. 'But then again, there's more to life than waves. I'm into this place because of the accents. And who's to say I'd just stay in one city? There's waves all the way up the East Coast, anyway. Oh, I dunno...'

'Dunno what?'

He thought for a moment, and then dismissed the conversation. 'Nothing.'

I found a parking spot just off Frenchman's Street, which would enable us to walk straight into the jazz hub of New Orleans. Marc was right about the accents. They sounded almost musical. I wanted one for myself.

'How am I for parking here?' I asked a passer-by, trying with little success to use what sounded like a local turn of phrase.

'Oh man you should be fine, but I heard those darn attendants are givin out tickets even on Sundays now. Not even the Sabbath is safe, man! What you gotta do is park back up towards Canal Street – in the central business district – around the IRS building or the casino. I can't recall which one but I know it's got free parking on a Sunday.' The man paused for effect. 'Always get 'em mixed up. IRS, casinos, banks – they all laundering money anyway!'

I laughed. 'Too right, mate,' I replied.

Marc had a better idea. 'Let's go in a paid car park. Fifteen dollars of faculty money sees us able to forget this thing until tomorrow. I need a mojito.'

Already the French Quarter was throbbing with music. Lone buskers sat in doorways of closing gift shops, wailing soulfully into the tropical summer air. On Frenchman's Street an eight-man brass band was standing next to a pathway that led over a rail crossing and up to the banks of the Mississippi, their music carrying over the main road and into an outdoor cafe opposite – much to the exasperation of a two-man outfit who had been getting ready to have a jam themselves.

The French Quarter was the original New Orleans, the only part of the city that is any significant height above sea level. It was here that the Mississippi Company (basically a French colonial exercise put together to serve France's interests in the Americas) chose to set up base, naming the new settlement after the Duke of Orleans. The French found this piece of land like an island, rising above the marshes and Mississippi flood plains. They probably never planned on their successors building outwards so far that they'd need levees to keep out water from the surrounding Gulf and Lake Pontchartrain.

As New Orleans turned into one of the New World's major ports, it became heavily involved in the slave trade. However, being run by slightly more lenient French masters (as opposed to downright nasty English and American slave-owners), New Orleans became known as the only US city to allow slaves to meet in public to play their native music. This is how jazz was born – a hybrid of various indigenous African and Caribbean styles.

The streets here were blissfully narrow, making most of the SUVs modern America drove very difficult to use. Architecture was European too. Rustic, colonial buildings, with shutters, wooden doors and fading coloured walls. I was at home here. You couldn't easily imagine one of the lavishly furnished, consumerist apartments portrayed in the New York-, LA- or Boston-based sitcoms existing within these structures. Instead I pictured the dusty, mildewed extremes of Henry Miller or Tennessee Williams stories, siesta culture and quaint European family scenes. This place was frankly not America as I'd ever known or envisioned it.

The streets were filling rapidly, so to get away for a moment from the bustle, and additional heat of the crowds, we strolled past the brass band, exposed beers in hand (which is supposed to be illegal in America), to have a look at the gigantic Mississippi river estuary on which the early settlers had been so dependent. Hundreds of yards wide, its banks were New Orleans's downtown waterfront.

What a river, I thought. You could boat halfway up the North American continent from here. This close to finally entering the ocean, it looked more like a shipping lane. The mighty Mississippi certainly had no equal back in measly Great Britain. Barges and other boats roamed freely with plenty of space. There was a feeling of dormant energy – as if the estuary were half asleep or basking, relaxed and confident in its wisdom and old age. Despite the volumes of moving water, it was a calm scene.

Nicknamed 'Old Man River', I imagined how important this passage of water must have been back in the early growth of the

New World. But then it occurred to me that when the bugger decided to flood, it could often take back much of the civilisation it had given life to. To our east, as night fell, I could see a building that looked like a dockyard warehouse, wrecked, just like the properties in Gulfport and Biloxi. Katrina had been here too, I remembered. With all the vitality on show, it was hard to imagine these streets, tranquil, trusty and decorated, but several metres deep in flood water.

We finished our beers and walked back to the noise and the people. I knew this was only a small part of the city, but the nucleus from which it planned to regain its status, its character. Tomorrow we would see another side to this wounded community, but for now you couldn't help but let the music take you.

Already a genre of music I'd never much cared for had found its way into my heart. But that was because it didn't sound anything like the pretentious, metronomic interpretation of jazz that you'd hear in bars at home. This music shook, jumped and bumped wherever it wanted to go. Its energy was constant, infernal and contagious. Bars were so hectic you felt almost guilty ordering drinks from frantic staff, while the streets filled to where you couldn't move without pushing people.

The tunes were so omnipotent you were pretty much breathing jazz. Some bars played their own from juke boxes and others had small two- or three-piece bands of their own. Others simply kept their doors open wide to let the street sounds in.

The music of New Orleans is truly its heartbeat – an electric charge that can be felt all around. The shaking, rocking, helplessly conductive sound of superbly ad-libbed, traditional jazz makes it easy to suddenly find yourself awake at four in the morning and still not even considering lying down to rest. The most popular clubs in the French Quarter were long sold out, but the streets were the place to be anyway.

I kept looking at every bar for one called 'Jimmy's'. One of my all-time favourite albums, Sublime's *40 oz to Freedom*, had plugged it in the thanks dub on the last track. It legitimised the place for me – to know that a band so well known among surfers had come here too and played. Oddly enough, that was one of the few surf bands Marc had liked, too.

I knew without asking that the music we were hearing right now was blowing his mind – even if it wasn't anything like Metallica. His face said it all.

The eight musicians we'd seen on the way to the riverbanks were now on Frenchman's Street, attracting a large crowd. I pushed towards the front as one of the band began singing in that husky tone of the great Satchmo himself, while all but the two drummers took a break to wipe their brows and drink water. Even when the music took a rest, it was still there – the percussion rolling for a minute, as the rest of the band readied themselves for another burst of flowing brass sound. Next to me were the cops who, content they'd now safely closed the street to cars, were enjoying a quick break of their own. I couldn't imagine their night's work being that testing around here – there was plenty of love in the air. You could smell it, smoothly blended into the humid night and its other aromas of spicy soups, street grills and alcoholic spirits.

As much as for the band, the crowd were gathering to see a small black boy with tight curly hair, dressed in a shirt, waistcoat and dicky bow. Red umbrella in his left hand and a whistle between his teeth, the boy cleared a circle in which to dance. At first he began lightly swaying, tuning in to the rhythm of the band, and then, with a quick twist, he dropped into the splits, flicked the umbrella through the air, and began to move instinctively to the rolling tunes of the band – every member was now playing again together. One moment the trumpets led, and then the percussion, but whatever the sound, the kid was in perfect sync.

Hoots and whistles of appreciation fired out from the crowd, and the boy upped his dancing. 'C'mon lady, c'mon!' he called, pulling at the hand of a passer-by who reacted as if she'd just been invited to dance with a megastar instead of a ten-year-old.

The band's bucket was filling with dollar bills. I looked at the individual members: elderly men, black men, white men, youngsters. The musical connection between the members ran deep – instinctively they knew where to go next, when to solo, to stop playing, to clap hands or sing. It was so infectious even the crowd could feel it. If you'd given me a trumpet right then I could have sworn I'd have been able to start playing it.

A double-bass player was holding the band's next movement together as the boy released the woman back into the crowd, blowing his whistle and pirouetting. Two of the players' T-shirts bore topical messages. One was a picture of a man armed to the teeth with a grin on his face and a speech bubble which read: 'Katrina: Great day for a hurricane'. The other said 'FEMA evacuation policy: Swim goddamn you!'

Somehow, the vibrations of the brass and percussion had completely nullified Katrina's ability to put fear into you. The T-shirts weren't in bad taste – they were defiant, proud. As if to say, 'take another shot, Katrina, we *dare* you!'

Just as riding waves could wipe my soul clear of problems, the music of New Orleans was doing the same for its followers. People were simply lost in it.

On our way back to Lopez Street, and India House, late at night and a good mile out of the French Quarter, we saw another two kids who'd attracted a much thinner bunch of onlookers. The dancer had no waistcoat this time, but crushed Coke cans duct-taped to his shoes so that he could tap. His friend played a trumpet, while those still brave enough to be walking the streets occasionally dropped quarters instead of bills onto the rag laid down as a money coffer. They obviously had less talent, but I still admired their entrepreneurship. Away from the French Quarter, with nothing to compare themselves to, it was worth a go.

Marc gave them a twenty dollar bill.

'Thanks mister!' the dancer yelled as we walked briskly by, barely even making eye contact.

'No worries,' Marc called back, before turning to me and looking up the road. 'How far is Lopez Street now?' he enquired. I knew what he was thinking. It was late, dark, empty and he was throwing money on the floor in a city we'd been told to treat as a crime-ridden hellhole.

It didn't matter though. Like he had said before, it was all about attitude, and tonight ours had been spot on. Buoyed by the night's sounds and energy we kept walking, and made it home, unsurprisingly, without any trouble.

'As I knew we would,' said Marc. 'Now all we need is for the car to still be there in the morning.'

Savaged by mosquitoes and sweating, I didn't stay asleep much later than about 7.30 the next day. Marc was already up and reading what looked like an academic paper of some kind, which seemed brave after the quantity of alcohol he had drunk the night before. Around us, the rest of the dorm snored and dreamed. There was a thick air of beer breath around, and I had a headache.

'Son, I hate dorms,' Marc whispered. 'Tonight, I'm sleeping in the car instead.'

I suggested he'd feel better after breakfast and coffee.

The long-haired Texan-Louisianan was sitting, half awake, in the lounge as we tiptoed through. Rhythmically, he gently pushed the rocking chair on which he sat.

'Hey man,' he nodded to me. 'What a night, huh. The kinetic energy is still in the air. Can you feel it?'

'Yeah, sure. Er, we're going for breakfast,' I told him. 'D'you wanna come?'

'Not this time, man, but go around the corner, head down Canal for about two blocks and just next to Rick's Pawn you'll find this little cafe... I forget the name. Awesome pancakes. Two dollars.'

I thanked him, and walked out into a muggy and already sickeningly warm Monday morning. 'He's changed his tone,' I commented to Marc.

'Cause he's off his bloody 'ead, that's why.'

With that assessment taken into account should we have been surprised that there was no 'Rick's Pawn', no cafes and nowhere to get breakfast within walking distance on Canal Street at that time? Perhaps not.

'Fruit loop,' muttered Marc. 'Nice guy though. I do like him.'

I couldn't walk into town again, not in this heat and with a head like mine. So we were forced to eat a McMuffin, hot cakes and syrup from a McDonald's two blocks away. Things must have been desperate, as Marc usually wouldn't even walk along the same side of the street as a pair of golden arches. Unlike me – I loved their food, often to the exasperation of fellow travellers. I knew it was hypocritical of me, supposedly being into ethical issues, buying fair trade where I could, and even writing about that stuff from time to time. But then again, I supposed, you had to moderate too – everyone was human and Big Macs were tasty.

Their breakfasts weren't bad either, as Marc reluctantly agreed through a mouthful of food and a swig of coffee.

'If you're gonna get McCaught-out though, son, then brekkie is the best time,' he admitted. 'This shit is actually edible. Although don't get me wrong. It's still minging and we're only here coz I got a bloody hangover, and there's like a mile of thirty-five degree humidity between us and the car.'

'Whatever you say,' I grinned. He'd made as much of a concession as his pride would let him. 'I'll have you in a Starbucks yet,' I added, 'and then we can go to church too.'

The silence he replied with made me squirm, so I changed the subject.

'Hey – wanna look for that Jimmy's place again?'

We didn't have to walk that whole mile, which was just as well as it would have probably killed us anyway. Thankfully Mr Missouri saved us, as he dashed off to the first day of work in his new life as a local of *N'Awlins*.

'Have a good night?' he asked as small talk.

'Yeah,' I replied, even smaller.

In the passenger seat of his 1993 Volvo estate sat a young-looking guy, who pitched in his own ice-breaker:

'Where you guys from?'

'Wales,' Marc said with pride.

'Sick. I'm headed there in December,' he responded – with an Australian accent. 'Or even sooner once I get the sack this morning.'

'The sack?'

'Yeah – meant to be in work at eight, but only woke up at nine. Fifth time this month. Worth it though. Frenchman's was going off last night, eh.'

We were at our car.

'Good luck,' I wished the Aussie, before thanking Mr Missouri for the lift.

'Not at all, dude, not at all.'

And then the Volvo pulled off, leaving us to walk into the car park in search of the Betty Ford.

As I spotted its dusty rear bumper from between two bigger vehicles, Marc stopped walking.

'I tell you what, let's not bother getting the car now. I'm not into sleeping in that dorm again. How about we go for another walk around the French Quarter and then get going. You know, back towards the surf, like. We're not gonna top last night anyway, so why try?'

I didn't object. He had a point. That was one good thing about travelling with Marc – he made choices early, and clearly. I wondered whether that trait would suit the no-ties life of a drifter, if his comments the night before had been in any way serious. Without waves, or definite places to be, Marc got restless very quickly. It hadn't happened yet on this trip – but we both knew it would eventually.

'Let's get lunch somewhere loud,' he suggested, 'and then hit the road.'

'Jimmy's?'

'If it exists.'

I was now starting to think we'd only find it by asking someone. But I was convinced the place would probably turn out to be really famous – somewhere everyone apart from us had heard of – and that I'd therefore look a complete tool in the process. Asking wasn't an option. We looked around for it one last time and saw no sign of it, before giving up and sitting at the same open-air cafe at which two musicians had been brutally trumped, pre-gig, by that eight-piece brass band last night. The pair had returned again today, and they were actually quite good. The guitarist wore a metal slide on his finger which he put to work on a well-loved twelve-string, while singing in a deep, incomprehensible voice. They were more melancholy than what we'd heard last night, but held the audience on their every note all the same.

Unfortunately though, storm clouds gathered within two songs, promptly turning into a burst of rain that canned their little performance yet again. We had a flimsy parasol above our table, which completely failed to keep us dry – although neither of us minded. Soaked to the skin was better than dying of heatstroke.

Filled with gumbo soup – a local blend of shellfish and peppers sumptuously spiced to almost weapons-grade – we started on a winding route back towards the car, via downtown.

By day the French Quarter was full of tourists and shops selling tat – usually voodoo toys. Voodoo was also part of New Orleans's heritage, journeying out of Africa with the slaves, to the Caribbean and then flourishing in Haiti. One of voodoo's most powerful women ever, Marie Laveau, was native to the city during the nineteenth century – hence the presence of a museum dedicated to her (which was still struggling to recover from the months of uncertainty that followed Hurricane Katrina).

One shop was also selling books on the storm itself which, along with the promise of yet more air conditioning, was enough to get me through the doors. I decided to ask the thin, short-haired black woman in her early forties behind the counter if she thought it would be appropriate for us to drive through one of the damaged areas on our way out. She lowered her oblong glasses and looked at me, firm but friendly.

'Appropriate? I'd say it's *essential*,' she replied.

Feeling awkward, I moved eye contact away from her, to the books again.

'This one's the best one; paints the most accurate picture of what went on,' said the woman, moving over and lifting up *Hurricane Katrina: The One We Feared*. The book's cover showed a 'before' and 'after' photo of the city – bird's eye view. I was drawn to the image of the Superdome, the 70,000-seater stadium that was home to the New Orleans Saints NFL team.

'Is that dirt?' I asked, looking at the patches on the roof in the 'after' photo. 'Or is it...'

'No – the roof got ripped off in several places. By the winds. You know, that was the worst wind damage I heard about from Katrina – the rest was caused by the flood. If you do decide to check it out, then you gotta also drive through Biloxi, Pass Christian, Gulfport – that whole coast. They were where the centre of the storm hit – lot of people don't know that. Katrina actually missed New Orleans.'

I told her we'd seen those places already.

'OK – that's good! So you saw what the hurricane did. Now you gotta go around the Lower Ninth Ward to see what *mankind* did – with a little help from a storm surge...'

'Mankind?'

'Yeah. You think pouring the Gulf of Mexico over the poorest people in Louisiana was a natural disaster? Uh, uh. It was man-made. You gotta look at who made the levees, why those people were chosen to make the levees, and a whole load of other questions. Here. I'd better check that book out for ya. Sounds like you need it.'

You had to love that Deep South accent. It made every voice warm, friendly, hypnotic.

She took *The One We Feared* off me and scanned it. A price of eleven dollars rang into the till, which began printing noisily. She began writing directions on the back of the receipt.

'So you best start off out by the Lake Pontchartrain. Head up Canal Street, pass the cemetery and then you need to find Lakeshore Drive. Got that? *Lakeshore.*' She opened my newly purchased book and showed me a photograph of a sign bearing the name of that street, submerged in flood water right up to a few inches below the words.

'That's what it looked like up there during the hurricane. You'll see how big a rise that is when you get there. Once you check that out, head east and then cut back into the residential areas. You'll see it all soon enough.'

'So what happened to you during Katrina?' I asked, hoping it wasn't an intrusive question.

She had no problem replying.

'Well, I was lucky coz I missed the storm. I got outta town earlier than most of the other people. Went to Houston, Texas; stayed with my cousins. It was a year and two months before I returned though.'

'Wow. Did you lose your house, then?'

'Yeah,' she smiled back.

'Yes?'

'Yeah. I lost everything. No insurance neither. Not that it'd have meant shit – everyone got screwed by the insurance companies anyway. But that's life. I was lucky. Thing is the French Quarter was fine and the looters left the shop alone so I still had my business, although losing almost two years' trade was hard. I had to return, though.'

'For the shop?'

'I guess, but also for New Orleans. We have to get the city up and running again. If you lived here your whole life you'd soon see why it can't be let to jus' drop off the face of the earth – like *some* might like it to.'

Who those *some* were I didn't want to ask, but they wouldn't be getting their wish – not considering the strength and resolve shown by the people we had met.

'You know,' she said, in a dreamy tone. 'I can't really complain about my situation. Not when you see what happened to a lot of other people who lived with me in St Bernard. I mean, I got my health, my sanity. What more can you ask for? I save my pity for the people who had to sit in that wretched Superdome...'

'The Superdome?'

'Yeah. I knew people who were in there and it sounded like the apocalypse! First, they took all the drugs and medication people had off them before they went in – so schizophrenics and all sorts were running wild in there. People were killed in that goddamn Superdome I tell you, sir.'

'Killed?'

'Yeah. Mugged, stabbed – and worse!'

'Weren't the police overseeing the whole thing?'

'From up on the second level, yeah. Jus' pointing their guns down and telling people to keep still. They were way too scared to go down there and try to sort out problems themselves. There was so much panic in there. And it was hot too which, when you think about the fact there were no working washrooms, ain't pretty. No food, no water. People I spoke to genuinely thought they were going in there to die. In fact, a lot refused to go there and stayed in their flooded homes instead. Which pissed the rescue workers off – hell, in some cases they stopped delivering food and water to people who refused to leave their houses.

'I knew early though. If this thing hits it's gonna be Armageddon. That's why I decided *Armageddon outta here*! Took three changes of clothes with me to Houston, and ended up staying six months. Coz then Rita flooded the city again. I tell you, our luck was *out* that year.'

This was the flipside to the treat some other residents of the Gulf – the surfers – had talked about so nostalgically. In one year three hurricanes – Katrina, Rita and Wilma – had marched, or rather spun, into the record books as some of the most powerful in known history. It was the year of the tropical storm; more hurricanes than ever, more landfalls, record-breaking wind speeds and two horrific hits on New Orleans in one month.

People had died, while others had surfed. I hadn't really given this stuff much thought when, in the rains of a South Wales summer washout (which at the time seemed a rough hand to have drawn), I decided to go storm chasing with Marc.

Storm chasing? That wasn't really what we were doing was it? We were only thinking about the swells that came off them. This was a bit of a wake-up call for us both.

And one that wasn't over yet, either.

Marc, for the first time on the trip, decided to drive the Betty Ford. 'You navigate,' he said.

We left the parking lot on the northern outskirts of the French Quarter, and took a right up Canal Street. The Louisiana Superdome passed by quickly to our left, its white roof gleaming, new and strengthened, in the afternoon light. No evidence of the horrors we'd heard about; instead just box office booths selling pre-season Saints tickets, or passes to the Hall of Fame. Both seemed more inviting to me than where we were about to go, but I knew we owed it to the place to see this with our own eyes.

As Canal Street took us further out of town, I noticed several of the buildings derelict, or under construction. On the way in to the city yesterday, my eyes had been so fixed on the road that this stuff had escaped me.

I looked at the map resting on the dashboard. 'OK, so Canal Street will turn into Canal Boulevard by the cemetery,' I said.

This whole area had been completely underwater after Katrina, including the graves (we were right on the location of one of the biggest levee breaches).

'Man, imagine someone got buried like a day before Katrina,' said Marc. 'That soil would have taken water like a box of Kleenex. Coffin full of stinkin' flood run-off. I read about all the sewers bubbling up around here, too – that's the stuff we don't think about when you deluge a city with sea- and lake-water. The whole sanitary system gets blown out. You drink from the taps back at India house?'

I had.

'I did too – but then someone's got to eh?' Marc looked a different man behind the wheel of the Betty Ford. More relaxed. In control rather than just staring at the map and plotting routes, or waiting for chances to correct my general knowledge.

Once we'd gone under another freeway bridge, the storm damage had spread from sporadic to total. Houses levelled – sometimes destroyed even beyond the foundations, which had been lifted or washed away by the surge. Neon-lit motel signs blown out, a gas station boarded up, Shell logo ripped off its post and the pumps covered with plastic refuse bags. Behind a plastic sheet you could just make out an old sign: 'We do five-minute oil changes. Storm season is here; be prepared now'.

On Lakeshore Drive itself several of the houses were new. Rebuilt by the owners whose insurance had paid up. I felt angry thinking about that – companies welching on paying out insurance after something like this was inexcusable. The beauty for insurers is that a natural disaster can lead to all sorts of get-out clauses for people who didn't take out the top-drawer packages: Act of God, flood exemption, even negligence if they looked hard enough. I knew these were the lucky few, and that in the poorer neighbourhoods where the less scrupulous insurance brokers peddled their trade, there would be a lot less reconstruction going on.

Here, besides the US flags, home-made billboards on stakes driven into the ground displayed statements of pride, and recovery:

Coming home!

We've rebuilt!

But in one instance:

Empty and for sale.

Some had trailers parked outside, which families were living in while their properties got repaired and rebuilt. Other houses were being placed on stilts, so if there was a 'next time' the water might run underneath instead.

A couple of miles further over we crossed into those less affluent neighbourhoods, heading south again towards St Bernard and the Lower Ninth Ward – the places that hadn't had the same opportunities for evacuation and recovery. Skeleton warehouses lined France Road, alongside ruined shopping malls. More rubble followed, which was once someone's home – a veranda in tatters. The residents had moved to a caravan with a lifebelt tied cautiously to the rear.

Public, private and state notices were everywhere: on lamp posts and roadside fences. Their tone was rather different:

**House levelling. $999.00 – any one-storey
blocked-beam property: Call 1.800.203.FLAT!**

No loitering.

NO TRESPASSING!

You're *not* crazy: 1-800-729-T-A-L-K.

We are back – The Abundant Life Church.

**Make levees not war – Get the Republicans
out of Louisiana for EVER!**

**Do *you* know your HIV status? No needles – just
confidential results in 30 mins.**

Some of the empty and abandoned properties had been spray-painted with even more macabre statements, which nobody had yet bothered to erase. 'Has been searched,' or 'Dead body inside'.

The vastness of the damage done by the Katrina and Rita floods was beyond what two young men from a small European seaside town could process. Perspective must have been so hard to hold onto during those first few desperate days, in the ruthless sun, while all around disease-ridden water washed away everything precious. Wherever you looked, people's livelihoods had simply been destroyed. The basic infrastructure of what had once been a fully developed North American city was all under repair – roads, cables, landscaping, roofs – everything. Next to uprooted trees, fly-tippers had been busy leaving fridges, microwaves, televisions and other household items.

The golden arches of a McDonald's sign were ripped back to their skeleton, and the building's doors pulled off. A row of basic condos appeared in our vision with HELP still painted outside the top windows. This was how many had died – racing the floodwater up to top floors and attics, only to get trapped and to drown in the filthy, lukewarm surge.

Every few blocks we would come within sight of another canal. These were all part of the flood defences and run-off system that had failed once Katrina's raised sea levels had pushed Lake Pontchartrain to bursting point.

As Marc drove, I looked again at some of the accounts in the book we had bought back in the French Quarter.

'Hurricanes,' said an interviewee for the foreword, 'often come out of Africa, like our ancestors. They then make their way through the Caribbean, just like the slaves did, before ending up in the southern United States. There has to be something spiritual about that route – God is trying to tell us something, although I don't know what.'

I didn't, either. This was too much. My mind had started to imagine the water pouring down the streets, over everything. Instead of life, refreshment, cleansing, it had taken on a sinister, depraved personality. I began thinking about how much we were at the mercy of the planet's oceans, and for the first time it felt wrong. I'd always loved the idea of being so insignificant, but that might have been from a naïve belief that perhaps the sea held some sort of affinity for me, that the ocean was benevolent.

Not at all. How had I managed to think that for so long?

What we had seen this afternoon was cruel; as simple as that.

★　★　★

'We're still totally in harm's way,' I remembered a plump man telling me back at Satchmo Fest the night before, the usual Louisiana smile welded to his face. 'So we might as well enjoy this way of life while it lasts. Coz next time it'll all be gone. The French Quarter, the business district – the whole darn lot.'

'D'you think?' I had asked, wanting to hear more.

'Think, sir? I know! Buddy, are you aware what kind of storm Hurricane Katrina was?'

'A Category five hurricane, the most powerful there is,' I replied.

'Now, you see, that's what most people say. But it ain't right. Back when it was over the Loop Current it might'a made Cat five, yeah.'

It was amazing the detail of knowledge residents of New Orleans had acquired since the disaster. The Loop Current? I'd not expected anyone but Marc to tell me about something like that.

'Yeah, out to sea she was a nasty piece of work,' the man repeated. 'But Katrina never came ashore as Cat five. No way. She was a three at best – a weak three. They get those things running aground in Florida all the time. But here, that's a different story.'

He took a bite of chilli-cleansed pepperoni pizza before continuing. 'And I'll tell ya what else. This ain't no secret neither. Katrina *missed us* anyway. Ya hear that. She missed us. The eye of the storm hit Biloxi dead on, not N'Awlins. No, sir, we got all but wiped out – the oldest and bestest city in the United States – by the *storm surge* from a hurricane we was *supposed* to be protected from. I ain't never gonna believe the Man from now on. We weren't safe then, and we ain't safe now.'

Typical of New Orleans, he went from delivering grave information about horrific events to revelling and enjoying life in merely the turn of a sentence.

'The music's good tonight – you boys are lucky to see this one. Lot of the good eight-pieces ain't out that often these days. Good for y'all to see N'Awlins is still alive. Tell others to *spread the word*!'

Minutes later, the man was dancing in the street – lost to the sound of that infectious, everlasting music.

CHAPTER SIX

OFF-TRACK

Republic of Cape Verde (Portugal), Atlantic Ocean, 500 miles west of the African Mainland.
Pressure: 1028 mb. Hot, hot, hot – and calm.

My Dad once told me about Cabo Verde. He went there before I was born, on a renegade surf mission with a couple of halfwit mates who knew nothing more than the name of the airport before arriving. They went, he thinks, in the month of February. 'Sharky', barren and windy – that was his verdict, from a memory that doesn't often miss much out.

By the time I'd got into wave hunting myself, a lot more was known about Cape Verde and its significance in surfing circles. Going there was not necessary – it could still have its effect on me, especially if I was on the Right Coast come late summer: desert climate, in the middle of the ocean. Who would want to be exposed to the elements anyway? In midsummer that meant heat and stillness until the first tropical weather front of the year at least. Once that arrived, things moistened a little, before the rains bore west. Most of these fronts got caught in complicated 'shear' processes, getting absorbed into the Bermuda or Azores High – the predominant weather system of the North Atlantic.

But occasionally, in just the right (or wrong) conditions, tropical squalls or thunderstorms could become something else – something worth paying attention to throughout the Atlantic Basin. And the hotter and calmer the preceding days, the more that 'something else' could intensify. Anticipating that event – the early formation of a tropical cyclone – had always been a high-stakes game. If such conditions showed up from July onwards, monitoring of this area would always be the top priority of the US National Hurricane Center.

What would it have been worth to Marc and me to know that, as we had been sleeping off that night out in New Orleans, one of their data planes was now taking its first serious flight of the year across the Cape Verde islands? That it was taking particular interest in a persistent pattern of showers and thunder, just west, over a very warm patch of Atlantic water?

Would it have made us do anything different? Who's to know? The rapid changes in Atlantic air pressure would get our attention soon enough – even before they named it Dean.

THE CAROLINAS AND NEW YORK

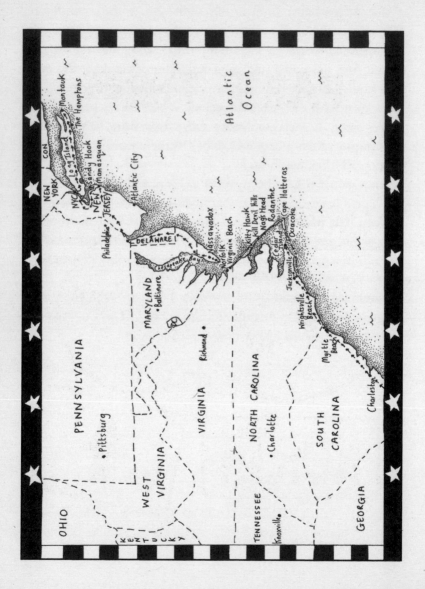

PART THREE

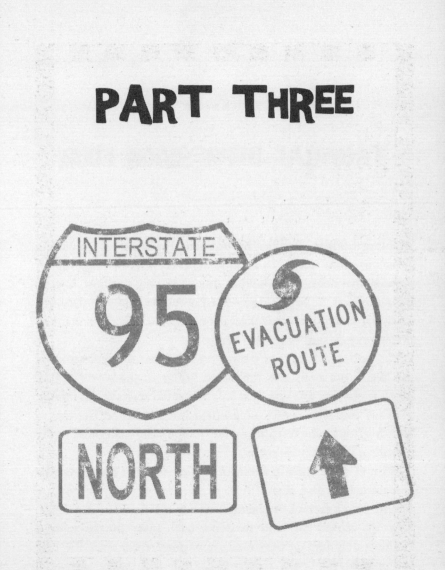

CHAPTER SEVEN

TROPICAL DEPRESSION FOUR

Building bridges (in the physical sense at least) is something Americans have always been good at. Everywhere you go there's a bridge that holds some kind of unique record: thinnest, lowest, highest, safest, riskiest, oldest – least necessary. They all deserved a title for helping us cross the various expanses of water that had made forays inland from the oceans.

The northern exit road from New Orleans, we were told by the key to our map, was the *longest* bridge in the world. Of all possible plaudits that was an accolade that did seem worth noting. Halfway over you could see nothing but buttressed freeway to both horizons, which made me feel temporarily marooned in the middle of Lake Pontchartrain.

'Want to drive again in a minute?' Marc asked. 'I'll pick out the best route back east, then.'

'OK,' I said, feeling like being back behind the wheel anyway.

As we waited for land to come back onto the horizon, I couldn't help feeling nervous at how powerful a force the lake had once been.

'I suppose this bridge was down after the storm too?' I commented to Marc.

'Yeah, it was. Most were. Good it's up and running again though, eh?'

I had the impression a real priority had been made of restoring bridges. They were surely one of most complicated aspects of the reconstruction job, and yet every one we had seen had been rebuilt and was flowing with traffic.

Back on dry land, after swapping seats and refuelling the car, Marc reckoned that there might be a short cut back to the main freeway if we went towards the more thinly populated towns of Mandeville and Chinchuba.

Besides getting fuel, it had also been time for me to change the first spark plug of the trip. This was an amazing feat considering my stepfather Dave had expected one to go every two or three hundred miles. Then again, given the ease of the interstate systems, the Betty Ford had basically been asked to go in one straight line so far, so I decided to blame Marc's driving.

'Funny how it finally starts misfiring the minute you get behind the wheel,' I said.

He didn't reply. It was so hot where we had stopped that it took all our energy just to concentrate on being able to see straight. By the time I walked to the rest room to wash the black engine oil out of my fingernails, I was so covered in sweat you would think I had just been swimming. Inside the service station the air conditioning moved over me in waves as my head throbbed.

Away from the coast, Deep South heat was a daunting prospect.

It didn't let up in the slightest as the afternoon passed away. With Baton Rouge dropping behind us to our west, open windows offered no relief at all against the humidity. Today's drive was an endurance exercise – eased only slightly by the Louis Armstrong cassette I'd picked up for eighty cents in one of the French Quarter's small markets.

We passed several roadside outlets, and each time I felt like stopping just to wander through an air-conditioned building again. The Tangier Mall claimed from the roadside to have over fifty outlets, including: Linens 'n things, Football Fever and J J Maxx. I remembered what Jonathan Raban had said about American department stores in *Hunting Mr Heartbreak*, one of my favourite books. He thought they were places where you were 'taught the social values of the age', but right now all my imagination could do was turn them into wide, high-roofed emporiums with perfectly chilled atmospheres. Somehow, Marc had managed to get to sleep, but I woke him at the sight of a prison.

'Wow,' he mumbled. 'You'd be tamping if you got sent to jail here. Imagine the yard – must be like a fuckin' sauna. Even light exercise could probably lead to a heart attack in the heat. Then again, I'd probably prefer a heart attack to doing a stint in there.'

Around us the landscape was flat, plain and, today at least, bone dry. This was the Mississippi flood plain. We passed a large factory, and a lone billboard for a 'workers comp' scheme. Not long after that we saw an army compound, before the trees began rising up either side of the road, masking the Katrina-ravaged areas we'd seen on the coastal road in. This highway would now run dead straight, all the way to the Atlantic Ocean – if we could keep driving for long enough.

Five more hours had been enough time in the car for one day though. Once we'd made it back into Florida, the heat and the energy of New Orleans the night before sent me into a sticky slumber – one which lasted eleven hours.

It was nearing midday the next morning when I wandered out of a motel room into yet more fierce sunshine, thinking only of strong coffee and getting ready to kill yet another day without waves or rumours of waves.

That, though, was when we realised it was time to make some important decisions.

After breakfast, Marc went online again, flagging up the following:

```
FOR THE NORTH ATLANTIC - CARIBBEAN SEA AND
THE GULF OF MEXICO
A VIGOROUS TROPICAL WAVE HAS EMERGED FROM
AFRICA OVER THE FAR EASTERN ATLANTIC OCEAN.
CONDITIONS APPEAR FAVORABLE FOR GRADUAL
DEVELOPMENT OF THIS SYSTEM - AND A TROPICAL
DEPRESSION COULD FORM DURING THE NEXT DAY OR
TWO AS IT MOVES WESTWARD AT 15 TO 20 MPH.
```

He told me his verdict immediately.

'Now *that* has every chance of being the real deal. It's absolutely bang in the middle of Hurricane Alley. I'm not sure what the winds around it will do, but it's over the warmest patches of water, and if it moves west it'll continue to be fuelled pretty much the whole way. We should be ready for this one to do anything.'

'What are you saying?' I said. 'Are we likely to get caught out here?'

'What d'you mean "caught out"?'

'Stuck too far from the beach when a storm appears.'

'Bloody hell. Don't let anyone in New Orleans hear you talk like that. "Caught out" in the case of a major hurricane usually means stuck *on* the coast!'

'You know what I mean.'

'Yeah, I do. And no, we won't. We're not far at all from the right places anyway. And it has to become a tropical storm before it gets named. Only then will it start to produce swell. We've got time.'

Again, a low pressure would be just another bit of swell, nothing more. But give it a name, call it a tropical storm instead, and I had the feeling every surfer on the coast would suddenly be looking ahead in anticipation – canning work, family or romantic engagements.

'OK – so what's your advice then?' I asked, seeing as we didn't yet have that oh-so-special name to follow. 'Where shall we go?'

'Well – it's anyone's guess.'

'I see.' It was unusual for Marc to say things like this. I'd become a little dependent on him to make the calls. Seeing his expertise seem in any way fallible was a bit like the first time a parent tells you they don't know the answer to something – it's just not what you need, or want, to hear. But I admired the way he could seem so confident, correct and full of himself, before just casually admitting he was winging it at times.

He went on to explain it was the weather patterns that were unpredictable though: 'That system could do anything from where it is. But if a tropical depression did form in the East Atlantic...'

'We'd be on for good surf?' This was all I wanted to know.

'Good surf? Just slightly. If it tracked the right way, we'd be looking at some of the best waves we've ever seen in our lives.'

Finally an answer I liked the sound of.

I had the idea we should just head straight west before waiting on the next bulletin – which I anticipated would be Marc's favoured plan too.

'Well,' he said, 'you may think that, but the Outer Banks would be one of the best places to be if good surf came along. And that would only mean angling north just a little. But for being in striking distance of everywhere, we shouldn't go much further up than that. Until we see what the swell's doing, of course. We can always change direction if we need to.'

It all sounded very random. But it wasn't. As I said before, our course had been set for us months ago – by another party, who was yet to properly exist. He would, though. The fertile ocean was beginning its conception process, and with it our trip's purpose would soon sharpen.

We arrived back on the coast at Savannah, Georgia. It turned out to be a nine-hour drive when we tried to cut across the state via Valdosta, during which Marc decided our route by using a classic – and perennially reassuring method – the coin flip.

'Right, we've got Florida and North Carolina. Which one's heads?'

'North Carolina,' I said. He tweaked the coin a few inches into the air, before dropping it down the side of his seat. Clumsiness came naturally to Marc at times.

'Got to read it where it lies,' he insisted, squirming almost upside down to look at the coin. 'It's tails. That's Florida isn't it?' He sounded a bit dismayed at the result.

'Best of three,' I said.

'No – it can't be best of three. That's basically saying you don't want to go to Florida. If you flip a coin to make a choice but end up realising you wished it had landed the other side, then you know what you wanted to do anyway.'

There was a pause.

'So best of three, then?' I said.

'Aye. All right,' he laughed, before reaching for the coin and flipping it again.

'It's Florida again. How about best of five?'

A few miles further up the road, Marc proposed going straight across Georgia as a compromise: 'There's a road coming up that will do that,' he said, peering again at our map. 'We get to the coast about a third of the way between Florida and the Carolinas. We can look online again then and go wherever we fancy.'

This sounded reasonable. It didn't matter that it was dark when we got there, after nine hours of near constant driving, or that we couldn't find anywhere to stay and ended up getting a rough night's sleep by the roadside.

Still waiting for swell, our mornings were getting slower by the day. The tiredness didn't help either. Again, all I could think of to start with was coffee – a dependence I knew would take hold sooner or later here. At home I rarely drank the stuff, but every time I'd ever been to the US or Canada my love of caffeine would flourish.

It had been a lazy start in central Florida yesterday, but now we were waking much nearer to the Atlantic Ocean, with minds firmly set on getting about the business that had brought us here – good surf could be just days away.

This was a small town called Darien, which immediately reminded me of Loxley, Alabama – so much so that I questioned if New Orleans and the rest had really happened at all.

This was a problem I'd noticed with living on the road. Things passed so quickly that you struggled to retain their significance. Already the people we'd met in the last few days were impossible to recall with any empathy.

'That's what happens here,' said Marc. 'Life runs so smoothly people don't think about what's going on in other states thousands of miles away – even if it is meant to all be the same country. I mean – look at this place. When you wake up here everyday does it matter what goes on in the rest of the world?'

Darien was a small, well-organised town of criss-cross roads, cute houses and a main street filled with every shop you could ever need. Tall trees surrounded the shady residential streets, which probably catered for people who worked in either Savannah to our north or Brunswick, the next city south. The 4x4s were as pestilent as they had been in Loxley. In the car park of the town's superstore, the Betty Ford was dwarfed by yet more F-350s, Dodge Rams – all the usual suspects.

This was probably the reason why, for a town about half the size of where I lived in Wales, Darien had three times more filling stations. There was also a gun shop and several pawnbrokers. My favourite thing about Darien, though, was the name of the supermarket where we bought breakfast: Piggly Wiggly. There were diners on the main street, but none were open. The town seemed oddly tranquil considering its proximity to the interstate.

I drove along the main street and came to a bridge over a river. Some mudflats followed, and then another river. Things had got very rural within a few hundred yards. Ideally, we wanted to find a public library – to see the latest on our little tropical disturbance.

Darien's library was a tiny building that looked like the welcome lodge to a national park. Inside we took advantage of air conditioning, and half an hour's free web time.

We made straight for the tropical weather update. Subtle details were emerging:

```
A VIGOROUS TROPICAL WAVE IS STILL LOCATED
OVER THE FAR EASTERN ATLANTIC OCEAN ABOUT 300
MILES SOUTH-SOUTH-EAST OF THE SOUTHERNMOST
CAPE VERDE ISLANDS. CONDITIONS HAVE REMAINED
FAVORABLE FOR DEVELOPMENT OF THIS SYSTEM –
AND A TROPICAL DEPRESSION IS NOW EXPECTED TO
FORM DURING THE NEXT DAY OR SO AS IT MOVES
WESTWARD AT 15 TO 20 MPH.
```

According to Dr Rhys this was enough for us to head north without delay.

'OK. To the Outer Banks?' I asked.

'Too right. Let's get going.'

The Outer Banks of North Carolina, besides Sebastian Inlet, was the most famous surfing destination on the US East Coast.

As kids, Marc and I were drawn to Sebastian Inlet by the way it resembled that wave we had at home – The Wedge – but it was the Outer Banks that would jump to the front of most surfers' minds if you talked about Atlantic hurricane swells. To many the name immediately recalled video footage of dark, sandy tubes, breaking shallow and ferocious, in water as warm as a bath. A thin finger of sand, miles out to sea off the coast of North Carolina, the Banks were famous for maximising the ocean's power.

As for Georgia, its coastline wasn't much use to surfers. It was the opposite of the Outer Banks. Marshy river deltas led to gradual beach drop-offs and ill-formed sands. All around us the land was as flat as any of the Mississippi areas, nestling in a kink in the coastline that sheltered it from swell.

Shortly after the South Carolina state line, we turned off onto a smaller two-lane highway, the US 17, with towering pine trees either side. A truck crawled along in front of us – a real feat of slowness considering the Betty Ford was usually the one causing the queues. Its snail's pace ensured we got to read the statements the driver had fixed to the trailer.

Around a Stars and Stripes was written, 'Support Our Troops Wherever We Go. No Aid Or Comfort To The Enemy – *No Way!*'

'For fuck's sake,' said Marc. 'You can tell this is the south all right, eh?'

Most of the conversation that afternoon kept returning to hurricanes, though. Our rants about southern politics, or arguments over directions were only passing comments amid more talk about the storm we hoped would soon send us surf.

'Did you know, by the way, that if one causes exceptional damage its name gets retired?' Marc asked me.

'No.'

'Well they do. So no storm will ever get named "Katrina" again.'

'Really? I didn't know they got reused in the first place.'

'Yeah. Normally names get recycled every couple of years. So the next storm to occur this season, I can tell you now, will be called *Dean*. Then Erin... and I think the one after that will be Felix.'

I told him I already knew the next names on the list: 'I've been ticking them off as they occur,' I explained. 'There's a piece of paper in the glove box somewhere.'

It was news to me that these names had been used before, though, and it seemed unfair to have two Hurricane Deans. How could the new Dean avoid the reputation of its predecessor? Was a name only a name? Maybe *our* Dean could still start with a blank slate.

'Imagine if you were from New Orleans,' said Marc, 'and you saw there was a Hurricane Katrina in the Gulf. It'd be pretty grim, eh? That's why they retire names.'

I asked if he knew which other storms had been 'retired' like this.

'Well, Katrina, Rita and Wilma of course,' was his first thought. 'And Andrew too. Let me think... Charley – you know, that one the girl at New Smyrna was talking about. And Betsy, the one that flooded New Orleans in the sixties. All the famous storms to lay into Florida are gone – Mitch, Floyd, "Ivan the Terrible". In fact, it's pretty safe to say that any you hear about in the news will be out of use. It's a long list – and the Katrina year was the most names added in one go. I think they put five to rest that season.'

I tried not to think about what my desires would be for Dean this time around – didn't want to tempt fate. Pushy parents sometimes got rewarded with rebel kids – if you catch my drift. Better sit back, keep hopes and expectations to a minimum, and be grateful for whatever came along.

'D'you think it'll be easy to forget what we saw in New Orleans?' I asked. 'You know, when we're cruising around places like the Outer Banks scoring hurricane surf?'

'I think it's a risk, yeah.'

'We should try not to though, eh?'

Now I thought about it, we hadn't seen an Evacuation Route sign on this part of the coast for a while. In Florida and the Gulf states they'd been everywhere. Instead they'd been replaced by notices inviting you to visit family-run food stores or diners, and billboards supporting local politicians. The multinational chains that lined the interstate had yet to move in for the kill here.

'Hang on,' Marc called out. 'There's a place selling home-made booze there! Pull over!'

Picket fences surrounded a trio of houses, the closest to the roadside being a shop: The Carolina Cider Co jams, stuffed olives, pecan syrup, tomato relish, benne wafers, boiled peanuts, apple butter and heaps of hot sauces – all home-made. It seemed the perfect place to stop for a break. 'Come on in, it's siesta time,' the building seemed to say to you. White wood walls supported hanging baskets and potted plants, with rocking chairs on the veranda. There were lizards darting occasionally across the parking spaces out front, making flies fear for their lives. An open-plan showroom of fine foods was fanned instead of air-conditioned. All around pine trees reached for the heavens, keeping us cool.

'Try some of our ciders,' the attendant, who was the owner's son, suggested. 'This one's peach cider. It's non-alcoholic, so you can drive safe anyway.'

I asked the boy how long they'd been in business. A sore topic.

'My family's run this place for generations. But we're coming under pressure now. They want to widen this road. Let trucks pass more easily.'

'Trucks?'

'Yeah – this road's so darn risky right now. Charleston's a port, and the delivery drivers pass through here on the way south. Trucks are supposed to go west to the interstate and then go north or south, but they all come through here instead. It's a short cut.'

I looked around. It was all clear for now.

'Where y'all from anyway?' the guy asked.

'Wales,' said Marc.

'Cool. They love this stuff in England, huh?' He gestured his arms around the store. I looked quickly for something to say – before Marc had time to retaliate at the slur of being called English.

'So they're going to widen the road?' I asked. It worked – immediately the moment defused.

'Yeah. Well, unless we can stop 'em. Lots of protest around here to it, so we might get somewhere. Drive through here next time and my Pop'll be around, probably. He'll talk about it *all day*.'

Loaded up with olives and peanuts, we expressed our solidarity.

Once I was driving again, Marc gave an opinion.

'*They* are the busiest people on earth.'

'Who?'

'*They*. Think about it. We always hear about them. *They* are going to widen the road. *They* plan to rebuild the dodgy levees. *They* made one place a national park and another a NASA space station. I just think it's a funny turn of speech. *They*. Kind of excuses them doesn't it? Makes whoever's responsible for something sound like some Orwellian, headless organisation.'

'*They* probably are,' I said back.

'Oh, I'm in no doubt you're right. But it still annoys me.'

As I pondered it, the idea of knocking down the Cider Co to extend a road out of Charleston seemed disturbing. It was a rare building in that, along with the two neighbouring houses, it had tried to coexist with its surroundings. Of the America we'd seen so far, it was much more common for humankind to want to build *on*, against, or in spite of, natural habitats and landscapes.

Fitting, then, that it was *Charleston*'s traffic that could become the cause of *them* wanting to further flatten the forest and traditional architecture – in this case in order to make the US 17 a bigger road. When we got to South Carolina's second biggest city it was the best illustration yet of the construction philosophy I'm talking about. Gargantuan bridges soared over the estuaries, surrounded by industry and military activity. Behind one smog-breathing tower, a US flag the size of a tennis court billowed in the sea breeze, its white stripes radiant, as if the cloth had just come out of an aircraft-hangar-sized laundry machine.

Side roads broke off the freeway, suspended in mid-air by battalions of concrete pillars, with ramps rising in and out of the sky. Cost had obviously been no issue when building the highways around the city. Any intersection or turn-off here could have been a record-breaking spaghetti junction back in the UK. Charleston also had more churches per capita than any other city in the States – and many were majestic, palatial complexes.

'If it hadn't been for dreams of basilica glory, these churches could have probably solved the country's homelessness with the savings,' Marc fumed. 'But I bet that wasn't ever on the agenda. I'd love to see how they'd all react if a homeless person walked through the 4x4s one Sunday morning to ask for a bowl of soup.'

Some more discreet buildings of worship did occasionally dot the side of the road, but they were rare. Residential properties were also well maintained and super-desirable – until we took a wrong turn at the end of a flyover into the downtown area, straight through a run-down suburb and a ramshackle square of wood houses – some with smashed windows, others overgrown with weeds. The Betty Ford was at home in this neighbourhood – I could feel it from the way her engine had temporarily eased the rattling sound that was starting to accompany deceleration and braking.

A few blocks later we were in the heart of the city.

'Let's park up and take a walk,' I said. 'Those snacks have made me hungry.'

It was early evening with a steady flow of young pedestrians moving towards the marina area. We followed, and came across a small grid of high street shops, bars and restaurants. Most of the people in the vicinity were white couples in their late teens and early twenties, who all looked as if they'd dressed for a high school photo. Outfits were timeless, hair fluffily shampooed and I started imagining them all to have names like Cory or Bethany. I wondered how many of the young couples here would be churchgoers, too.

And then there were the soldiers, or sailors. Every few blocks we'd see stiff, frowning, uptight young men walking in full military regalia – freshly pressed white uniforms and caps with straps that rested over the front of the chin. Some held their arms out elbow first, with their leading wrist dipped, so their lady friends could hold it like a handle.

As we approached a crossroads two such soldiers arrived alongside, wearing a pair of girls like bracelets. No smirk, no smile, no emotion showing behind the chin-strap and cap.

'Fuck it. I can't resist,' whispered Marc, looking for trouble. As the four strolled past us he innocently asked, 'Fancy dress, eh, boys?'

We almost didn't find anywhere to stay that night. Marc reckoned it was because all the motels were afraid we might be a gay couple again. I hadn't given much thought to the possibility of that happening before we came to the south, but it seemed as plausible an explanation as any. Each time we looked at a motel it would always look empty – no cars anywhere – only for the receptionists to either ask for hundreds of dollars, or tell us there was no room. It fell to a trusty Econo Lodge to save us from a night roughing it in the Betty Ford – an event we were hoping to put off until absolutely necessary.

The place was manned by a young Indian guy, who was more interested in talking cricket and Premier League football than checking us into a room in a hurry. His family had moved over from London as his dad was a lecturer at Charleston University.

'What does he lecture?' Marc asked.

'Business and finance.'

'And he runs a motel too – on the side?'

'Yeah.'

'That works.'

'I know. So what team do you guys follow?'

'Wales,' Marc replied.

'No – which Premiership team?'

'Oh – whichever one's got the most Welsh players. At the moment I like Fulham and Blackburn.'

I stepped in: 'Arsenal. I'm an Arsenal fan.'

'Arsenal? Honest truth?' The boy looked excited.

'Yes. Honest truth. Supported them since I was a kid.' (Again, Wales had needed to be marginalised for the greater good of relating to people.)

'Well in that case the room will be ten dollars cheaper,' he smiled. 'I *love* the Arsenal.'

Marc frowned.

'Your dad's taught you well,' I laughed. 'He a Gooner too?'

'Of course!'

'Good to hear. Nice to know there are followers here in the US. Maybe we'll meet him tomorrow.'

The hospitality of our new Indian friends was indeed extended further at breakfast, when they wheeled in a television with Sky Sports for us to watch.

'There's a cricket game on! England against the West Indies! I bet you boys are missing cricket over here eh? What with all this bloody baseball.'

This was another sore point with Marc, who felt Wales should have their own cricket team too.

'How did you guys get Sky Sports?' he asked, turning to the boy.

'Oh – it gets arranged through the university. It got wired up for us as a gift when he agreed to move here.'

'Really? Someone must have really wanted your dad to work here then?'

'Nah, not especially – it's easy to do now that they've brought cable to the street behind us.'

They again. Marc was right – *they* were indeed the busiest people in the world right now.

They hadn't been so kind over the course of time to Myrtle Beach – a seaside vacation town a few hours north. The first time Marc had mentioned the place I knew it sounded familiar for a reason, and my memory was jogged as we arrived at the sprawling outskirts early afternoon the next day.

Marc and I had once spent a week or two on a surfers' Internet forum winding up American posters about US foreign policy. Marc had a quiet period in his studies and I'd scored a bit of temping work that basically involved sitting at a desk and occasionally answering calls, or filling staplers, while mostly wasting time online. By mid afternoons, when most of the US was awake, we'd have people at each other's throats for hours. Then Marc had a new idea.

He invented a teenage character called Lyle, who had right wing views that would make Attila the Hun seem like a cuddly toy. Lyle soon had a cult following of genuine characters (we think), all thrilled to hear of his desires to see the US invade France, stop and search people 'of colour', cut all foreign aid and sanction stem-cell research at its earliest possible stage.

In the 'where from' column, Marc had picked somewhere at random: Myrtle Beach. (Because it sounded about right, he'd said.) Our creation, this gun-toting, jaded teenager with plans for US world domination, hailed from a town we never expected to visit, but were now driving right through.

Late summer bedlam was in full flow. Traffic ground to a halt several times, and every faceless source of tourist entertainment was doing a year's worth of trade in a day: water parks with plastic fire-breathing volcanoes and dyed water, zoos with no real animals and shopping precincts that sold nothing of value or taste.

'A surf check and then out of here,' Marc reckoned.

'Definitely. Before we meet Lyle.'

Most of the beach access was private, so we didn't even get that far. We elected instead to push on for another two hours into North Carolina ('The Birthplace of Aviation'), hitting the shore again at Wrightsville Beach. As in Florida, Wrightsville was an island of coastline which you got onto by crossing another bridge over an inlet.

There was a bit more luck in the air. The parking meters had just stopped needing to be paid off – as it was five o'clock, and many families were leaving after a day on the beach. We found a spot right next to the old wooden pier, and ran across to the sand, gazing out to sea in hope.

The waves were a trickle – but crucially it was possible to surf them, if you were very desperate. And we were. Several days of driving makes you ready to surf anything.

'I don't care how small and windy it is,' I stated. 'I just want to get wet and paddle around.' The Welsh surfer in me was coming out.

For once Marc couldn't agree more.

When you're driving big distances, finally arriving at surf is a surreal feeling – especially when the water's warm enough not to need wetsuits. The changeover of moods is instant. It took us about two minutes to be in our shorts and running onto the warm sand.

I stretched a few times, as the shoreline lapped around my feet. It's easy to forget how bad sitting in a car all day is for your back. I twisted to the left, and then the right – whereupon several clicks echoed out of my spine. Feeling more limber, I also pushed my neck to one side. Again a cracking sound burst out, freeing me up, ready to surf.

The water was heavenly – still warm but no longer oppressive like the Gulf. In the tiny but fast-breaking peaks, we surfed for almost an hour. With no wetsuit weighing you down it was still possible to squeeze some speed out of the knee-high waves, and the more I paddled and rode, the more my energy was coming back. I'd forgotten how good a simple go-out in innocuous summertime slop could sometimes be.

Further up the beach I could see somebody surfing really, really well – to a high professional standard. Tiny waves weren't getting in the way of allowing the guy to blast any little ramps of water he could find. Seeing someone really ripping is always reassuring – it means you're in a proper surf locale. If there was going to be a swell, then most of the coast from here on up would be sure to turn on.

With the sea virtually at body temperature, you could sit and wait for waves, too, without losing any energy or flexibility. I would have taken this session over bigger but colder waves any day. Once you'd finished a wave here, you could dive through the shore break to paddle back out, and feel the water run down your back – warmer than the air itself.

The horizon had now gone grey and it felt like night would fall quite early. In the poor light, I rode a few last waves to the beach, feeling pretty pleased at managing to squeeze in a few turns myself over the crumbling sections of white water. Jogging back up the steeply sloping sand, I was refreshed and ready to drive as close to the Outer Banks as we could get that night. I'd just realised how important it was to move surfing back up the agenda – to the top. After all – that was why we were here.

To show how quickly things can change in the south, by the time we reached the Betty Ford, it had begun to rain. Dripping with fresh water from the showers, I stood in the parking lot, not wanting to open the car in case the inside got wet. This vehicle was home for the moment and needed to stay dry. The short-lived squall was then followed by the smell of oil as the rains evaporated off the tarmac, and the once humid air thinned around us. As we cruised over the bridge back out of Wrightsville I could hear, through the open windows, our tyres squeaking on the moist road surface.

'This is the first time I'm not minding that this car doesn't have air conditioning,' said Marc. 'I bloody *love* the rain sometimes.'

He'd get his wish. A few miles later drops started falling on the windscreen again. Drops which soon turned to another torrent.

'Windows up,' I ordered.

Within minutes the car had misted so much that it was nearly impossible to see outside. Added to that the fact that the wipers weren't very good, driving was becoming hard.

'How far now are we from the Outer Banks ferry?' I asked Marc.

He pulled the map out from under the seat.

'I make it about an hour... Oh shit! We forgot to book a crossing time.'

'Where are we then?' I asked, leaning over.

'Coming up to Jacksonville. We need to get to Cedar Island for the ferry. That'll take us to Ocracoke and then it's another little boat hop on to Hatteras Island.'

'Well, how about we call it a day on the driving then,' I said, wanting the surf to stay in my thoughts for as long as possible. 'We can stay in the next place with vacancies, get some food, watch a film or something, and call to arrange a ferry before going on tomorrow.'

'OK,' said Marc. 'Let's keep our eyes peeled.'

Several glades of trees followed before we passed a square and some shops on our left, and then a giant emporium called Saigon Sam's Military Surplus. A hundred yards or so after that there was a motel: The Ocean Breeze. The name was enough to make us stop, but its location next to an army shop was the clincher.

We checked in and went for a walk over to the shops beyond Saigon Sam's. Walking on the verges of American freeways can be weird – you're covering areas that aren't really meant to be done on foot. Suddenly it seems like such a slow mode of transport, and even parking lots and small junctions strike you as vast patches of open space. There was a Chinese takeaway still open, next to a pizza place, although the whole region seemed deserted – except for two trucks parked at the other end of the row of shops.

I bought Schzechuan prawns in extra chilli sauce and washed it down with a Diet Coke – absolutely fine for post-surf munchies, and less than five dollars for the lot. Outside, I tried to call my mother in Toronto while Marc finished his crispy beef. The payphone wouldn't play ball with me – some operator woman interrupted my call when the line at the other end had only rung three times. She told me to put more quarters into the machine.

'How do you know I need to put more quarters in?' I asked.

Humourless, the response was a blank, 'seventy-five more cents to connect this call, sir'. In the background, and through the same line, I could hear Dave answering the phone.

'Hello? Hello? David speaking. Anyone there?'

I banged the receiver down with an aggression that surprised me. Feeling guilty, I asked Marc to let me call them for half a minute on his mobile – just to explain what had happened with the payphone. I told them we were in Jacksonville, North Carolina, and that the Betty Ford was going fine (several new spark plugs and 15 litres of oil later). Dave told me that it might need an actual oil *change* at some point, and said my mother was out for the minute, but expecting a postcard and another call when I could manage it. He added that a hurricane was expected in the Atlantic too, according to the news reports, but couldn't remember details. I promised to do what I could on the oil, postcard and phone call requests, said goodbye for the moment and went back into the Chinese to wait for Marc. He'd put too much hot sauce on his food and was making heavy work of it.

Eventually he finished and said, 'I think I saw two pubs at the end of that road. We could go for a drink. This place seems perfect for going and getting into a conversation with some locals.'

I knew what he meant – perhaps we would have a chance to meet the kind of people you wouldn't really run into in a surfer hostel, or in the seat next to you on a flight.

Next to Saigon Sam's was a hairdresser named Kut N Up Barber Shop, which advertised haircuts 'both military and civilian'. An ageing 4x4 in the shopping parking lot, one of the only two vehicles in sight, had a 'US Army Vet' sticker on it, and there were several banners at the side of the highway that extolled the virtues of 'Freedom' as well as the common slogan 'Support our Troops'. To me this stuff seemed eerie – especially on a dark, wet evening in the southern United States. But then again, Marc had a point. It was a waste of time constantly locking ourselves in motel rooms and watching news and weather channels – HBO or ESPN. Perhaps my reservations about this weird little roadside settlement were all the more reason to go in search of a bar. Drop your prejudices, I ordered myself, some of these people could easily be good friends.

We walked another 50 yards down a lane away from the main road. A collection of residential caravans filled a small field at the start of the road, before another street went off to the right – called Puppy Lane. It was all silent and only sporadically illuminated by small lamps. Opposite the junction was a small, square building with its front lit up – like a Hopper painting – but with a board outside that announced that it was 'Karaoke Night, featuring N TACT'.

There were no windows to the premises, and the front door was corrugated metal. A miniature label read 'Welcome to Le Pub – please do not bring drinks inside'.

'Is it open?' I asked Marc.

'Dunno – give it a shove.'

The door squeezed ajar, leading into a dark, open-plan bar with a pool table, jukebox and dance floor. There were about half a dozen youngsters inside, several of whom were dressed in gothic regalia. As we walked in, each person in the building stared at us.

'Two Millers, please,' Marc asked the barmaid.

We sat, squirming, awkward, out of our element.

I looked at the wall – decorated caringly with images of various armed forces. Warplanes cruising at altitude, groups of soldiers posing on duty and head-and-shoulders shots of youngsters in full uniform – like those we'd seen in Charleston.

A little further along the wall were embroidered badges of various military campaigns – as well as memorial notices and statements of condolence for lost lives – presumably people who had been local or known to the pub.

Eventually, a guy with a shaved head, wearing a red shirt and uber-baggy jeans, decorated in chains and studs, asked me if my accent was Irish.

Funnily enough, this kind of comment would cause no offence to Dr Marc Rhys – who everyone knew could begin to have heart palpitations the second anyone mistook him for being *English*.

'No – close though. We're from Wales, matey,' Marc smiled.

'Cool. What the fuck are you doing in Jacksonville-North-Carolina then?'

'Ah – well, my buddy and I have driven from Florida. We're going up the East Coast. We're surfers, see.'

'Sick – I bodyboard sometimes. You going to the Outer Banks, right? Hatteras? I go there sometimes. You got to make sure you surf Rodanthe. I'll write it down for you. Rodanthe – got that?'

'Rodanthe,' I repeated. 'Thanks – yeah, any tips we can get will help. We're hoping on some waves off a hurricane actually.'

'Shit, man, you get a hurricane swell at Rodanthe you're the fuckin' luckiest guys alive! Although you might not actually be alive at all if you surf the low tide close outs.' He winked, knowingly, and nudged me on the shoulder.

'I'm Marc anyway,' Dr Rhys introduced himself. 'And this is Tom.'

'Good to meet you guys,' came the reply. 'Sam.'

'Sam?'

'Yeah. I'm Sam.' We shook hands.

'So Sam, let me buy you a drink,' Marc insisted.

'Uh – jeez, OK. Get me a rum and Coke.'

'No worries. And one for yourself,' Marc added to the barmaid. He was really turning the charms on. It was working at breaking the ice, too. One of Sam's friends had made his way over, and soon we were talking about football – *US* football, that is. A topic Marc knew a fair bit about.

Meanwhile, I asked Sam's mate, Cregg, where he was from.

'Originally born in Pennsylvania, but I've lived all over since my parents served – California, Arizona, Georgia and Idaho. I'm now living here though, of course, so I guess you could say I'm outta North Carolina right now.'

'Your parents served?'

'Yeah. Army. Both of them. That's where they met.'

'Oh, tidy.'

'Tidy?'

'Sorry,' I said. 'It means cool.'

Over a few moments' silence, a thought occurred to me. I looked over and saw Marc, deep in conversation with Sam, whose girlfriend had also now walked over and joined them. The other few kids were over by the jukebox, selecting tunes. Were they old enough to all be...?

I turned to Cregg and asked.

'So – are you in the army?'

'Yes sir, I am.'

'Which part of the army?'

'I'm in the Marine Corps, like Sam.'

'I see. And is everyone else in this pub in the Marine Corps too?'

Cregg looked around, and then, with a matter-of-fact expression and a shrug of the shoulders said, 'Yeah.'

'There a lot of Marines in Jacksonville then?' I asked, wondering whether Marc had also found out the same information by now.

'About sixty thousand of us. You want a beer?'

I looked at Marc, still talking away about the plight of the Carolina Panthers NFL team.

'Sure,' I said. 'Why not.'

CHAPTER EIGHT

HURRICANE FLOSSIE

So there was Sam and Cregg to start with. Cregg was from 'all over' and Sam, I soon learned, hailed from Alabama.

Sam's girlfriend was actually his wife, even though they both looked about twelve, and he was beautifully frank about the thought behind it.

'If I die – get killed in action – and we're married, she'll get some money outta the government.'

The reason the group were out tonight was that Sam was going to Iraq in two days' time – for his first Middle Eastern tour of duty.

'I've only ever been to Okinawa before.'

'Okinawa?'

'Yeah.'

'What were you doing there?' I asked.

'We were watching and waiting for Korea to step outta line.'

'Korea? *North* Korea you mean.'

'Yeah – I think. It ain't really my job to pay attention to that kind of detail. I just do what I'm told, when I'm told and how I'm told to do it. No questions.'

Fair enough. So what was he going to do out there?

The answer was that he'd been trained in spotting bombs and ambushes, and would be driving out front, up ahead of military convoys to probe for devices or possible attacks.

'So you're right in the line of fire.'

'Yup!' He smiled, a gulping grin of acceptance. Such was life. 'I got a lot of responsibility too – gotta keep the others safe. The job's only done when every last man is back alive and healthy.'

Another guy sitting near who'd been listening cut in:

'*Fricken AMEN to that, dude!*'

He and Sam started talking about the upcoming mission in more technical detail:

'What vehicle ya driving out there?'

'Hummer,' Sam replied.

The two mumbled something detailed about the various vehicles that made up a convoy. I'd forgotten that Hummers were originally designed for the army. Mention one to me and the first thing that comes to mind is David Beckham. Back home, these were the most controversial of all the indulgent gas guzzlers. At war, though, I guess you could see the use for them.

The other guy, who'd been to Iraq twice already, thought Hummers weren't much cop under fire and told Sam in the same direct manner that he'd be burned alive if a rocket hit him while driving one.

'You scared?' I asked.

'I'm fucking crapping myself,' he replied. 'But who isn't?'

None of the people here were over twenty-four, I realised, and Sam was barely twenty. He'd been in the army since he was sixteen. I thought about how middle-class kids his age might shed a tear over the thought of moving to university, or going on a foreign-language exchange. This was serious though – he was going to be a soldier in a country which was claiming American lives almost daily. And his resignation to that fact was total.

Another girl within the group introduced herself as Katherine. She had straight dark hair and wore thick, wide-framed glasses. I could see at least one tattoo on each arm, but this made her look weaker rather than tough. The lenses of her glasses magnified her eyes, making her look alarmed like a rabbit in headlights. This was exactly how she came across in person. Gushing, honest and open, she told us very quickly that she'd lost her fiancé in Iraq, and that her current husband was there now. She was in the Marine Corps too, but hadn't yet been sent anywhere dangerous.

Katherine was the only member of the group who had anything more than a surface interest in where we came from. After talking a bit about France, Germany and the sights and people of the British Isles, she said, 'You see – that's why I joined the Marine Corps – to see those kinda places. It ain't like that at all though.'

I asked her where she was from.

'North Carolina. Right here. When you live in Jacksonville being in the Marine Corps is what you do.'

I probably needed another drink.

Marc was doing fine, though, and when the karaoke started, he put his name straight down for a rendition of 'Hey Jude' – once Katherine had sung two old country and western songs in a soft, trembling voice. Even though they were her friends, the others talked and laughed all the way through her timid attempts, so I gave her a patronisingly over the top amount of applause, as if to say at least one person watched. She was touched by this, and put her name straight back down for two more.

Meanwhile, I realised that Marc was already wasted. As he slurred his way to *na-na-na na-na-na-na, hey Jude* the others started joining in.

Katherine went up again, and sang 'Prop Me Up Beside the Juke Box (If I Die)', to a little more recognition than before – perhaps because it was a much stronger attempt – starting out on her second number, 'Bohemian Rhapsody', alone. This couldn't be allowed, and so the other six juvenile soldiers all piled up to the microphone to help her. They swayed, cheered and chuckled their way through all of the nuances and movements; an archetypal image of everything right about the US armed forces.

Drinks were going down smoothly by now, and we felt like members of the group ourselves. Conversations were replaced by arm-in-arm drunken singing, and optimism had filled the room. Talk of dying or getting burned in a Hummer had almost been forgotten.

Until another kid in the group – the only male without a shaved head – took to the microphone to sing. He gestured to the others that he'd do the next song alone, and I soon saw why. He had an outstanding voice, and powered through an anthem-like number I'd never heard before. It was heartfelt, clearly known and loved by all the others, and about life as an American soldier. Like Sam's conversations earlier, it was frank, lamenting the eternal cost of being expendable and of being willing to lay down your life for a nation. The lyrics talked about how they didn't do it for the money, and loved the responsibility and being the ones in the firing line.

Two verses into the song the kid paused, turned his cap back-to-front and swayed in thought, waiting for the next lines to reel across the screen.

In the last part of the tune, Sam's girlfriend broke into tears and dashed to the washroom. How could I forget how close to home these lyrics were for her right now? Then three others joined the kid on the little raised platform to sing the last chorus into the microphone together. A few lines later everyone joined in – even me and Marc, trying to guess the tune as we went along. It was easy enough – just repeating the words 'American soldier' until virtually everyone was choking with emotion.

From here there were a few lighter moments but the mood mostly swung towards the sombre again. Katherine made us all laugh by saying her impression of Canadians was that they 'can't drive for shit', only for Cregg to start a wild rant about how much he hated the French and felt betrayed by 'Old Europe' over the Iraq debate.

As the group kept drinking around us, Marc and I started talking about what was going on.

'You know, son,' he said, 'I really respect the way they all see the army as their duty and don't get caught up in the politics. In Britain we're quite supportive of our troops, coz I suppose we don't really see them as being the ones who pick the fights. But something is different here.'

'Perhaps it's coz America's more divided over it?' I said.

'Over the war?' said Marc. 'I dunno. I don't reckon any of these guys could tell you of an unjust operation.'

'Nicaragua, Panama City... Vietnam!' I began.

'Yeah – but are those stories taught to these guys? How many of them d'you reckon did history in school for any longer than they had to?'

I thought about this. Probably none – not if they'd managed to get on the frontline before even turning twenty.

'You know what,' Marc whispered closely in my ear. 'These guys are just fuckin' kids, man. They come from such different backgrounds to the arseholes making the decisions. Think about it – d'you reckon the local councillors, congressmen and governors would ever send their kids to war? Reckon the chief exec of fuckin' Halliburton's son will do anything but go to Princeton or Harvard? The only time that little shit will hold a gun is when he goes grouse- or deer-shooting for sports!'

I wondered what kinds of upbringing these kids had. Scared, drinking away one of the last nights before one of them went off to Iraq to drive in front of a convoy that would be a target for all sorts of attacks. Sam didn't deserve to die. He seemed like a really kind-hearted person.

None of them seemed to know what had brought them into this situation. They were just there. Doing what should be one of the most prestigious and honoured jobs available.

The night bottomed out with more karaoke from Katherine (this time back to her painful worst), and everyone starting to yawn from a very down kind of drunkenness. We said goodbye to the soldiers, swapping contact details and swearing to stay in touch. But I knew it would be unlikely. Before walking back to the motel we were hugged by each of them.

Silence hung over the whole walk home, past the half-lit shopfront of Saigon Sam's with its banners proclaiming the necessity and heroism of serving in the armed forces. Stuck to the front wall of the building was a plaque, illustrated with yellow ribbons around a statement displayed proud and clean:

A Marine's Creed

It is my destiny to serve in obscurity most
Of my life awaiting a crisis that may never occur.

It is my trust to know the solution if the
Crisis does occur.

It is my duty to constantly give all that
I have for my Corps and Country.

We paused, swaying slightly, reading it.

Marc groaned – not in disapproval, but a sound that suggested being haunted by something.

'Man!' he exclaimed. 'I've got total respect for that – for all of them. It's more than I'd be capable of. I'll admit that.'

We walked away, both of us looking at the ground.

★   ★   ★

Getting to the Cedar Island ferry wasn't going to happen in any hurry the next morning. My head felt like it had been to outer space and back when I woke up (including the exploding bit). All I managed in almost an hour was to reach for the remote on my bedside table and flick on The Weather Channel, which soon enough delivered a tropical weather update:

Good morning. The forecasters who predict hurricanes have repeated their beliefs today that the eastern states should be on the alert for above-average activity this year. There have only been three named tropical systems in the Atlantic Basin so far – but the National Hurricane Center is sure that several more will follow. Meanwhile, it's now thought the Pacific is going to see a below-average storm season. The reason for this? A little known phenomenon called La Niña. Now you may have all heard of El Niño... well scientists think that we've been moving out of an El Niño cycle these past few months and into a La Niña. La Niña is a kind of reverse of those circumstances. A cooling of equatorial waters that reduces the number of tropical systems able to form in the eastern Pacific. This lack of activity kills off the wind shear that can tear apart developing storms in the West Atlantic and the Caribbean.

Although hard to follow in my state, this stuff was really interesting to me. A few years ago I'd actually been to the point where the El Niño cycles began – on the Peru-Ecuador border. I'd gone there on a mission to try and ride the world's longest wave – just beyond the fishing village of Puerto Chicama in northern Peru. I got the wave doing its thing all right – and revelled in the experience of riding for several minutes at a time. In fact, it was the only surf trip I'd ever been on which made my legs ache more than my arms. But that wasn't the main memory. After one long wave I'd seen an incredible bird on the beach – with bright, icy-blue webbed feet: the blue-footed booby (one of Darwin's discoveries). You see – the water at Puerto Chicama was incredibly cold. You had to wear wetsuits there even though it was on the equator, because the Humboldt Current ran near by – the same one that made the Galapagos wildlife unique. And it was that same current that controlled El Niño. Fishermen in Puerto Chicama could warn you it was coming before any weather men – just from putting their hands in the sea.

This patch of freezing South Pacific water had not only helped make the world's longest wave though; it could cause worldwide weather havoc whenever it stopped flowing or by warming up. And now I was hearing about how it might affect the hurricane season as well. I tried to sit up as the presenter moved to point at the ocean off West Africa:

Add to this the fact that Hurricane Alley – this area of water that extends from out of Africa right across to the Gulf and the Caribbean here – is getting warmer each year due to climate change, and we could be on for one oversized whopper of a storm season.

A pause was added here, presumably for effect. And long enough for me to remember Kevin in Fort Walton Beach; another local waterman who, like the fishermen of Puerto Chicama, probably could have told the forecasters all of this months ago.

Moving to the current situation. We'll start with the Atlantic, where experts are now very closely monitoring two systems that could affect the East Coast in the next week or two. The first is a collection of thunderstorms in the Gulf of Mexico, which is nothing in itself – but it's starting to show some organisation with winds said to be increasing around the centre of the area. Right now hurricane hunters are looking for signs of an "eye" – a focal point for a storm to grow. We'll keep you posted on this band of weather, which is expected to develop into a tropical storm by the end of the week. Of much more importance at the moment though is this tropical wave out of the Cape Verde Islands that we talked about yesterday.

I sat bolt upright. Immediately I could sense there was about to be some news for us. The presenter continued:

Well, the system has continued to show significant organisation, and right now all predictions are that this little mass of cloud that you see here in the East Atlantic is going to develop into tropical storm status within two to three days, and will most likely go all the way to becoming the next major hurricane of the season. It's still a slow moving one – so it's gonna be a good few days before any warnings need to be issued as to possible landfalls, but all eyes will be on this system from now on.

I yelled to Marc: 'Wake up! They're talking about that storm off Cape Verde.'

He groaned. The weather man carried on:

Moving to the Pacific, and although we just said activity will be reduced this year, that's certainly not the case right now. Hawaii is currently on a blanket alert, as Hurricane Flossie moves towards shore...

'Did you hear that? There's a major hurricane in the Pacific right now too.'

Marc wasn't interested. He wanted to talk about the Marine Corps again:

'Didn't you find last night just a little bit disturbing?' he inquired. 'It was... well... *harrowing*. I mean – those guys were *kids*! It's totally changed the way I see the American army. They were really, really nice people. Friendly, kind – a good laugh, like. But they haven't a clue what they're doing! It makes me really angry.'

'Yeah. It is kinda creepy,' I admitted. To tell the truth I didn't know what to make of it yet.

I carried on talking to him about Hurricane Flossie and the rest of the latest weather bulletin instead. This time he listened a bit more.

'So Flossie's looking to wallop the Hawaiian islands one side,' I told him, 'and the Atlantic Basin is pregnant with twins.'

Marc laughed – a sneering, dismissive laugh. 'Twins! Whatever. God, I'm glad I don't have to stick a literary slant on everything! It must get so tiring. Anyway, what did they say about the Pacific staying quiet?'

I tried to explain about El Niño, La Niña and all that as best I could, but Marc took over.

'La Niña is even harder to predict than El Niño,' he told me. 'But it's actually very simple: if the Pacific is cooler, then it's calmer, and will have less pull on Atlantic systems – making our side of the continent prone to massive storms at any time. It's good for surfing, but it also means it's very likely that somewhere will get really, really *slammed* by a hurricane before November.'

'How long have people known about El Niño and La Niña?' I asked.

'Ages – but they're very popular topics of study these days because everyone's climbing over each other to establish a link between them and global warming.'

'And is there one?'

'No – or rather nothing indisputable. There's no concrete link between *anything* and global warming.'

I hated these non-committal scientific answers.

'OK. So no concrete links may exist,' I agreed. 'But what do *you* think, Marc?'

This was like trying to get a personal opinion from a hospital consultant – impossible however hard you tried.

'I think... that... it's possible,' was the best he could do. 'They have proved that El Niño is getting more frequent. Or at least that it's at its highest frequency since records began – although that is only a few hundred years, and only a few decades of anything accurate.'

Even if it seemed waffly to me, dishing out some oceanographical knowledge had calmed Marc down and, in its own way, had made me feel much more at ease too. The status quo of our relationship had been restored. He was the expert, the realist. I was the one looking to live out a story.

I suggested going to look in Saigon Sam's Military Surplus.

The place had been open for an hour and inside it was dark and musky. My eyes had to adjust to the lack of sunlight – it was already blindingly bright outside. There was the smell of mildew and tent canvas. Various gun accessories hung off the end wall, gathering dust.

The knives looked like they'd kept their age better though, gleaming even in this half-light, as did a lot of the army-issue camping gear. In the last aisle before the till, there were rows and rows of badges for sale from all the various operations the US armed forces had undertaken through the ages. It kind of reminded me of the way storms got named. Like a tropical depression, a military move was worth so much less until brought to life with the 'Operation' tag: 'Operation Just Cause'. 'Operation Desert Storm', 'Operation Enduring Freedom'.

'Can I help you with anything?' the man behind the counter asked. He was a stocky, grey-haired guy with a small, well trimmed goatee, and a tight T-shirt bearing the name of the store.

I wondered for a second what level of technical detail he could go into if I asked him about knives or guns. Having worked in a surf shop myself, I remembered the way I used to impress novices by talking about the rail and rocker contours of certain boards, fins and other bits of specialist equipment. What if I did want a knife? Would he tell me that this one cuts deeper than that one, as might a certain tail shape better suit a faster wave?

'Oh, I'm good thanks,' I said. 'Just interested to have a look round. I had a few beers last night with some of the Marine Corps.'

'Camp Lejeune?' asked Saigon Sam.

'Sorry?'

'They were probably from Camp Lejeune. That's the base near here.' He had that same direct tone we'd seen last night – concise, polite replies to anything you asked. He was a former soldier, I suspected.

'Did you ever serve yourself?'

'Yes, sir, I did. Marine Corps. Twenty years. Even went to England.'

'Really? I'm from Wales. Did you ever serve with our soldiers?'

'Oh yeah, the Welsh Guards are famous here.'

I saw Marc look up from the badges. He hadn't said a lot in here so far, but this had pricked his attention. Saigon Sam carried on:

'I loved the Brits. They're good soldiers. Good friends of America.'

'Thanks,' I said, before telling him about our own Sam from last night, off to be a lookout driver in Iraq.

'Makes sense,' was all that came in the way of reply.

'Yeah. Sounds a dangerous job, eh?' I asked.

'Well,' said Saigon Sam, 'he's actually got one of the safest jobs.'

'What?'

'Yeah. He's not going to be a target.'

'At the front of the convoy? How d'you mean?'

'Well, any attacker would want to hide from the front of the convoy. They hit him and then the whole group that's coming up behind will shoot the shit out of them. No, he's the one person in a convoy the enemy *don't* want to kill.'

'Really?'

'But he's also the guy with the most responsibility. If he misses something he's putting lives behind him in imminent danger.'

Although he was stern and emotionless, I still couldn't help liking Saigon Sam. Like the guys from last night, he was honest, straight talking, and you felt he was motivated by a desire to uphold the good, the true and the just. Again, I thought, all great reasons to enlist – if they actually meant something to the people who posted you somewhere.

Marc was getting humbler by the hour. Warm comments about US troops this morning, followed now by doing something he usually avoided stubbornly out of principle: souvenir buying.

'Yeah, but it's an 'Operation Iraqi Freedom' mug!' he protested.

We turned back on to Highway 17 to head out to the beaches and away from this world so new to us. Had we stayed on the road a little longer last night through the outskirts of Jacksonville, Le Pub's clientele might have been a lot less of a surprise to us. We passed the edge of Camp Lejeune – a high-fenced, sprawling compound of barracks, obstacle courses and mock battlegrounds. And then came the housing estates the soldiers were living on. Simple, red brick semi-detached homes in suburban cul-de-sacs – except they too were surrounded by wire fences. Highway 17 was now called Freedom Way, and for hundreds of yards either side of the entrance roads, banners were hung out either celebrating soldiers returned home or wishing luck to those heading out:

**Welcome home Sgt Williams, Captain O'Hay
and Captain Eccleston!**

Thank you 3/6 Platoon.

My hottie, my hero, Sgt Donovan.

Welcome home DADDY!

It made for heavy reading.

Beyond the city outskirts signs of civilisation dropped away, and all that remained around us was marshland and a winding road that didn't seem to be going anywhere in a hurry. The Betty Ford was running her smoothest yet, not needing to pull herself up and down any inclines, and the flat landscape meant you could see other vehicles coming from miles off. Marc stared quietly, reflectively, out the window while I put all my effort into cornering across the whole road and driving as fast as possible.

'The ferry must be somewhere around here,' said Marc. 'The map makes it look like it sails from behind these marshes and lakes.'

'Well, this is the only road in the area, so we must be going the right way.'

In the ferry terminal's waiting area an hour later and tingling with histamine after suddenly finding that mosquitoes bit by day here, I bought a copy of *USA Today* and flipped it over to the weather page. The story of the day was Hurricane Flossie in the eastern Pacific. Apparently it was set to come closer to Hawaii than any storms for over a decade. The Big Island to the south was preparing for the possibility of landfall from a system packing winds of up to 140 mph. The statisticians were out in force, comparing its potential to the 'achievements' of Hurricane Iniki, which ran past the chain during an El Niño period over fifteen years previously, killing half a dozen people in Kauai and leaving over two billion dollars worth of damage. Safe to say, Iniki was retired from the naming lists.

The Atlantic, according to the forecasters, was still asleep for the moment, although that Gulf of Mexico system was being monitored for signs of development. There was no mention at all of the storm we were hoping to hook up with. I asked Marc what he made of it.

'Well, it probably went to press last night, and things can change really fast when it comes to hurricane prediction. What did they say on the telly this morning?'

'They said the clouds and rains off Cape Verde would almost certainly become the next major hurricane of the season.'

'Well – that's good enough for me. We're doing the right thing going here,' Marc confirmed. 'Unless you dreamt it.'

I read on. Flossie, the paper claimed, was already being nicknamed 'The Un-Forecastable', because everything it had done so far was against prediction. It had rapidly intensified in the past three days over waters that didn't have any significant warmth, and had since sustained its strength despite every six-hour prediction giving it no hope of surviving much longer. All of Hawaii was now in Flossie's 'cone of uncertainty' – a zone containing the possible routes the eye might take. The article concluded by saying the following: 'The forecasting of hurricanes remains one of science's key weaknesses, and no storm has made this point more eloquently than Flossie.'

A Category 4 described as 'eloquent'? That surely wasn't written by anyone at the National Hurricane Center.

A world away from Flossie's terrifying eye, we now lay sunbathing on a ferry that was cruising smoothly through calm, tepid, blue ocean towards the serenity of Ocracoke, the southernmost of the Outer Banks and the place where Blackbeard the pirate was known to have retired after cutting a pardon deal with the Carolina authorities. (He didn't live happily ever after, though. The Governor of Virginia was uneasy about a retired plunderer living so near, and late in the autumn of 1718 he sent an assassin squad out for him. The crew were successful and returned with Blackbeard's head after killing him in Ocracoke inlet.)

The Betty Ford was resting below deck, and our torturous bites had finally begun to subside. There was no way of knowing what the swell was doing at this stage, as the waters between the mainland and Outer Banks were essentially a lagoon and not exposed to the rhythms of the Atlantic Ocean. The journey wasn't much more than an hour, and before long the boat drew slowly up to Ocracoke Island from the western shore, docking in a bay of quaint wooden houses, quays, well-kept motorboats and seaside bars and restaurants.

'It's bloody Amity Island from *Jaws*!' said Marc.

As we crept off the boat, the Betty Ford's engine pistons again sounding unusually well-behaved and compliant, I looked around. Spread out before us was a community of small businesses and a sense of freedom from the branded, franchised and cut-throat life of urban America. A fifty-something man sat with an open beer in hand, manning his stall of rental bikes, while young waiters and bar tenders walked, skated or cycled to and from work. Most wore their mini aprons or employer-branded T-shirts with pride, but no shoes.

Schools were due back in most states in a few days' time now, but the last push of holidaymakers was still firmly in control of the island. Families, tanned, relaxed and nearing the end of their stays, walked serenely along the quays, browsing menus and gift stalls. I got a sense of being totally removed from Flossie's threats of landfall, or the bustle of the cities. As far as this place was concerned, many of the world's worries simply didn't exist. Although for the surfers on the island, glued to the National Hurricane Center's website, the Atlantic disturbances certainly did.

The further north you got now along the Eastern Seaboard, the less and less the chances of landfall were worth worrying about. The Outer Banks did get hit from time to time, but rarely by any of the major storms. Still, as I bought a leash from a surf shop on a street corner, the cashier was able to tell me vividly about how he remembered the whole of Ocracoke virtually underwater from a hurricane strike.

'Oh, we get them,' he said, rubbing hair out of his eyes. 'Only nowhere near as much as Florida. They get swell, followed by landfall – but we just get the swell. It's a sweet deal.' He looked at me for a second, before his fringe fell back down again. The downside to shampooing overly sun-bleached hair, and an obvious sign he hadn't been in the sea lately.

I asked if he knew anything about the storm rumoured to be brewing in the Atlantic, off West Africa.

'Yup – there's sure as hell something out there. Could really go off if we're lucky. Right now it's a long way from giving us a decent swell – not properly formed.'

'But it will?' Marc asked.

'Yeah – they say so. Still, a lot can happen though.' Another attempt to push his disobedient hair back up. 'We'll most probably get some waves off of it, but you'll know if we're gonna get *pumping* waves once it gets to the Bahamas. If it's intensified by then, everyone starts trying to get the week off work and we get like a year's worth of waves in a few days.'

'Really?'

'Yeah – although if the storm turns into the Gulf or the Caribbean, then the angle means this coast only gets waves off the eastern wind-fetch before it goes below the islands to the south and then out of range. That could well happen this time. Best place to go then, I tell ya, would be Long Island.'

'Long Island, New York?' I was surprised by this. I looked around – sometimes surf shops had maps of the local coastline. I wanted to see why Long Island would be well placed to get swell from a storm travelling south of it.

'Yeah – Montauk,' I saw, from behind that flippant fringe, the guy's eyes light up. 'Should see the beach breaks there. Place fricken *pumps*.'

'Anywhere else?' I was interested to see how far your average Carolinas surfer travelled within their own country.

He thought about my question for a second, again rubbing his head. 'Well, yeah. You can go to Rhode Island even – that place gets like the most swell ever when a storm passes by to the south. And even Nova Scotia. But you're talking serious cold. I'll go all the way south, and I mean *all* the way, but anything north of Jersey and Long Island is too cold for me. Ain't been to Rhode Island. Ain't been to Maine neither. Can't see it ever happening, if I'm honest.'

We could. Marc and I were ready for anything, and if that meant racing a storm to Maine, we'd do it without hesitation.

'Anyways – we're all staying mighty positive right now,' the cashier continued. 'Been one of the worst summers ever for waves, and we really deserve this one. I'm praying we can all stay put. Unless it slams into land – like Isabel did.'

'Isabel?'

'Yeah. But it was cool. Look at this place,' he instructed. Behind me, back out the door was the little main road, and the quaysides with rows of clean, well-loved boats waiting to help

155

their owners relax. 'It's paradise, man. We all survived – ain't no N'Awlins here.'

A few kilometres north of the town, we parked up and walked over a dune to check the ocean.

It looked menacing – dark in hue and groomed by a light offshore wind blowing off the vast lagoon to our west. The sand was more gravel-like, and no palm trees in sight. Reeds and dry shrubs sprang up from place to place. Two people swam in the shore break, while half a mile north I could see another patch of about ten people on the beach.

'This ain't Florida any more,' said Marc, as a patch of the surface got ruffled by a gust of wind.

The landscape had changed drastically, he was right. 'There's still not a lot of swell, mind,' I warned. I could think only in terms of waves now. I'd had some fun ones at Sebastian Inlet and New Smyrna, a novelty paddle around on the Gulf Coast, and a grovel in warm, but really sub-standard conditions at Wrightsville. Like the surf shop worker said, we deserved some good surf now, considering the amount of effort we'd put in.

'It's coming,' said Marc. 'Still a bit off that horizon, but it's out there.'

CHAPTER NINE

HURRICANE ISABEL

Ocracoke didn't face quite so directly into the Atlantic as Hatteras – the biggest and best-known of the Outer Banks. We'd have a good chance of riding something that evening if we drove on. To get to Hatteras you needed no ferry reservation, and all of Ocracoke could be covered in not much more than half an hour.

The dock for the Hatteras boat had a real end-of-world feeling. You drove down a tiny finger of sand for miles and miles – nothing on the horizon and ocean on both sides, before coming to an abrupt stop in the road, where a small group of cars were queuing, seemingly for the chance to drive into the sea and off the edge of the continent. A mist had now formed, so there was no chance of seeing any of the boats running between the islands.

'Remember in the Narnia books, when that little mouse, Reepecheep, is that his name, sails off into the mist?' said Marc. '*The Voyage of the Dawn Treader*, isn't it? Awesome book. Read it when I was like five. And I still remember it. Anyway – doesn't this place make you think of that? We're gonna drive into bloody oblivion here.'

'Sounds fun.'

'Too right it does. At least then I won't have to go back to work.'

We waited a few moments, still no boats in view. Then Marc asked:

'D'you know anything about the Bermuda Triangle?'

'No.'

'Pretty big area actually. Goes from Miami to Puerto Rico and the Bahamas – if you drew a triangle between them. Lots of unexplained disappearances of boats and planes round there. Probably just a coincidence. The Gulf Stream is strong in that neck of the woods for one. And compasses don't work in the Triangle, either.'

'Don't they? Well that's got to be odd?'

'You'd think – but that's one thing there is a simple explanation for. A colleague of mine, Ben, wrote a paper on it. It's one of only two spots on the planet where a magnetic compass will point towards true north. Everywhere else they're a bit off. If someone's navigating the area and doesn't bear that in mind, they'll get lost – pre-GPS, obviously. Add a hurricane to that and it's easy to see why lots of people get into trouble there.'

'Yeah.'

'Did you know Columbus was one of the first people to get into shit there? Or rather one of the first *accounts* of someone getting into shit there. And probably coz of a hurricane then, too.'

Often, when Marc started to stream his talking like this, you knew he had something on his mind. He was finding comfort from something, hiding behind his banks of facts. His worry couldn't have been riding a small ferry barge between two giant sandbars, even if we were on the edge of the Bermuda Triangle, as he had always been a pretty fearless waterman. My guess was the mention of work. Maybe he was feeling guilty for being away from his world of equations for such a nebulous reason. Was I wasting his finite and expensive time by dragging him around the East Coast chasing an uncertain swell source? Or was he dreading going back to it all – to his Dr Rhys alter ego, which I'd kind of hoped he was finally abandoning back on the mainland.

'So you don't think there's anything, you know, fishy about the Triangle then?' I asked.

'I hope not. Some people would say we're currently *in it*! Ben told me about a few of the theories though – laugh-out-loud stuff. Time warps, Atlantis, aliens – all bollocks, of course. Studies have accounted for most of the incidents. But people will still let their imaginations go.'

'And why not?' I asked.

Marc smirked. I knew we wouldn't see eye to eye on this. He wandered off to find a drink, and returned red faced and fuming over something else anyway.

'Bloody fucking Yanks calling me English again!' He'd had a conversation by the vending machine.

'That bloke over there. What an idiot. From Ohio, he said. Called me English twice, then said he thought Wales *was* England.'

I laughed.

'It's not funny!'

A full day of travel, perhaps? No solid waves since New Smyrna, and headaches from a load to drink the night before. Not to mention the dozen mozzie bites each that itched from time to time. It was obvious from the mood in the car that we both needed good surf.

The second boat ride gave us that reassuring rock from side to side that tells you there's a bit of swell running. We docked to a crisp, golden evening on the island of Hatteras. The mist had gone, and with it all traces of wind. We rolled straight off the boat and onto a street that cut through the main town at the south end: pretty wooden homes painted with colours that reflected the late sunshine, and clean, paved roads, which all led to a main highway that would run the length of the whole sandbar, eventually arriving at the bigger settlements of Kill Devil Hills and Nags Head to the north – whereupon you'd almost be in Virginia.

The lighthouse at Cape Hatteras had always been a landmark for surfers who knew anything about the Eastern Seaboard. This was one of the most exposed breaks in the whole of the country and, like Wrightsville Beach, it stood an excellent chance of having surf most days. There was a playful, one-day swell coming in from a local storm that had run out yesterday. Speeding through the forest that occupied the wider land towards the cape, we passed other cars with boards on or in them coming back from the beach – their owners looking wet-haired and satisfied. Then the trees gave way for us to see the iconic, towering, black and white, ten-storey-plus lighthouse, and we knew surfing was just moments away.

A jetty just north of the lighthouse was organising the small swell into wedge-like left-hand peaks, doubling it in height, a little like Sebastian Inlet in reverse. The sand was soft-packed, and made the waves churn over with impressive, raw power. The other good thing was that, unlike Sebastian, each set would break in a different place – meaning the considerable crowd could get their fill (instead of the best or most knowledgeable surfers always getting the pick of the best waves).

The water here was still soothingly warm. You needed no wetsuit at all – not even a neoprene jacket – and I felt loose and comfy sitting around waiting for waves. There were some very talented young riders out too and, as in Wrightsville, it motivated you to surf well. Everyone was buzzing after waiting through the recent flat spells, and the disappointment of Tropical Storm Chantal.

'This has nothing on what we'll get if the hurricanes work out next week, man,' a deeply tanned surfer with grey hairs mixed amongst the sun-bleached browns told me, as we chatted in the line-up, waiting for a set. 'Once you put a serious swell on this place *everyone* will get tubed. Even grandma over there.' He was referring to a middle-aged woman, probably another ten or fifteen years his senior, who was cruising a longboard right through the pack of energised youngsters, wave after wave.

The soft sand also meant you didn't mind getting thrashed by the chest-high waves. A fair few sets would close out, sometimes violently. A good kicking over a forgiving, sandy seabed is healthy for the soul though, and Marc and I had an hour and a half of pure fun before it got too dark to see anything more.

In the cooling evening, we got out and ate a tea of olives and peanuts – leftovers from the South Carolina Cider Co, and then prepared to spend our first night in the Betty Ford.

As an estate the car had plenty of room, and so we moved our belongings and boards into the middle, making cosy little private compartments. I opened the windows and blasted insect repellent everywhere. It made us cough at first, before easing off and leaving just the sounds of the beach, cicadas in the trees behind and the odd passing car.

The other good thing about sleeping in your vehicle is that you are guaranteed to wake at first light. In a flash, sleep was over and we were surfing again, this time with the dawn light rising out of the sea in front of us.

It was the same routine again: random A-frame-shaped waves were breaking up and down the beach. And for this second session there was a strong offshore wind grooming them into hollow cylinders – offering the odd tube as reward for being in the right place at the right time. Waves good enough to stop you thinking about anything as you rode them, relying on oceanic kinaesthesia to tell you what to do instead – a deeply personal sense of where and how to move that surfers had to earn through years of trying to stay in tune with the rhythms of the seas all over the planet.

As a surfer you're never more reverent of the ocean's energies than when sitting in the midst of a new swell on a new continent, absorbing its unfamiliar rhythms. A human body, don't forget, is mostly made up of water – which is why we are so easily picked up by it and feel such a natural affinity for waves. When you ride a wave some of its energy goes through you – through your water. For that fleeting moment you are part of that volume so vast merely its edges can reduce rock to sand, and whose movements and cycles are so all-conquering we rely upon them for survival. Almost everything a surfer cares about is completely at the will and whim of water and tide – beyond simply the waves alone. Sea breezes or offshore breezes – so important in shaping the surf – both follow oceanic weather patterns. And weather in turn can hold the whole human race – modern civilisation as we know it – to ransom. Here, at the edge of the US mainland, we weren't only frolicking in America's Atlantic frontline – we were playing with and tapping into forces that guided the entire globe's way of life.

The Outer Banks were the newest and most geologically active part of the East Coast. The land was moving west at such a rate that only a few years ago *they* (that is government of the state of North Carolina) had decided to move the Cape Hatteras lighthouse inland almost a kilometre. Sounds ambitious for an object 200 feet in height and weighing 900 tons, but in a matter of months the entire construction was raised, placed on rollers and towed to its present resting place behind the parking lot in which we were now sitting and unwinding after a morning surfing.

The Hatteras lighthouse was an important one. The Banks had often been dubbed the 'Graveyard of the Atlantic', with over 600 known ships having been lost around here. Galleons, war boats, pirate vessels, cargo ships and explorers had all come to grizzly ends along these islands, quite a few of them in hurricane conditions.

By midday a nasty sea breeze had come up and was tearing the last movements of the swell to shreds. This was probably it for good waves until the system we were waiting for took shape.

'What next?' Marc asked.

'Dunno – a trip back into the town? Lunch somewhere? How about getting online to see what's happening out to sea?'

'Yep. That all sounds like a plan.'

We edged out of our space and made for the exit to Cape Hatteras's parking lot. I looked at the cars and where they were from: Virginia, Delaware, New York and New Jersey. For a Brit nearly five hundred miles would be a long way to drive for a holiday – but it didn't bother people here.

'D'you know,' said Marc, 'that a gallon of petrol here is about a third of what it is back home? That's insane, eh? We could probably get to Chesapeake Bay for the same price as it costs me to drive to work and back.'

'Bigger engines though,' I noted.

'Yeah. Look at that one!'

An enormous six-wheeler was parked at the edge of the lot, with glistening, polished bumpers. It had to be three times the size of my car at home.

I was more interested in the SUV next to it, though, because of its bumper sticker – 'Hurricane Alert' was printed in a snazzy font across a copy of the red and black flag that would be flown on the beaches here in the rare event of a storm threatening to make landfall.

'Must be a surfer, that one,' I said. Either that or someone with a particularly macabre sense of humour...

Despite landfalls being less likely here than in Florida or along the Gulf, there was still a pretty rich hurricane heritage in the Outer Banks. The place was proud of this and had a wild side to its identity as a result.

In Hatteras town, we drove past a row of tiny wooden show homes – the kind that looked as though they could be flat-packed, driven off and reassembled by nightfall. Each was coloured differently: purple, pink, lime green, banana yellow, orange, pastel blue – with little white verandas.

This was the Hatteras Sands Resort. A middle-aged woman greeted us. She had a pair of glasses hanging around her neck and a short bob of neat blonde hair, which went well with her clean white T-shirt and neat appearance. She had emerged from the reception door a couple of minutes after we'd walked through the entrance gates.

'Can I help?'

'Er, yeah – are those houses for rent?' Marc asked, pointing at the multicoloured row of cabins.

'They sure are! In fact they just cleared out of the last reservations of the season. How long are you looking at staying?' She beckoned us into the office.

'No idea,' Marc shrugged, walking over. 'Could be a few days, could be two weeks.'

'Well, give us a hundred dollars and you're good for three nights.'

Marc started talking over some finer points to this arrangement, while I walked around inside. The reception joined onto a dining area and games room. Someone had a liking for jigsaw puzzles around here; about twenty were framed and displayed, all on patriotic themes. There was the bald eagle, the Twin Towers of the World Trade Center, US flags, a transcript of the national anthem. The tablecloths were made up of stars and stripes. Flags and pendants adorned everything they could possibly be stuck to or hung from.

I walked back over to Marc, who was still chatting to the lady. 'Yes, I'm a university lecturer,' he was saying. 'Physics, but my research involves computer programming too.'

'Oh jeez, you should talk to my grandson – he wants to study computer modelling. Car design, I think. That sound right to you?'

Marc usually hated talking about computing if it was anything other than the few obscure areas of the discipline in which he was almost professor-proficient. So it was surprising how tolerant he was.

'Yes – there's a lot of mathematics to what I do, but your grandson sounds like an artist.'

'Oh he is. Ain't that right John?'

'What?' Her husband was walking in, keys in hand.

'This boy's a college professor. In *Wales*!'

Now I realised why Marc was being so friendly.

'Wales! My goodness, what a beautiful *country*,' said John, also passing the same trial with flying colours.

'We're from California originally, so that Welsh weather is just so cute to us.'

Cute? Hardly. The lexicon Americans used to describe weather certainly had the propensity to be a little odd at times. Perhaps it was because of the size of the country – maybe that was why they pulled out these words that seemed to belittle Mother Nature (or Gaia, if you like). In its way, I suppose calling the utter drudgery of a soaking, dark, determined Welsh winter 'cute' was a bit like describing a life-threatening hurricane as 'eloquent'.

The next thing John did was hand us plastic, button-sealable wristbands, to show that we were guests of Hatteras Sands. The bands, surprisingly enough, were also patterned with the Stars and Stripes.

'Now we *are* in America, so we're going to be patriotic,' he said. We locked them onto our wrists, smiling. 'Good,' said John.

I spotted an interesting aerial photograph under the glass of the counter. It showed Hatteras Island, thin and straight as usual, but split in half by the ocean. The patch of water in between had been labelled in Tipp-Ex handwriting as 'Isabel Inlet'.

'As in "Hurricane Isabel"?' I asked John.

'Of course! Now, let me tell you about that! That picture there is of the New Inlet, or Isabel Inlet. This part of the island here...' He pointed to the left of the photo. '... got cut off by the storm and became Little Hatteras for a couple weeks. A long time ago that was how the island was anyway, split into two. Eisenhower or someone – I forget who – started building a bridge between them. But then a hurricane filled the whole section with sand and the bridge pilings got buried. That was when they decided to just build the highway back over the new sand. Lasted decades, until Isabel hit and removed the sand again – and the road too! Returned things back to how they were – except the pilings that were the start of the old bridge were still there.'

They again. Busy as usual – although hurricanes seemed to still be a step ahead.

'What did you do during Isabel?' I asked.

'Me? Oh, I walked on the beach in the storm. It was *beautiful*!'

I liked these guys – even more so after they told Marc to just fire his computer up on the spot for a wireless connection.

'You can go into the house in an hour – I'm just gonna get it ready.'

'No worries,' said Marc. 'I'm not fussy.'

'There's going to be another hurricane soon, isn't there?' I asked John, as his wife disappeared with a broom.

'Of course,' he said. 'There's always going to be another hurricane. The season's here. It's a matter of time. Now you guys have a nice day.'

CHAPTER TEN

NAMED

When we wandered through the lounge area the next morning, John had some news for us.

'Yeah – there's a storm out there.'

I told him we knew because Marc had checked the forecast for us last night.

'But I wouldn't worry,' John continued. 'They think it's gonna hit Florida from the way it's building out there.'

'What?'

'Yeah – lookin' like takin' a swipe that way. Erin, I think it's called. Or is that the one in the Gulf? There's two of 'em out there – I know that. But I really wouldn't worry – we'll get plenty of warning if either of them are gonna make it up here.'

'I'm not worried,' I said. 'We're interested in getting the surf off them.'

'*Surf*? In a hurricane? Wow! I don't know about that.'

John wished us luck and made his way back towards the office. Marc, meanwhile, was arriving at the official low-down.

'Dean,' he said.

'What?'

'Dean. That's the name of our storm. Erin's the one in the Gulf. It's funny, coz Erin was actually the first one to form, but then Dean got to tropical storm strength earlier. They were both only named this morning, though.'

I had butterflies immediately. It had happened. Dean had come to life. From now on, there would be a third party involved in all our decisions.

'So what's going to happen?' I asked Marc, who was still as blank in tone about the whole thing as the Hurricane Center's ticker tape commentaries.

'Well, Erin is the more immediate one,' he explained. 'But only because it's threatening the mainland first. It's no use to us down there in the Gulf though. Unless you want to rue the fact we aren't there instead, that is.'

'Should we be?'

'Er, tomorrow we should, yeah. I think old Kevin back at that surf shop in Fort Walton is in for classic surf. But you never know – if we'd gone to the Gulf we might get like one day of waves from Erin, and then get totally caught out by Dean. Dean's definitely got the most potential coz it's out in the open Atlantic. Now let me see...'

He clicked through a few more pages.

'Well its winds have reached enough speed to get named, and the whole thing is still smack in the middle of the ocean. Right now as we speak it's generating swell, so whatever happens from now on we know there's something to chase.'

'How long?'

'I'm not really sure. Three to five days?'

Three to five days on the Outer Banks was an easy stretch to watch disappear – for me at least. But for Dr Marc Rhys it was a different story. We had come up against one of his oldest demons: time to waste.

Marc simply wasn't comfortable with down time. He had this restlessness that none of his close friends had ever really been able to understand. 'Status anxiety' was what his mother once called it when he was preparing for his PhD viva. This comment offended him so much that he took the cup of tea she was drinking out of her hands and poured it down the sink before storming out of the house with a board under his arm, and going in the water for twenty minutes.

He always loved his surfing – of that there had never been any doubt – but while the rest of us had given in completely and entirely to its lures, Marc saw it more like an addiction he'd been afflicted with. Like all addicts in recovery, he used to try to go dry from time to time. Moderation, it seemed, was not an option. He quit going to the beach during GCSE exams, and again during A Levels. Approaching his degree finals he chose to have non-essential knee surgery so as to force himself out of the water for two months (it worked – he got a record-breaking first). But his years in London were the most perturbed of all.

While working on his PhD, Marc had found this girlfriend – from somewhere in the Home Counties – who the rest of us utterly loathed. The reason for our hatred was because it was clear to all of us she only loved Dr Rhys. His alter ego – the fallen surf bum, the wannabe nomad and anarchic beach layabout – was barely known to her.

Through those few years I'd only see him on New Year's Eve, and perhaps occasionally in summer, when we'd surf tiny, high-tide Rest Bay amongst crowds of swimmers and beginners (while two miles away the wave we'd lived for in winter as kids, The Wedge, hibernated). But as Marc researched areas of physics so intricate they made my head ache, he wondered whether he could have done things differently:

'You've been to some pretty silly places in the last few years,' he said once, 'and some good ones too. I have not. And it is a regret I may have to live with.'

It was a regret that the girlfriend from the Home Counties could not live with though, and when he landed a series of lectures and some research work that would bring him back to South Wales on a semi-regular basis (semi-regular enough to buy a house down the road from the dishevelled apartment I shared with the singer of a local punk band), she asked him to declare his intentions. Apparently, Elaine found meeting his mates one of the deciding factors. After a weekend they spent in Porthcawl with no surf in sight, but plenty of beer, she had found herself unable to reconcile the complete lack of interest in careers shown by his core crew of old school friends. If he moved back, he could do it without her. And anyway, who wanted to leave West London for Wales? Oh, the thought! She demanded he put his cards on the table: was the other woman – in other words, the sea – going to be there in the background, or was he ready to declare himself fully reformed from his surfing addiction?

Marc didn't fully commit to either option, and in a flash the girl was gone. Surfing was clearly the more steadfast of the two.

He never really acted that gutted about the break-up, but flung himself into research like never before. He toyed with 'string theory' – forming ideas of how the universe may have come into existence – and stumbled on computer modelling techniques that could simulate the movement of water better than any yet developed. He won awards, helped local campaigners beat a wind farm proposal that threatened a surf spot, and rode waves on and off in between, although never with the same drop-it-all-if-the-right-swell-showed-up level of commitment as the rest of us. Elaine was rarely mentioned again, thankfully.

However, we knew that being rejected like this had bothered Marc. When we were young he used to get restless on a rainy afternoon, but post-Elaine he was unstoppable. A hung-over Sunday cup of tea was too slow a pace of life for him, and on the solo, commercial surf trips he did go on (one of which was to the exclusive Maldivian resort of Tari Village), he was always rumoured to take along work – a few papers to review at the very least.

And now at this temporary base, Hatteras Sands, his anxiety at staying put and waiting for swell returned with a vengeance. We'd check the surf and eat breakfast, but then Marc would withdraw into himself and work online, not wanting to waste the days, while I drove around the island by myself. Up until now he'd been fine because we'd been constantly on the move, but I should have guessed he had the potential to get like this when he'd wanted to bolt from New Orleans after just the one night.

Worst of all, though, he was starting to make me feel guilty again – could I have done something more useful during all the days I had spent waiting on waves in the last decade? He'd created a scientific legacy between swells, while what had I done beyond pursuing a hit-and-miss writing career? I had learned to play poker, memorised every line from the film *North Shore*, studied surf mags to the extent that I could name a wave in almost every country, and had managed to finish inside the top ten for *Surfer* magazine's online *Fantasy Surfer* game. (My one and only foray into geekdom – too bad it didn't earn me a penny.)

As I drove over the Outer Banks for the next few days, my mind began to work too hard. It was Marc's fault. I even felt bad for leaving him to it. I knew our friends back home would think I was failing in my mission – not succeeding in coaxing the old Marc out again.

Although the winds were always about, the odd moments in which they dropped off gave me the occasional peak to surf while we waited on news of Tropical Storm Dean – who I was relying on to kick-start the trip's momentum again. We needed this storm to deepen. Our entire plan was at Dean's mercy.

Erin, meanwhile, had begun to aim for Texas (the TV channels had, with almost deflated tones, ruled out any chance of it hitting New Orleans again). As a tropical storm this meant that the Lone Star State would have to contend with immense rains, even if the winds themselves weren't that big a threat. It was big news throughout America. The surfers I came across, though, were mostly marvelling at Erin's potential to give waves to the famished communities of Florida's Panhandle and Tampa areas.

Meanwhile, during his first few days in this world, the young Dean's intentions remained a mystery.

In a surf shop not long before the turn off to Cape Hatteras, three days after the storm's christening, I had a chat with another attendant about hurricanes on the Outer Banks. Again, the advice was: if the hurricane didn't track up, look to the northern states for the best chance of scoring.

On the walls of the shop, satellite photos of great storms were pinned to a cork panel by passionate collectors. Isabel was there – her eye almost directly over Hatteras and Ocracoke.

'The one we all remember best around here was Kyle,' said a slim guy standing behind the counter. He looked to be in his late twenties, had the usual permanent face tan of a surfer. His short hair had lost some of its colour to the sun, although it still remained firmly brown rather than blonde. 'A few summers ago, the fricken thing just kept comin back to life and sending more swell. And it never killed no one – far as I know.'

I took a moment to peer at the hypnotic shapes of the various circles of cloud. Some were rough swirls around a still forming centre, while others looked like thousand-mile-wide buzz saws of white water vapour drifting ominously through otherwise clear atmospheres – bellicose, menacing and with minds of their own. I imagined them looking around, as they hovered over the ocean, thinking about where best to strike. And the bigger the storm, the more defined the little black dot in the middle. A fully formed hurricane was a compelling site from space – and studying different ones in a series was something I could have carried on doing for hours. Each had slightly different nuances of mist, patches of cloud. Like snowflakes, but of a much less benevolent nature.

'Did you know that in the eye there's like no wind, no cloud, and super-fine weather?' the cashier asked me, his voice calm – as if thinking about it as he spoke.

'Yeah – I'd heard that.'

'I was in the eye of one once – everything just went real calm for like an hour and a half. And then it just went fuckin' crazy – the gnarliest winds and rain I ever saw. And waves like the size of your house, dude.'

Alongside some of the photos, other paper clippings related to hurricanes had been pinned; postcards of paintings, ancient native drawings of vapour spirals. Some were going orange and fading as if they'd been pinned up for years.

'People in America have known about hurricanes and tried to understand them for centuries, man,' he added. 'They should surf. Then they'd get more out of them.'

I asked about the places to surf on the Outer Banks this year. Sand movement was so constant that surf spots would come and go over a matter of weeks. I'd even heard of local pros having to re-spray their cars to avoid people recognising them parked up, and then knowing where the best waves were happening. Fair enough, I reckon – why should they do all the hard work of finding a spot, only for the lazy ones to benefit anyway?

'Oh, man. It changes so much.' The guy gave me a knowing look. The same code meant I wasn't going to get thrown a bone either.

'Hard to say – especially as there ain't been any surf lately.' I was aware you had to earn local knowledge. He was entitled to keep tight-lipped – especially since it was done in such a friendly way. 'That's gonna be the hardest thing if Dean sends us swell, you know – workin out where to surf. You been out at Hatteras – the lighthouse?'

'Of course.'

'That's pretty consistent – the jetties keep sand in place more there. Same with Rodanthe – you know, or s-turns as they're also called.'

Rodanthe was the spot Sam had told me about during our night in Le Pub. I'd already surfed that a few times too – and he was right. A couple of peaks north of the pier – towards the s-turn in the main road – had given me some playful afternoon sessions. Marc had even come along once too.

The latest shot on display in the shop was Tropical Storm Barry – from June of this year.

Would there be another commemorative portrait on the cork board in a few weeks' time, I wondered, one by the name of Dean, perhaps?

After another quick paddle around in the lee-waters of the Hatteras lighthouse, I gave the Betty Ford a quick on-the-spot spark plug change and oil top-up, and headed for home.

When I got in I spotted Marc's blonding mop of hair by the poolside, where he was sunning himself and reading a copy of *Time*. His laptop was still beside the lounger, but I knew something had changed because he suddenly looked at peace.

'How were the waves?' he asked.

'Nothing special.'

'That's what I want to hear. If I get this one last paper reviewed I'll have no outstanding work, and it should mean I can stay away longer.' He gestured towards the sleeping laptop. 'Tropical Storm Dean is really on the move now. I've been looking at it today.'

He sat up, draped his T-shirt over his left shoulder, grabbed the computer again and motioned for me to walk with him towards the reception room. Hours on the sunlounger had made his freckles come out, and left a latticed imprint on his reddening back.

'Right – should be a signal here... OK. Got it.'

He clicked a few times, knowing exactly where on the National Hurricane Center's website to look.

I leaned over to see the report. Its familiar tone was so deadpan in the way it delivered news that meant so much to so many:

```
THE CENTRAL CONVECTION ASSOCIATED WITH DEAN
HAS MORE OF A BANDED APPEARANCE THIS LUNCHTIME
- INITIAL MOTION IS STILL SLIGHTLY UNCERTAIN
- DEAN SHOULD ENCOUNTER WARMER SEA SURFACE
TEMPERATURES ALONG THE FORECAST TRACK - AND
THE VERTICAL SHEAR IS EXPECTED TO BE LIGHT
DURING THE FORECAST PERIOD. THE INTENSITY
GUIDANCE CALLS FOR STEADY STRENGTHENING -
AND SO DOES THE INTENSITY FORECAST IN BEST
AGREEMENT WITH THE ICON CONSENSUS. GIVEN THE
FAVORABLE UPPER-LEVEL WINDS AND WARM WATER
- THERE IS A POSSIBILITY THAT DEAN COULD BE
NOTABLY STRONGER THAN FORECAST.
```

Neither of us said anything, as Marc waited for me to re-read the report.

'Good, eh?' I asked.

'Good? It's fucking unreal! The only trouble is the current prediction cone has started suggesting it's far more likely to go into the Caribbean or the Gulf. Remember what that lad on Ocracoke was saying about going north to somewhere like Long Island or New Jersey?'

'Yeah.'

'Well, it does make sense. We'll know more in the next six hours, but the Outer Banks might actually be a bit close. How do you feel about driving again?'

'Whatever we need to do,' I told him. 'The Betty Ford has to go back up north eventually anyway.'

'Well – I'll keep looking. But it may be that we will need to move again – even as early as tomorrow.'

'Like I said, that's fine,' I said. 'Did you do any work at all today? Or have you just been looking at storm models?'

'A bit.' Marc smiled. 'It's hard, mind – working in this weather. And with so much at stake...'

Leaving the laptop in my hands, he turned and ran across the Hatteras Sands parking lot and back up to the edge of the pool. He promptly performed a running bomb, plunging loudly and violently into the middle with a titanic splash and alarming a teenage couple who had been enjoying a clandestine cuddle.

Positive developments, I thought. Besides Dean, it looked as though Hurricane Marc was also starting to organise its priorities.

CHAPTER ELEVEN

TROPICAL STORM DEAN

Something odd happened to me the next morning that left me disturbed and confused: I slept late! So late that I woke feeling groggy, missing any chance of catching a surf before the wind came up.

'Bollocks,' I groaned, rolling over and looking at my watch. It was almost ten. I was devastated, and Marc was nowhere to be seen.

I lay on my unmade bed, wanting to move but not quite managing to send the right signal to my legs. A crushing bout of tiredness had crept up on me. I hoped it was just the amount of sun and surf I'd been getting, and not anything else. I had been eaten alive by an army of mosquitoes a few days ago after all – although I was sure they were probably nice, clean ones here in the USA.

Eventually, I heard Marc wandering around outside.

'Why didn't you wake me, you bastard?' I called out. 'I've missed the wind.'

'Coz we're leaving,' he called back. 'I've checked us out.'

He'd been looking at the charts since before dawn and was even more certain that, because of Tropical Storm Dean's path, we had better head north.

'They might get some swell here on the Outer Banks,' he explained. 'But the angle isn't as good as it could be. And Florida, meanwhile, is actually on the edge of the "cone of uncertainty", so going there could well be too close.'

As with Erin, the media, meanwhile, had begun to seize on the slim chance that the storm could end up taking a swipe at New Orleans again.

'Do they say that every time a potential hurricane appears on the map?' I asked.

'Without fail. At the formation stage they'd have reason to as well. This thing could go anywhere.'

After late morning surf check up at Cape Hatteras, we convened over a supermarket-bought breakfast of bagels and cream cheese. The agenda was deciding a route.

'We might be able to ride a few along our way up north,' said Marc. 'Do you know where we can catch some waves between here and Long Island?'

I told him we could punctuate the trip with stops at Virginia Beach and Atlantic City in New Jersey – as well as the strip of coast immediately south of New York.

'I've heard rave reports about Manasquan Inlet,' I told him. 'As well as Sandy Hook – the furthest north beach along the Jersey shore.'

'Sandy Hook? How have I heard of that place before?'

Before I could answer, Marc remembered. Sandy Hook became famous in the surfing world for a photograph taken in the early morning of September 11, 2001. The day of the attacks on New York's Twin Towers, according to *Surfer* magazine, had also coincided with the arrival of clean swell lines from a so-called 'perfect storm'. A photographer had stepped onto a groyne at Sandy Hook during the swell and snapped a picture of surfers gorging themselves on pristine autumn point break waves, while in the background the Manhattan skyline billowed smoke into the heavens. The guy hadn't known the significance of these images at the time, and could have just as easily stood and shot from shore. If he had, we would never have heard of Sandy Hook.

Marc explained how before Dean got to the Windward Islands a hurricane swell would be forming nicely, but from too far west to catch the Outer Banks, Virginia and Jersey Shores. Instead, the best chances of good surf would occur where the USA ran out eastward into the North Atlantic. Here the south-facing shores would pick up the brunt of Dean's energy, which would by then have been groomed into perfect, long range sets of fast-moving waves.

'So ultimately,' I said, 'New York is where we need to head?'

'Yeah,' said Marc. 'The work's done then. We can hop all over New England and Long Island, playing it according to wind and whatever else we want to do.'

This sounded like a done deal, so we turned the keys for the show home over to John again and set off along the Outer Banks – this time to drive all the way to the end of Hatteras Island and on towards the state of Virginia.

We passed Rodanthe, the furthest up the banks I had been so far, after which all we could see was a long, straight strip of highway that ran close to the ocean on both sides. Dunes often masked the open Atlantic to our right, a dam of sand build-up that could defend the precious carriageway from eroding winds and storm surges. You could only guess the range of surf spots that lay behind them.

'Nuts to think the Outer Banks are moving slowly westward,' I said, remembering how the lighthouse at Hatteras had been literally pulled across the beach. The banks were in motion by up to 15 feet a year in places, apparently. I wondered what implications this might have on property in the area.

A lot of the wooden houses had raised bases propped up by stilts, which would protect them from floods and encroaching seas. When we did pass small towns, most of the properties were lavish and gorgeously designed with winding stairs, balconies, extensions and verandas of all sorts. Even though they sprawled out like Escher paintings, the dwellings always looked really homely with their quaint wooden exteriors and gardens that ran straight onto the dunes. I tried to imagine what they were like inside, guessing which ones were occupied. Coming home from the beach to one of these would be a real treat – a wonderful fantasy, until the prices crossed your mind.

'It's like bloody southern California here,' Marc observed.

This was the start of the heavily built-up sections of the Outer Banks – the towns of Nags Head, Kill Devil Hills and Kitty Hawk. It was here that Marc decided we needed to stop again.

'Trust me!' he exclaimed. 'I need to send an email. Forgot to do it back in Hatteras.'

'Forgot?' I pulled a pained expression. A look that said, 'Do we absolutely have to?', but Marc insisted.

'I won't be more than ten minutes. You can drop me off at one of the coffee shops. They'll all have wireless around here.'

A few blocks of retail buildings with communal car parks appeared at the side of the road – which included a little Internet cafe. Dr Rhys disembarked, memory stick in hand. As is the case throughout the States, a petrol station was only a stone's throw away as well, so I went to fill up.

There was heavy traffic in Kitty Hawk. Two-lane highways streamed with cars, coming and going to the demands of rows of traffic lights hung high over the intersections on US 158. We stopped at a gas station, which would only accept pre-pay or credit cards. Mine didn't work for some reason, so I walked in and used cash to order twenty dollars of unleaded, a Nicaraguan coffee and some sweets – a strawberry and liquorice twizzler and several neon-coloured chews in a thick, white bag. Marc could get his own snacks.

Once the gas nozzle clunked dead, I hopped back in the Betty Ford and drove to the edge of the forecourt and sat watching the scene for a moment while I drank my coffee. Within a few minutes it had gone cold, and it made me feel anything but rehydrated. I felt shaky and sticky. Why hadn't I bought chilled water instead? It was another really humid day, so to feel more comfortable I started trying to remember British weather – winters in which I would shiver to sleep, only to wake the next morning to find every joint frozen and creaking like those of an eighty-year-old. I thought about the layers of wetsuit we would be wearing in five months' time, and how loose you felt surfing here in just a pair of trunks.

At the far end of the street I could see a dune. Just beyond it was the ocean. I wondered if it would have waves, and turned the car up to go and look.

The oceanfront street was one-way, and every parking space belonged to privately owned homes. 'Towing in operation!' warned sign after sign.

I found a road that was going to head back down to the US 158, with a few non-permit-holding cars pulled up along it. Worth the risk – it would only be for a minute. Leaving the Betty Ford wedged against a pile of chippings and sand, I ran back up to look over the sea defences at the ocean. It had changed drastically. The clear waters off Hatteras were no more. It was now thick, brown, wind-chopped and devoid of swell. Lifeguards patrolled like prison wardens, and hordes of tourists ran amok across the damp, sludgy sand. There was no way anything worth surfing could be breaking along this coast today. We were off to Virginia for sure.

I was worried Marc would be annoyed when I got back to collect him. I'd said five minutes and been gone for nearly half an hour. He didn't even notice though.

'All done?' I asked.

'Yeah. Message sent, and I even had time to look at the rugby news.'

'Fair enough. I bet you looked at the latest from Tropical Storm Dean though too?'

'Of course.'

'And?'

'Well, it's going to be *Hurricane* Dean any hour now. In fact, it's starting to get a bit worrying.'

He pulled the link up for me to see.

'Yeah, it's, er, going to be a belter by the looks of things.'

Marc pointed at the screen:

BASED ON WHAT WE THINK WE KNOW ABOUT INTENSITY CHANGE – THERE DO NOT SEEM TO BE TOO MANY INHIBITING FACTORS TO AN INTENSIFICATION OF DEAN. GLOBAL MODELS UNANIMOUSLY DEVELOP A LARGE UPPER-LEVEL ANTICYCLONE NEAR THE CENTER OF THE STORM AS THE SYSTEM TRAVELS INTO THE WEST ATLANTIC. IN COMBINATION WITH VERY DEEP WARM WATERS – THIS PATTERN WOULD FAVOR THE DEVELOPMENT OF A VERY POWERFUL HURRICANE. THE OFFICIAL INTENSITY FORECAST IS HIGHER THAN THE PREVIOUS NHC FORECAST AND IS IN GOOD AGREEMENT WITH A CONSENSUS OF SHIPS – GFDL – HWRF – AND LGEM MODELS.

'It's got potential to be a natural disaster,' said Marc, abruptly. 'Category five is seventy per cent likely. That's one *hell* of a storm. And if it did turn towards Louisiana with the Gulf as warm as it is now, the implications could be catastrophic.'

I didn't know what to say. It certainly wouldn't be that easy to live out the carefree life of a surfer against news of New Orleans being deluged again – and that was only one of many possible scenarios.

By far the worst places to get hit by major hurricanes would be countries in the developing world – and we both knew that the Caribbean and Latin America were full of those. A big walloping from a Category 5 hurricane could set places like Honduras, Haiti or Cuba back a couple of decades. With brittle building materials and homes of corrugated iron and basic wood, just a few hours of oceanic fury could flatten a whole town beyond recognition. I thought about all the media images I'd seen in my life of people fleeing such storms across the world – wading away from their livelihoods and property with stoic expressions – as if to say 'this was always going to happen to us anyway, being as we're poor'. Was it just my selective memory, or did that kind of thing only seem to happen in the countries that could least afford it?

Then again most of the famous land-falling hurricanes, when you looked them up, had hit Florida, Texas, Georgia, Louisiana or other states. Was that really the case, or did the American and European psyches have difficulty committing to memory the storms that did damage elsewhere? From the comforts of an Internet cafe on the touristy coast of the Carolinas, I hoped that we wouldn't be about to find out. I couldn't think of what to say – should I just keep a brave face and ask Marc about the surf situation? Or would he too want to talk about Dean's implications elsewhere in the Atlantic Basin?

'Well, let's hope it stays out of the Gulf, then,' was the best I could do on the spot, 'you know, if the water really *is* that warm.' But Marc didn't seem to mind my lack of sensitivity:

'Well, it's gonna do what it's gonna do,' he said. 'Let's get driving.'

CHAPTER TWELVE

TROPICAL STORM ERIN

'Idiots!' I screamed powerlessly out of the window at the light blue PT Cruiser which had just cut us off horribly as we tried to turn onto the bridge from the Outer Banks to the mainland. More annoying than anything was the fact that the car had a roof loaded with surfboards. Surely this was wrong; surfers weren't supposed to cut each other off like this. We were brothers and sisters, weren't we: the shoeless, jobless tribe of nature lovers against the slick 4x4s and comfort cars of rich America.

'Bullshit,' said Marc. 'Those bloody cars are the ones the surfers drive these days. When was the last time you saw someone pull up to the beach in an old 2CV with their longboard hanging out the sunroof? Only in *Endless Summer*, buddy! Did you get a look at some of the knobheads in the line-up at New Smyrna? Bloody dyed hair, middle-class punks. Kids driving jet-black pick-up trucks with 'Four More Years' stickers on the bumpers – probably blaring shit like Limp Bizkit from the stereo. Spoilt brats, son, I'm sorry to say!'

Marc thought the cost of living near the ocean had priced a lot of people out of surfing these days. He probably had a point, when you thought about the amount of good beach we'd seen fenced off as private property so far.

Traffic for the rest of the bridge off the Outer Banks was more accommodating. We descended onto flat ground, the US Mainland, and a sign indicating the way to Virginia. Then there followed a sweet, but short-lived cruise through some rural lowlands – before concrete began to encroach again.

After a few miles of peaceful countryside, farms and agricultural fields, we were soon crawling along on thick, smoggy four-lane freeways. The closer we got to the ocean the slower the roads became, until finally we rose up onto a coastal carriageway. I felt queasy from the smells of seawater and fast food coming together in a polluted onshore breeze. Casinos, hotels and seedy nightclubs overlooked yet more filthy water. Cars were everywhere, although that didn't seem to deter drunks and tourists from wandering across the road as and when they pleased.

Between a couple of groynes there wasn't much of interest going on in the ocean at all. Undeterred, a hopeful crowd of almost fifty surfers bobbed up and down in the mucky water and tiny waves. It was windy too – really windy.

Alongside an expensive car park, scaffolding was being erected. You wouldn't have guessed it from the conditions, but a big surf contest was due to be held here in a week or so – a World Championship qualifying event with a hefty pot of prize money. I wondered if the organisers would be looking at the news from the National Hurricane Center.

'Where else can you surf between here and New York?' Marc asked promptly.

'What – apart from Sandy Hook?'

'Yeah.'

'Well – a few places along the Jersey shore,' I announced, gingerly. 'I was thinking Atlantic City – it's meant to be one of the first places people surfed along the Eastern Seaboard.'

'Really? Well I don't care. Let's give it all a miss. It's a massive detour to go there, isn't it? And if it's anything like this...'

I thought about how different this place might look in less than a week's time if Hurricane Dean sent swell its way – just in time for the contest probably.

It was decided that we'd try to get over to the northern part of Virginia by nightfall which, given that the day was now thickly overcast, didn't feel very far off. 'I really, really, want to cross Chesapeake Bay before it's dark,' said Marc.

And so we turned our backs on Virginia Beach. On our way out we got stuck in even more traffic, before learning we'd spent almost an hour doing a full revolution of the Norfolk ring road in the wrong direction.

Our map wasn't detailed enough for us to spot the right highway, and there were no landmarks or signs besides an endless run of equidistant traffic lights – each punctuated with enormous emporiums and fast-food chains. We were being bombarded by brand names, flashing lights, logos and slogans. The promise of food was especially taunting. I'd counted four Taco Bells since the coast, and each time they looked more inviting.

When the Chesapeake Bay crossing came into view, though, I realised why Marc had wanted to reach it during daylight. In a country where bridging inconvenient inlets of water was a national pastime, here was yet another astounding feat of engineering. I saw the sign:

The Chesapeake Bay Bridge/Tunnel

'Hang on – there's a bridge *and* a tunnel?'

'I know,' said Marc. 'And we're going to use both.'

'You what?'

'Yep – after a mile or two of going over the water this bridge plunges *into the sea*. It's a shipping lane, see, Chesapeake Bay. Wouldn't be much use to build a big fuck-off bridge across the whole thing, would it? You can sail right up to Baltimore from here, man! So they made a bridge slash tunnel...' He chopped at the air, giving added drama to the slash.

I couldn't see how such a thing was possible. But it was. As the freeway swung eastward, now well out to sea, there was a man-made island of boulders through which the road dropped out of view and into a deep underground passageway illuminated by bright orange lights. I felt a sense of eeriness in being below such a giant mass of water. On descending to a level that made my ears pop, the road began to rise again, climbing back out into the rapidly absorbing dusk. Land had now disappeared from view apart from a few twinkling lights made either by small boats or humble waterfront buildings on the coast to the north. Ahead of us, two flashing lights showed where the road was going to go subterranean again – through the middle of another man-made island.

'Isn't that fucking awesome?' Marc exclaimed, clearly in awe.

'I bet building this was an absolute mission,' I said.

'Yeah – I've got a book about it all at home,' Marc replied. 'It was a big challenge. Built it in the sixties, they did. It won an award from the Yank Society of Civil Engineers, and then became one of the Seven Engineering Wonders of the World. Quicker than taking the bloody ferry, eh!'

'Seven what?'

'Engineering Wonders of the World.'

'Bloody hell – can something man-made be a wonder?'

Marc frowned. 'What are you on about? All the wonders of the ancient, medieval and modern world are man-made! Of course it can. How about the Pyramids, the Empire State Building, the Eiffel Tower or, more important than any, the Millennium Stadium! Makes my eyes water with national pride every time I pass it.'

'So the New Orleans levee system didn't make the list?' I noted, sarcastically. 'That seems unfair.'

The bridge made landfall on a stretch of flats called the Delmarva Peninsular. From here we would pass through both Maryland and Delaware, but not tonight. We were now permanently stuck behind trucks (which must have been going *seriously* slowly to hold us up). The road was down to a single lane with driveways turning straight onto it. Reaching the bridge felt as if the day's goal had been met.

The end of our long drive came soon. A sign just visible from between a cluster of loblolly pine trees was the only hint that one of those classic, post-war-type motels was waiting just off the highway to drag us back into another of the many time warps that lurk along some of the US's oldest major roads. Four words were printed in steel lettering on burgundy, lozenge-shaped panels stacked lopsided like an abstract logo for a pop band. As with the best of the diner and motel signs, the displaying of the name alone rung of nostalgia for a time and a land that I had never been to, and yet knew so much about:

Rittenhouse Motor Lodge. *Vacancy*.

It appeared so suddenly out of the dark that we missed the gravel driveway and had to make a u-turn a hundred yards on. We got it right the second time and I tentatively steered the Betty Ford up to the doorway, under a canopy of forest. Outside the car cicadas whirred, their sound amplified by the wall of tree trunks around us. With the engine off, our headlights seemed an intrusive, unnatural source of light.

I knocked on the front door, through which I could see a large room of antiques. A dim, oil-burning lamp flickered, while faint, blues-based rock 'n' roll music could be heard emanating from another room.

A man in his sixties came into the room and opened the door, smiling. Immediately he took interest in our trip and wanted to know details – before we'd even agreed to stay.

'New Orleans? Ain't been there in years. How was it?'

'Scarred,' Marc replied. 'Deeply scarred.'

We moved on to arranging a room, emptying boards and anything else of value from the car and then took a walk over the highway to a Food Lion supermarket just up the road. This night-time dash for sustenance could have cost us our lives, as trucks tanked past at terrifying speeds. There was no pavement, and to avoid one set of oblivious headlights I literally jumped into a ditch of tall grass – and all for a bland-beyond-bland pre-packed pork sandwich and a packet of crisps.

In the absence of any nourishing or fresh food, I also bought a cheap gallon of red wine – only three dollars. I waited for sleep, lying supine on the freshly made bed and watching a pee-wee baseball game live on ESPN. The kids were really going for it – more competitive than the major league games I'd seen before. When the last inning ended with a catch, delivering victory for the team from St Louis, parents stormed the diamond cheering and jeering, while the defeated Oklahoma youngsters left the field in floods of tears. After that came pre-season NFL. I searched for the Weather Channel, but only got adverts, unrecognisable films and generic sitcoms.

By dawn the channel had become available again. With the remote still on my bedside table, I was able to switch the TV back on as soon as a wall of harsh daylight poured in to the room and woke me. It was early and I couldn't get back to sleep. I lay in bed for almost an hour, hypnotised by the bulletins, before Marc woke up.

Willing the presenters towards giving us some info on Dean, we didn't have to wait long:

This morning twin storms are still with us, both posing threats to the US mainland. Tropical Storm Erin is now making landfall in Texas, causing floods from its heavy rains. However, of far more importance today is this one: Hurricane Dean – now a Category 4 storm – packing winds of up to 145 miles per hour. This is becoming a very serious system and we won't know it's predicted path until Dean makes it to the Lesser Antilles. All interests in Florida and the Gulf states should keep an eye out for this one. Be ready – have kit, and make sure you know where to stay if an evacuation is ordered for your area. The Carolinas and northern states are probably safe, although the only thing we can be one-hundred per cent certain of right now is that this hurricane is intent on foxing us forecasters.'

'Aye – coz you're bloody crap – that's why!' Marc called out to the television. The report continued:

Moving to the Pacific now, and Hurricane Flossie. Here's another one that was doing all it could to throw our predictions off. Experts a few days ago were preparing Hawaii for a major strike. However, it turns out the system weakened as it passed just to the south...

Flossie had been a startlingly near miss. The anchor explained how 'the worst remaining effects are some high waves pounding the beaches', before telling Hawaiians to stay out of the water until the rip currents and waves died down. 'Nobody wants this one to claim any lives now,' grinned another well-dressed expert with perfect teeth. 'Not after the storm has passed!

'Bet the surfers are going nuts over it,' claimed Marc. 'Red flags everywhere probably, but who cares?'

The owner of Rittenhouse was offering us breakfast but, having woken pretty early, we opted to do an hour of driving instead and look for a diner somewhere along the road as we headed north. From there, at a leisurely pace, we could be riding a few waves in New Jersey before dark and then go through New York the day after – whereupon the real swell should be imminent.

We wanted to eat in Nassawadox, just because the name sounded so cool, but everything was shut.

'Go about four and three-quarters of a mile north,' said a passer-by, 'and you'll see a diner called the Sunrise Grill. Awesome breakfasts.'

After that Marc got the idea of trying to go off the main road to see if we were still anywhere near to the west-facing coast of Chesapeake Bay – which was now running up the country somewhere to our west and parallel with the Atlantic. This part of Virginia was a peninsular after all, with water on both sides. The early autumn sky was clear from horizon to horizon, and it was a wonderful way of tracking slowly north – a real break from interstate monotony. The bay hid most of the time between swampy inlets, reeds and picture-perfect snapshots of rural Virginia: a decades-old red tractor parked in a glade, farm sheds, houses shaded by trees – their branches pronate like hands releasing a bird into the wild. At one point we stopped the car to look around, with no idea where we were, other than that it was between Chesapeake's west coast and Highway 13. There was no human activity anywhere. No engines. Not even a plane miles above in the cloudless sky, silently ebbing towards Washington or Baltimore to our north-west.

The sound of the Betty Ford starting up again was almost intrusive. Gently, we crept through a maze of nameless roads.

Bungalows and simple homes – probably self-built judging from little incomplete touches on some – were spread at intervals, rarely with any fences or walls to show where the land was officially divided between families. Most had cars parked up as if everyone was at home, and they were often humble models such as Honda Civics, Ford Escorts (like ours) and the odd Volvo estate – older 750s or V40s. Here we were in true farm country and the choices of vehicle seemed more European in size than anywhere else we had been so far.

When we got back onto the main route north we had already crossed Maryland, and were halfway through Delaware, the First State – as it was the earliest of the original thirteen states to ratify the US Constitution.

Then, not long after passing Dover, we turned to drive parallel with the south-eastern border of Pennsylvania. Within miles the greenery and farmlands ended, buried again by huge freeways and trading estates. Like a warning, or countdown, a series of billboards brought us on, back into urban America:

Don't Phone and Drive!

**Jimmy's Diner. Good home-cooked food:
Not a fancy place.**

Buckle up. It's the law.

Become an organ donor. Give your heart to Jesus today.

And then:

Interstate 295. New Jersey Turnpike ⇨

The tollbooth took a dollar off us and released the Betty Ford onto a road that bore directly towards New York City.

Within five miles, we were virtually stationary – roadworks reducing us to one lane. Marc was grumbling about how we hadn't yet managed to pass one major city without getting bogged down by works. Constant widening of highways, he claimed. Just as driving a car was meant to be something we all needed to give up. Another sign reminded us that, just in case it was possible to find the necessary speed, injuring or killing a roadside construction worker would result in either a $75,000 fine or fifteen years in jail.

It was going to be another down-to-the-wire race against the setting sun if we were going to get into the ocean tonight. The only thing on our side was the northern lengthening of daylight.

'We'll make it for a surf,' I promised myself out loud. 'I can feel it.'

Marc gave no reply – his forehead was resting against the glass of the passenger window, seemingly empty of thoughts.

The 295 started flowing again before Trenton, whereupon we were guided onto the 195 and more queues. At one point near the turn-off the freeway even widened to eight lanes – all of them moving less than 20 miles an hour.

'Oh, for fuck's sake,' I found myself saying. Eventually the stop-start motion had provoked a reaction in me. I could see how lives spent in cars could lead to all sorts of tense dispositions.

'What happened to your music, Marc?'

He looked up, still blank. 'Eh?'

'Music?'

'Oh, er, dunno. Lost my batteries. I'll have a look now.' He started fumbling below his seat, pushing 4-foot-square maps out of his lap and over my face.

'Watch out!' I yelled. 'I'm driving here – even if it is at about a mile an hour! You wouldn't want us to run over a worker, eh?'

He wasn't listening. Why had I suggested music anyway? I knew full well why it hadn't been on for a day or two – because his collection of metal and mullet rock had already worn thin. It was too late, though. The batteries to his MP3 player had shown up in the dark recesses of the Betty Ford's upholstery and within seconds Alice in Chains were heralding us on towards the coast.

The most consistent surf spot along this end of the Jersey Shore was Manasquan Inlet – a set of jetties and beach breaks that on the map looked not very far off.

Like the Outer Banks, Manasquan Inlet was a spot always well covered by the surf media during the Atlantic storm season. I'd seen pictures of it thundering with huge swells, surfers getting tubed like you'd expect in Hawaii or Indonesia. And it wasn't that rare an occurrence, either. Like the Hatteras area, Manasquan ran quickly into deep water, and the jetty helped form sandbanks that were ideal for peeling waves.

All we had to do now was find the place.

I steered us onto an oceanfront road to find a similar scene to what we'd left behind in Virginia Beach: grey promenade, a bit run-down, faded concrete colours – probably due to Atlantic batterings – and a few bars and shops. But this time the tacky stretch was much shorter. Within a few miles of the freeway things tidied up considerably, and we entered a gorgeous housing estate. This was the Beverly Hills of New York City's commuter belt, with perfectly manicured lawns (no need for sprinklers though, as the rain fell for real here) and towering architecture. Each house seemed to have more than eight bedrooms, drive space for four or more cars and multiple living rooms in which you imagined all kinds of futuristic home comforts. The wood-panelled exteriors were perfectly finished with overlapping single tiles or wedges of wood that were painted in soft shades of grey and polished like rows of scales. Given the weather, these would be very high-maintenance homes. Outside, Irish and Italian flags almost equalled the number of Star-Spangled Banners on show. And all were only yards from the beaches, some of which, again, had been sectioned off as private property.

In the network of plush suburbia that ran behind the coastline, Marc and I looked for somewhere to park. We needed to take a look at the waves. At the end of one road was a gate through to the sand, with no obvious signs telling us we couldn't use it. I nominated Marc for the reconnaissance mission.

'Just find out how much swell there is,' I said, 'and then get a look as far up and down the coast as you can. See if there's a peak anywhere with surfers on it.'

While he was gone, I had a look at the map we'd been using. With some help from surf mags and guidebooks, I'd dotted where I thought various surf spots should be found along the Eastern Seaboard. We were pretty much in the lee of New York here. Sandy Hook was only a few miles up from here, and from there you were pretty much riding waves into Raritan Bay. The street we had parked in was quiet though; no cars, and certainly no surfers.

Marc emerged back from the little alleyway, his pace and facial expression suggesting he might well have seen something rideable.

'So?' I asked him.

'D'you want the good or the bad?' was the reply.

'Bad.'

'No. I'm gonna start with the good. There's waves. And they look all right.'

'So the bad?'

'You have to pay thirteen dollars to go on the sand.'

'Thirteen?'

'Yeah.'

'Is it worth it?'

'It's a bit of a close-out, and then there's a few lefts running into a shore break a bit further over.'

'How far?' I asked.

'Two hundred yards?'

'And do we reckon this is Manasquan then?'

'How would I know?'

'Are there any surfers out?' I asked.

'About ten.'

I wondered why only ten people were riding fun beach break peaks in one of America's most populated areas – but then again there was a fee to even touch the water's edge. We agreed to drive around a bit more.

A few blocks further on we saw a man in his thirties wearing overalls and at work on a lawn that had been perfected down to the very last blade of forest-green grass.

I leaned out of the window and asked, 'Excuse me, is this Manasquan?'

'Not here,' he replied. 'Manasquan's the next town over.' The guy had a proper 'Joisey' accent – the kind you imagined New York's commuters would use when yelling at you to get out of the way. 'You gotta head back up to the main road. Take a right at the end of this street and go about four blocks back. You'll cross a railway, and then immediately go left again at the traffic lights. That's Manasquan.'

'I reckon he was the owner of that place, not the gardener,' said Marc. 'Nice guy. Mowing his own lawn. Good on him.'

Manasquan itself was a bit more discreet about its wealth, although you'd still reckon on needing at least a Supreme Court judge's wage to buy property there. There were less of the wide, landscaped gardens, more flags – all either Irish or Italian – and hardly any parking spaces.

At the very end of the road that ran parallel to the beach there was a wider road along the edge of a sea wall that flanked the inlet. Its houses were draped with yet more flags, as well as sports pendants, overhead cables and telecoms wires. Here, after three laps around the block, we found a car that was pulling out and slid the Betty Ford into the gap left behind, hidden from view by a Toyota Sequoia V8 and a Lincoln Navigator. It was free to park.

Leaving our surf gear in the car, we locked up and made for the sea on foot. Our luck was gaining momentum. The girl taking tolls for beach access was just finishing for the day.

This was Manasquan Inlet. We didn't need to ask. The swell was being pushed into a series of neat, very rideable peaks, breaking across a beach full of surfers. There were a lot of longboarders out and you could tell it would take a bit of patience to catch a good one, but patience we had. Patience was something we were good at.

Nightfall had to be only an hour off so we elected to get straight into the water. We walked briskly back to the car, whereupon another thought entered my mind.

'Marc, didn't you say the water gets colder north of Chesapeake Bay?'

'Yeah. Couple of degrees. Oh, good point...'

Was it still warm enough not to wear any neoprene? Marc decided it was, and donned his boardshorts as he had in Florida and North Carolina. I had a wetsuit jacket, which you could wear with boardies, and was glad of it when we got to the water's edge. One small eddy of lapping shore break moving through my toes was enough to notice the difference. The ocean here felt fresh.

I dived in and found myself gasping for air as the cold water poured through my shorts, making me start paddling immediately and briskly. Behind me, I heard Marc curse. 'Shit, it's freezing!'

It didn't matter. During the next half hour, as the sun set behind the rows of Jersey millionaire homes, we exchanged waves with the other surfers at Manasquan inlet. Some sets broke into fast, shapely sections, and others backed off a bit. We didn't care though. We'd made it to the northern states. The novelty of where we were was enough to make this session as good as any other we could hope for until the arrival of Hurricane Dean's now certain liberation swell.

In the water I heard a few talking about it. One woman was saying she planned to go to Rhode Island over the weekend, while others speculated that Jersey itself was already neatly placed to get something from the storm – although neither held the same appeal, according to one guy, as a trek all the way up to Nova Scotia.

Where to go next was far from the front of my mind, though. For now I just wanted to enjoy surfing again, grateful that our sessions were getting better and more frequent.

'There's just a hint of something starting to build now, d'you reckon?' Marc said, as we waited for a last post-dusk wave in near complete darkness. 'Nothing compared to what's on the way, but this is good fun, eh?'

After our last few waves, riding oil-black water as night fell almost completely, we walked back to the car, warming our feet with heat retained by the pavements and wondering what to do about a bed for the night.

'I can't see any signs saying we can't park overnight here,' said Marc. 'So if we go somewhere to eat, and return late enough, I reckon we can try and kip in the car. Right here. Next to Millionaires Row.'

For the first time in weeks, after drying off from the surf, I put on jeans, socks, sneakers and a jacket. This felt cosy after all the humidity of the South. It was pretty late by now, and after driving a few blocks we knew anything other than takeaway food would cost. We ended up walking into a Subway on the edge of a wide parking lot and several rows of shops, joined onto a Wal Mart.

Marc protested at first and stood outside as I walked in. But he gave in with little resistance once his hunger had caught up with him. 'They do all right food here,' I claimed. 'Subway pizzas are meant to be awesome.' The food looked simple, but trying to make sense of all the combos on offer was degree-level stuff. Not even Marc could get to the bottom of it.

'"Make a sub a salad for 99c." What the hell does that mean? A sub is bigger than a bleedin' salad – or does that mean you get both?' Continuing with a method he had been using for a while now, Dr Rhys simply ordered exactly the same as me – pizza; Hawaiian but with chilli flakes.

We opted to sit in the Betty Ford to eat.

'D'you know?' began Marc. 'The Chevy Suburban will never catch on in Britain. It's so... you know, *big*. Burns enough fuel to warm the Gulf of Mexico a couple of degrees with each journey – and it's shapeless too. In fact all those SUV-type things are.' He nodded towards a milk-white model with tinted windows, '... Lost', Volcom and NoFX stickers on the bumper, and gleaming alloy wheels. It was waiting for a kid who had just run in to Subway, while the *8-litre* engine purred almost inaudibly, running the whole time.

'I dunno,' I replied, through a mouthful of a pizza. 'Someone where we live will get one soon, I'm sure. All you need is for one or two people to get the idea. We only like small cars coz that's what we're used to.'

Marc thought about it. 'Hmmn. I'm not so sure...' He looked like he was ready to debate this point, but then a yawn seemed to interrupt his thought processes. 'Although I bet it's really comfy inside that thing,' he added, gesturing again towards the still waiting vehicle. 'Imagine we had a Suburban to sleep in tonight.'

We didn't, though, and between now and tomorrow morning this was unlikely to change. I didn't tell Marc I'd been having the same thoughts myself. Vehicle envy wasn't something I'd ever admit to.

It was easy enough to find Manasquan Inlet again, where the streets were now wonderfully quiet. Parking was readily available and enough towering trucks were still in place for us to slip, unseen, into a space which we hoped would do for the night.

I'm an expert at sleeping in cars – back in Europe I once spent over a month living out of my Nissan Micra. You need to cover the gear stick with a pillow – which was easier here as the Betty Ford was an automatic with a smaller handle to cushion. Then you put your surfboards across so they lean from dashboard to rear seat. This makes a little cubbyhole underneath, big enough to sleep anyone. Drop the windows an inch or so and you're all set. Nothing but the odd passing car and, in this case, a whistling wind running through the wing mirror a foot or so from my head. It offered as good a night's sleep as you could want, and a feeling of total freedom; nothing to tie you down.

Marc, who also reckoned he could get used to sleeping in cars, woke first, not long after sunrise. 'Awesome,' he exclaimed. 'I was sure the police were going to turn up just after we nodded off to move us on. But it looks like we're OK.' He stepped outside and went for a walk. I stayed put and stared at the faded roof lining, thoughts blissfully blank.

Half an hour later, he came back to get something to read. I asked him about the waves.

'They're way smaller,' he replied. 'Like a foot or so, and really strong offshore. Looks cold.'

It was indeed a chilly morning, and nowhere was open yet for us to get tea, coffee or breakfast. A few dozen surfers were already heading out – getting a few freebies before the tollbooths opened again to take money for the right to step on the sand. Marc had taken our map out with him.

'With this direction, Sandy Hook is going to get a bit more swell than here,' he noted, before adding a disclaimer: 'I think.'

'Really?'

'Well, it's a little point-type wave, isn't it? The sandbanks here are clearly crap for small swells. What have we got to lose? And besides, it breaks at low tide.'

'Yeah – it does. You're right.'

'Well, low tide's at twelve. That gives us time for coffee.'

'Nowhere's open, though, and what about the wind? It might come up by then.'

'I don't care about the wind,' said Marc. 'It's not as likely to blow every afternoon this far north, and that place on the corner opens in ten minutes. The beach starts charging in like half an hour too. I'm *not* paying to surf. Tried it in the Maldives and it's been on my conscience ever since.'

He meant that he'd been to a surf camp where you could pay for the luxury of being granted access to a private surf spot. It was an idea I hated, and one which I remembered berating him for at the time. I recalled telling him that is was cheating – paying to avoid all the dedicated surfers who would do a much better job of surfing the place. I know he liked it more than he let on – because he'd later recommended the experience to another mutual friend (unsuccessfully swearing them to secrecy – although he didn't know it).

'Whatever,' I said. 'At least you've been to the bloody Maldives. Unless I make some drastic career change, pay-to-surf places like that will always be out of my reach.'

He laughed sardonically. 'Oooh, my heart bleeds for you. It's not as if you've really suffered for it though, is it? Don't you start moaning to me about your bloody wave-count. People like me can't spend months mastering crowded spots by being there morning, noon and night. And anyway, I said I regretted it. I agree with you. Privatising surf spots – like that one in Fiji, what's it called again?'

'Tavarua.' He was talking about the world's most famous private wave. An island and reef pass owned by two entrepreneurial Americans. Not even Marc would be able to afford a trip there in a hurry.

'Yeah, Tavarua. It's wrong, wrong, wrong,' he lamented. 'As are all pay-to-surf places. Yep. Done it once. Wouldn't recommend it to anyone.'

It was my turn to laugh.

He did, however, have a point about spending months mastering spots. That comment cut to the very crux of the differences between the two of us. I'd always thought that if you wanted to ride the world's best waves you had to give up serious time to them – whereas Marc was convinced that clever planning and storm-monitoring could get you a result anyway. Over the years I'd camped out at some really famous waves, pretty much practising surfing them day-in, day-out. The most famous of these was Jeffreys Bay in South Africa – the place that had also turned me into a writer. I knew Marc would love to surf there one day, but a problem he'd face would be the competitive crowd that hit Jeffreys Bay every time it broke. Put simply, Marc didn't have the time to get fit enough to beat those kinds of surfers to a wave.

On the flip side, though, he had an incredible career, money, a home and something constructive to tell people he did for a living. It must have been a tough trade to make.

Refocussing our thoughts on the need to make a plan, we wandered back towards the pavements that ran alongside the inlet facing south over to Lake Louise and Point Pleasant Beach. Spaced every ten yards were benches, each of which bore memorial dedications to people who must have regularly sat on them:

Matthew Brady – You gotta do what you gotta do.

James Van Shoick.

Thomas Morrow.

Harry Strutz; a friend to all.

Gene Strutz; everyone's mom.

I tried to imagine the faces behind each of these people. At peace, watching the world go by – just what benches were designed for. The chill was lifting and it was now a wonderful, summery morning. As the day grew lighter and warmer, the promenade alongside Manasquan Inlet was coming to life. People were power walking, dog walking, buggy walking or simply leisure walking. Others rode bikes, skateboards or just stood and chatted to friends. Around us, through the bleating of seagulls, you could pick out the nasal tones of the 'Joisey' accent.

As the road sweepers came by, I noticed a baby rat sniffing innocently around the harbour railings as the wake of an Army Corps of Engineers ship rolled against the stone wall. The makers of the scandalous New Orleans levee network had a bad reputation here, too, for lax construction laws that had hammered the Jersey marine environment. As one of the government agencies involved in the management of harbours and coastal industry, they had handed out permits to dredge from several places along this coastline. This was despite objections from locals, who feared moving sediment around on the seabed could only be bad. For surfers, dredging had to be one of the most dastardly industries around – wherever in the world you went. Mind you, back on land Manasquan was being kept so meticulously tidy that you'd never have guessed its adjoining ocean was gravely ill.

The cafe nearest the beach was now open – Carlson's Corner. It smelled of disinfectant inside as a wet-haired worker (post-surf this time, I think) readied the place for the day ahead, mopping the floor.

'Wait one moment please, guys. Once this floor's dry, you're welcome to come in.'

In the windows were pictures of great waves breaking at Manasquan – thick, tubing and with hurricane ferocity. A poster advertised yet another contest, this one was a bit less prestigious than the Virginia Beach event and due to run in two weeks' time.

'We always get good waves for that one,' the man behind the counter said, seeing what I was looking at. We were OK to come in and order coffee and some pancakes now. In front of us in the queue was a girl in a red sports bikini, who had just been surfing. Her wet skin had been firmed by goosebumps. She was tanned and in perfect shape, and ordered a single doughnut with pink topping for breakfast. Her wet feet had already left sand and seawater on the freshly cleaned floor, but something told me the proprietor wasn't going to complain this time. I could see Marc trying to think of something to say to her, but nothing came to him and the chance passed. She walked out into the sunlight to skate home, board under arm. For a moment I spotted something behind his eyes – a slightly forlorn look, which right then I knew would resurface before this trip was over.

The noise of the milk-steamer blasting against a metal jug shook him, and he looked back at the counter.

'Waves are gonna get good here soon, aren't they?' I asked the guy serving us.

'You mean Hurricane Dean?' came the reply.

'Yeah.'

'I dunno. We might get something. Everyone's hoping at least. We're all putting out as much positive energy as possible. I think I saw like a fifteen-second swell period for Sunday – although pretty small.' (A 'swell period' is a means of judging power. Anything over a ten-second gap between waves meant strong, long-distance waves.) 'It's always like this in summer,' the guy carried on. 'We get surf on weekends only – when it's busiest and you can't find anywhere to park. We got good waves last Saturday too.'

'Did you?'

'Yeah, like a quick day-long swell. Dunno where from.'

'Did you get in the water last night?' Marc asked.

'Yeah. It was fun. Kinda dropped today though, huh?'

'I know,' Marc mumbled. 'We're thinking of going to look at Sandy Hook later.'

'At low tide? Could be worth a go. You'll have to pay to get in the parking lots though. Like fifteen dollars or something.'

'Ten.' Marc's monosyllabic reply was blunt.

It hadn't halted the amiability of the server, though. 'Ten? Well, you know more than me then dude. You guys'll have fun anyway. It'll be a blast. I gotta work. I'll probably get out around here later in the day. If there's any swell left by then.'

It was funny how Marc didn't mind paying for a parking space near the beach, and yet objected so fiercely to being charged to go on the sand. Unless you planned to only sit in the car, a parking charge was as good as paying to surf anyway.

I picked up a copy of *USA Today* from the counter and asked if we could take it outside with our breakfast and coffee.

'Sure. As long as you leave it behind when you go.'

The back page was what we wanted to see – the weather section.

The paper was a day old, so its information on Dean was a bit behind the last update Marc had read. The main focus was on the landfall of Tropical Storm Erin during the last forty-eight hours. For a system that hadn't even made Category 1 status, it had done some considerable damage.

As expected, the storm had come ashore near Lamar, Texas, and then turned to head north – in the direction of Oklahoma. It had killed around twenty people near the shore – piling heavy rain onto already saturated soil. It seemed such a small number of fatalities compared to something like Katrina but, feeling involved in the way I did, it was impossible not to wonder who each person was and how it had happened. Texas now had a severe flooding problem and desperately needed dry weather soon – otherwise worse could easily follow.

Erin had carried on from there, showing considerable staying power over land – a place where most tropical cyclones usually died quick, unceremonious deaths. After entering Oklahoma, Erin had *re-intensified* – sweeping west with winds of fifty miles per hour and more. There was a quote from the Oklahoma National Weather Service issued yesterday: 'This stubborn little intensification has resulted in what basically amounts to an inland tropical storm. Another instance of freak weather to add to an already strange year. At dawn, Erin still had an eye-like feature and a spiral-shaped band of rain and was producing gusts of over eighty miles per hour. It's another one for the record books all right.'

The storm's remains were predicted to go back east, through Missouri, Kentucky, and Virginia – where there was even a very remote chance of the whole thing coming back to life if it got as far as the Atlantic Ocean again. Marc said this wouldn't happen, though.

'That's the rarest of several really, really unlikely scenarios,' he said. 'They just put that in because the media need a story. You must have noticed by now how they always speculate towards the extreme?'

Sleeping in the car last night and driving all of yesterday, we hadn't checked on Hurricane Dean for a while. Would Erin's sibling, whose character was yet to show itself, show the same resilience as his sister, I wondered?

'Next time we get a report on the storm will be when we're in NYC, probably,' said Marc. 'Doesn't matter, though. The swell's already been created now – it's on the way whatever the hurricane goes on to do. It's gonna start building the day after tomorrow so we need to start thinking about where to pick it up – what local weather and wind those waves will be met with when they finally get here.'

'And what about having a surf today?'

'Oh – after that, of course. Come on, let's make a move.'

CHAPTER THIRTEEN

SANDY HOOK

Getting to the water's edge at Sandy Hook felt like a huge milestone in our journey. As we walked out onto the baking sand I properly recognised we were in the lee of one of the world's grandest human settlements.

It all seemed to come together at once; a dark blue NYPD chopper soared overhead, as the thought occurred to me that a clear day might allow us a view of the city. This was not an issue. Over a small dune, New York appeared so close it wouldn't have mattered whether it was clear or not.

To our left, just over the bay, was the entire Manhattan skyline – as you'd have imagined it. You could see the Chrysler Building and Empire State rising plum out of the middle of it all. Verrazano Bridge was pouring traffic in from the south-west, while over to our right was Brooklyn and the start of Long Island.

'Wow. What a backdrop for a surf!' I muttered.

'I know, man,' said Marc. 'So that must be the centre of it all there.' He pointed. 'You know, the full-on downtown bit. Funny – I thought it was further inland than that. Maybe it's coz Staten

Island is so flat – like as in the buildings are small. I mean, the sky scrapers over there are fuckin' huge.' He carried on trying to map the cityscape out, while even-pulse swell lines rolled down the beach, as if themselves being pulled towards New York City immediately north.

Marc carried on thinking aloud. 'So the Empire State and Chrysler are pretty similar, aren't they? Although Empire State's bigger. What a name for a building – "Empire State"! I'm not into it at all. Sounds like something from *Star Wars*. I bet whoever thought that one up was really proud of themselves at the time.'

'Imagine the amount of activity going on in between all those buildings,' I said. 'Like Times Square – it's right in there – just spitting distance from us. It looks so... so *peaceful*, doesn't it?'

We sat down on the sand. The beach dropped steeply into the ocean, almost forming a natural seat. I worked my feet into the wet ground. Like in Miami, the urban sounds stood no chance of travelling across the calm swishing of the sea.

I wanted to find the surf spot that existed here, but nobody knew what we were talking about. These beach-goers were all proper city types. Some were walking out onto the sand with deckchairs and picnics under one arm, talking on cellphones with their free hand. Everyone was wearing jewellery and there were very few of the life's-a-beach types of people you'd see in California or Florida – people who looked like they lived in and out of the water. Smells of suncream and hair gel were emanating from the busy shower areas, while the car park was as 4x4-friendly as you could imagine.

'We'll find it,' said Marc. 'There were only six lots, I think. We'll just work our way back.'

Sandy Hook was a 6-mile long peninsula at the top of the Jersey Shore, preserved – like Sebastian Inlet and New Smyrna – by state park status, with a ten dollar fee to get into the area. It was basically a spit of sand that bent off to the west at its extreme end, forming a hook shape. This bend had formed over the centuries to deflect wave energy along its shore, which was great news for surfers as it meant swells rolled from south to north with perfect 'peeling' potential. You knew great waves were highly likely somewhere in the park.

As I said before, to surfers from outside of the East Coast this would always be the place from which a surf photographer had taken a picture of someone riding a wave in front of the burning Twin Towers on 9/11. But Sandy Hook's more commonly known legacy dated back to the Cold War. Formerly called Fort Hancock, it had been home to missile silos – the early stages of America's nuclear deterrent strategy. Sandy Hook was an original part of the Star Wars defence system – designed to protect the people of New York and Philadelphia from attack. The launch facilities were all derelict now – or at least that was what we were being told. A sun-faded information board assured us that the still visible Nike Radar was a deterrent only. (Apparently the missile defences for this area were now 'hidden in the Midwest' – New Mexico was Marc's guess.)

At parking lot D we knew we'd found what we had been looking for. The surf stickers on various bumpers were evidence enough. We found a space and started waxing up.

'Is it breaking?' I asked the dripping wet occupant of the truck next to us, who was loading a longboard back into the rear cargo hold.

'Ehh, kinda,' was the reply. 'The tide is dropping so it should get a bit better.'

'How's the water?'

'Warm. No wetsuit.' The man hopped straight into the cockpit and pulled away, almost skidding as he went from reverse into drive, causing a horrible clunking noise as his automatic gearbox laboured to arrest the truck's backward momentum.

'No one's asking about our accents any more,' said Marc.

I hadn't thought of that but, now he mentioned it, this was true. Perhaps New York had so many foreign voices that we presented no novelty at all.

'Hey – at least it means they won't be calling us English,' I reminded him.

In our boardshorts, and with the car locked up, we made our way towards the beach. A series of fast-peeling, but crumbly, right-handers were breaking off a 15-foot tall mound of boulders towards a designated swimming area. Surfers needed to pull off waves halfway, as riding into the flag-protected bathing zone was a criminal offence. The surf wasn't at all bad – in fact they were perhaps the best waves I had seen on the East Coast so far. And all along the line we would be riding waves in clear view of the Empire State Building.

'Reckon there are any people up the top right now, able to watch us surfing out here?' I asked Marc.

'Probably. You must be able to see for miles from there.'

The bloke we met in the car park obviously hadn't just driven up from Florida and the Carolinas. Otherwise he'd never have advised against wearing a wetsuit. As at Manasquan, I gasped emerging from my first duck-dive and only noticed the putrid smell of the ocean as an afterthought. The sun, now virtually directly above me, was the only thing keeping it bearable in shorts.

There were a few others in the water, but this didn't really stop you being able to get waves. Since the place broke in sections, people got shut down halfway along the ride – so you could easily swing around and take off on what was left. I paddled until I was almost behind the rock groyne, the furthest surfer up, and therefore with the right to catch whatever wave I wanted. In some places a newcomer doing this meant locals would automatically drop in on you – riding the wave anyway just to show you that skipping turns in their break was bad etiquette. This was New York though, and I just kept thinking of the yellow cabbies. And anyway, it was Friday afternoon, late August. The only locals were probably in red lifeguard trunks, and more concerned with protecting swimmers.

Sure enough, someone dropped in: Marc Rhys! Grinning, he spun around and paddled for the first wave I took, shouting 'party wave!' as he jumped to his feet. I didn't really care and so we wove down the line, trying to avoid hitting each other as the wave warped awkwardly. Then another section came that cut me off, but just about let Marc through.

'Fucker!' I shouted to him.

As he paddled back up, I waited, watching the other surfers hopping along the wobbly wave faces.

'We should shout at each other more,' Marc suggested. 'Everyone else will see that we're together and not want to hassle us too much. It might mean we get more waves. In fact, let's try yelling in a 'Joisey' accent. Then they might even think we're the local crew!'

I laughed. It probably would have worked.

I could feel myself loosening up each time I cruised down the line. For the first time on the trip it felt as if I was nearing my surfing potential – paddling fast and over distance without tiring, taking off with a spring in my step and feeling agile. I was back at the stage where surfing my best was second nature, something I didn't need to think too much about. My board felt sweet and tuned-in, my natural sense of where to sit in the line-up had become automatic and it felt as if the ocean wanted to work with me – good news as it meant being able to make the most of Hurricane Dean once the proper swell arrived. Marc was making it count too – in a completely different dimension to the world in which he lived at home. The office, lectures, meetings and conferences meant nothing to him now.

Soon after, the idea came to me of trying to ride a wave while actually looking at Manhattan. You know – just one of those silly things that has to be done once you set your mind to it: catch a wave, get out on to the open face, and then lock my eyes on the New York skyline. I'd never really realised how much you needed to keep reading a wave as you rode. It took a couple of attempts – choosing a landmark while making sure you stayed ahead of the twisting sections was harder than you would imagine.

With so much else going on around us though, I realised how easily the act of surfing could become peripheral in a place like this. Mind you, who was I kidding? This was New York. Almost everything was peripheral. The smell of city run-off in the ocean should have told me that – we were in a place where every person looked after themselves, and where most probably never even thought about the ocean. As we practised an art that was all about living with the forces of nature, I was all too aware of immersing myself in a sea in which million-year-old sand grains floated along with traces of modern man-made plastics, metals and fuels. If I hadn't grown up used to Welsh breaks like the river mouth at Ogmore– only half a mile downstream of a sewage plant – it would have probably made me feel nauseous. The patches of silt that rose through the sunlit, sucking parts of the inside section could as easily be ground and powdered polystyrene as they could be quartz, sandstone, shells or sea-salt.

It didn't take away from the pure pleasure of surfing though. The soothing sound of the Atlantic slowly nibbling at the edge of a continent was all around and the cold water kept me moving, holding the tempo of the session high throughout. A rip current running off the groyne meant you were always paddling towards the top of the point, and could seldom take a breather. The surging, churning rhythms of Sandy Hook's waves were a fascinating puzzle to solve as a surfer too. A slight backwash from the sea defences would drift down the steep shoreline, throbbing through the shoulder whenever it wanted. You could never get bored riding waves like that. We were going to surf our brains out here, until either sore shoulders or hunger called time.

Or thunder.

The sky began to infuse with ominous navy blues a few hours after we'd started surfing. By now the energy of paddling meant we were warm even without the sun. But once it started raining tepid drops I knew the clouds dragging out from the west were cumulonimbus. It didn't bother me, or Marc. I'd surfed through blazing lightning before, but a few others in the line-up started worrying. Even before the first thunder clap.

'They must be from somewhere like Ohio, Montana, maybe Wisconsin or Indiana,' whispered Marc, as we waited in the rain between sets. 'Or city slickers with no idea. There's loads of other shit around here to catch a lightning strike ahead of us.'

Another, much closer thunder clap sounded, and some of the swimmers began screaming and running from the water like a scene from *Jaws*.

We carried on surfing, now getting the pick of the waves. The storm was bringing with it a heavy sea breeze, which was pushing the sickly smell of pollution inland. The weather front was also making the Sandy Hook right-handers much harder to surf, and wilder, containing a raw power that in the blazing afternoon sun had not been there. Dead low tide exposed a couple of algae-covered boulders, one of which would surface right in the middle of the wave if you took off too far up the beach.

It was with both amusement and exasperation that the remaining half-dozen surfers in the water responded to the lifeguards' announcement, which came within a minute of the first peel of synchronised thunder and lightning tearing through the darkening sky like a vein. The beach was being *evacuated*. We were to exit the water and return to our vehicles immediately – because of the storm.

'Yanks and their bloody weather!' Marc cursed. 'They just want something to be able to report on tonight's bulletins.' He frowned and started impersonating the many anchors we'd seen on TV so far. 'Panic in Jersey today as Sandy Hook was evacuated coz of a storm. No casualties, but a couple of surfers from "Wales-England" had to cut a great session short...'

We weren't as annoyed as the last people to leave the sand, though – a trio of scantily dressed women, who looked like they were sisters or even triplets, had been taking sexually suggestive photographs of each other straddling the boulders and stretching out their limbs so as to let the rainwater run off their soaking bodies.

'Just a reminder that we're in New York,' I noted, as people stared, confused at the vanity-inspired get-together. 'Lest we forget.'

It wouldn't have surprised me to learn that these three women had been waiting for just such weather – maybe even glued to the same TV stations as we had been – biding their time until the opportunity arose to get the shots they'd been planning. It seemed an awful amount of effort, but then you could see these girls *really* liked the way they looked.

The rainwater and the cold ocean had given me numb feet and chattering teeth by the time we'd got into the car. Through windows thick with condensation, I tried to spot the way out of lot D, but it was no use. We had to run the engine for ten minutes to dry the windscreen. Everything in the car, it seemed, was wet. Outside, meanwhile, the rain fell so thick that the fastest wiper speed wasn't enough to deflect the stream of water in front of me. I turned us out of the parking space, largely through guesswork, and began moving forward.

'Oh, sod it, I'm opening my window,' Marc exclaimed.

'What? Hang on!'

'It's fine. The wind's keeping the rain off my side.'

We weren't going anywhere in a hurry, as a queue of almost fifty cars lay in front of us, all wanting to return to the comforts of urban New Jersey.

In one of the sporadic gaps between brutal rain showers, I spotted the three poser women getting into a cherry red Mustang. The last car to leave, they turned to join the queue, ejecting a collection of rubbish out of the windows. Soft drink containers, straws, burger boxes, bags and some half-eaten fries. Either they figured the rain meant nobody was looking, or they didn't give a shit.

Suddenly I felt consumed by anger and banged the Betty Ford's horn hard, holding it for a couple of seconds. Several other cars replied – probably because they thought I was telling them to hurry up – including the Mustang a few places behind.

'What are you doing?' Marc berated me. It had been a pathetic gesture on my part really, and I knew it.

'Nothing.'

I opened my own window and stuck my head out into the rain. Immediately the waves of the past hours came back to the forefront of my mind. A smile crept onto my face, and the ocean's energy coursed through me again. This was all part of it, anyway. These were the moments surfers should appreciate better than anyone. We were getting closer to nature's more capricious side. The Atlantic was showing us what it could do – a smaller version of what was going on right now further out to sea. It reminded me that Dean was out there, very real, and getting busy.

Another long, drawn out rumble of thunder followed two flawless forks of electricity, cleaving the atmosphere behind us. A fresh wind rose again off the sea behind, lashing rain across the cavalcade of cars.

Patience, I thought, *patience, I need*.

CHAPTER FOURTEEN

NYC

'Right, that's it; now I'm officially giving up surfing.'

So Marc announced less than twenty-four hours later, as we got off a bus at Times Square. The ocean now felt a long way away, and the look of disgust on his face was genuine.

'Here we are, the heart of the capitalist world, the absolute epicentre of free-market conservatism, you know, boom and bust big business – and what's the first thing I see? *A fuckin' Quiksilver sign!*'

It wasn't necessarily the first thing I'd seen. In fact Times Square was so confusing you weren't really able to process sights and sounds with enough clarity to pick anything individual out, let alone work out what to do about it all. Perhaps that was the name of the game anyway, I suggested to Marc – total bombardment of the senses. This was, after all, the beating heart of world commerce. Surely it was this way partly to make us want to buy things.

'What do you mean by "game"?' he asked. 'Whose game?'

I didn't reply, but glanced over the road, the opposite way from the Quiksilver shop at a dominating mass of animated neon mosaic. Coming to life, it began to scroll from right to left:

GM: 23.27, IDC: 29.26, MSFT: 27.1998, INTC: 19.9661... ... ... DOW JONES... ...

That seemed to answer his question better than anything I could have said. The key player had identified itself – money, and more of it than we could ever imagine, circulating with every movement and sound. The world's biggest market.

'Right, I'm going to look inside. For a laugh.' He meant the Quiksilver shop. I followed. If this was all a game then we might as well play along a little.

'Hello sir, how are you?' asked a petite young girl in a perfectly fitted Roxy hoodie – brown with the logo scribbled roughshod along the front and an NYC heart on the shoulder. I doubted this girl had ever stood up on a wave – you could see it in her city eyes and prissy posture. Still, she was into the lifestyle, smiling, shaking her freshly shampooed and silky hair (further proof she didn't surf as it obviously never got immersed in the toxic waters of Sandy Hook) – and all to the rhythm of a hideous pop-punk tune, being played so loud the place felt more like a nightclub than a surf shop.

'Yes, I'm after a surfboard,' Marc said, patronisingly. I looked away. He was on his own with this one. One thing he certainly *didn't* need was another board, so I figured it better to stay clear of this latest unpredictable mood.

'Oh... OK, er...' The girl seemed caught out as Marc followed her to the other end of the shop.

The space was tiny, but that didn't matter. This recently declared blue-chip clothing behemoth had a flashing slot in the Times Square chimera now. That was worth whatever astronomical ground rent they had to pay on the place. I settled to watching a cinema screen made up of no less than thirty smaller tellies, showing some ephemeral footage of the Roxy girls goofing around in innocuous Fijian rollers – which I recognised immediately as Tavarua, the 'private island'. They were wearing reed hats and playing Polynesian banjos while cruising on longboards (something surfers never did where we came from!). Occasionally some middle-of-the road male pro rode a bigger wave at Cloudbreak, a reef that broke near to the island and which was also open only to resort clients. Simple, sexy, expensive and easy, this was surf culture as the masses now wanted to see it. The footage did involve people riding waves though, and as a result was just enough to distract my attention from what was going on around me.

Marc returned from the board rack, annoyed and amazed at once. 'They've got Al Merricks in there – nice ones. You know, boards that were made to *ride waves*.'

'What d'you mean?'

'I mean they've actually been shaped. You know, sometimes restaurants or shops might have blank boards as decorations – but these things... well, someone's actually spent time making them, you know, *surfable*.'

'I thought you were only looking to get the attention of the girl.'

'She's not interested,' he replied curtly. 'I asked.'

'*Asked?* Asked what?'

'If she's going for a beer later.'

I put my head in my hands, hoping this kind of embarrassment wasn't going to get more frequent. Better talk surfboards instead, perhaps.

'I see. So how much are they selling them for anyway?'

'Nine hundred and eighty dollars.'

'What's that in pounds?'

'Shit loads. I mean, who the fuck buys a surfboard in bloody Times Square anyway?' He paused, and then offered the answer to his own question... 'Some twat who's looking to use it as an ornament in his poncey studio apartment, that's who. What a fuckin' waste. Imagine walking around out there with an un-waxed Al Merrick 6'1" under your arm! Come on, let's go.'

We stepped back outside as Marc moaned about the music they'd been playing in the shop, too, saying the original surf punk sound had been hijacked. He could talk – he hardly liked the stuff himself when we were younger.

'Look at that place, man,' he lamented, turning to gaze back at the flashing logo, next to a lit shopfront picture of a perfectly breaking, warm-water wave. 'We used to dress like that and listen to similar music, and everyone in school thought we were drongos. We weren't drongos though – we were just thirteen years too cool for the in-crowd. And now here we are, grown up, I'm a fuckin' *physics lecturer* and finally Times Square is trying to tell people they should dress surfy to be cool. Mind you, now I think of it, I'm fuckin' flattered actually. Although, I'm still giving up surfing.'

'Really?'

'Well, after this bloody Hurricane Dean swell is over perhaps.'

★   ★   ★

After trudging slowly through the Jersey rainstorm the day before we had stopped just short of New York City, checking into a grubby and alarmingly empty motel in New Bergen – the closest you could stay to Manhattan before rates started to climb sharply. This place had nothing like the buzz of downtown. Here the buildings were run-down, the streets filthy and filled with fast, unsympathetic traffic. The air felt heavy and dirty. Just emptying the car outdoors was enough to make your face greasy and your nose itchy. A porter offered to take our things up to the room on a grand, gold-framed trolley, perhaps because we were the only customers he had seen for hours. At the sight of the surfboards though, he looked more reluctant.

'What you got in there?' he asked, pointing to the bigger board bag. I wanted to quip 'body' as a reply, but he would have probably believed me and called security.

The freeways had grown so thick by the time we turned off that at one point I counted fourteen lanes of traffic, all chock-full of cars going to and from the best-known city in the United States.

As the traffic got even denser than in Jersey, so had the roadside slogans, some dangling the lure of saving (and then spending) money, others feeding off need:

Divorcing? Mediation saves money and time.

Ultra Diamonds: Up to 75% off.

**KG Insurance: Rates based on driving records,
not credit scores.**

As in Norfolk, Virginia, our map just wasn't detailed enough to provide any clue as to where we were going. But just after a sign explaining that 'Coke Zero tastes so much like Coke we're thinking of suing ourselves', I realised why queues were forming as fast as they were. The Lincoln Tunnel was up ahead, and beyond that would be the prospect of trying to drive through downtown Manhattan during late rush hour – something to avoid for sure.

The next leg of the journey could wait, I'd decided. We knew where we were going now, anyway. Our pursuit of Hurricane Dean's swell would take us out to Long Island in the coming days, which would mean needing to drive over Brooklyn Bridge. Even if Rhode Island or Cape Cod were our ultimate destinations, a spin up towards the beach breaks of Montauk and the Hamptons would surely be preferable to the heavily urbanised crossing into Connecticut.

'There are ferries from Montauk over to East Connecticut anyway,' Marc pointed out. 'And I reckon Long Island ought to get waves first. It's well placed for the southerly swell.'

With all of these factors adding up, we elected to look at the swell's timescale before going any further. The last mile had taken nearly forty minutes.

As I listened to yet more rain beginning to fall outdoors, Marc opened his laptop. It felt refreshing to have spent three days without either of us going online – as if we'd been giving the storm time to breathe and think for itself. We'd been liberated for a while from the need to keep plugging in to the latest titbits of information – even if it meant we were a bit behind on what the waves were doing.

Dean had really begun to shift during the last twenty-four hours, and at a worrying rate. This was the latest information from the National Hurricane Center:

DEAN REMAINS AN EXTREMELY DANGEROUS CATEGORY FIVE HURRICANE ON THE SAFFIR-SIMPSON SCALE – HEAVY SQUALLS ARE SPREADING OVER JAMAICA ALONG WITH HIGH WINDS – AND A HURRICANE WARNING IS IN PLACE FOR THE CAYMAN ISLANDS – PREPARATIONS TO PROTECT LIFE AND PROPERTY SHOULD BE RUSHED TO COMPLETION – INTERESTS ELSEWHERE – INCLUDING TEXAS AND THE YUCATAN

PENINSULA SHOULD CLOSELY MONITOR THIS SYSTEM
AS IT MOVES WEST-NORTHWEST NEAR 17 MPH - 28
KM/HR - SINCE OVERALL CONDITIONS STILL FAVOR
YET FURTHER INTENSIFICATION.

'The storm's done its best for us before going out of range,' explained Marc. 'But there'll be too many islands in the way for it to send any more swell now. Whatever is going to come will have been made and sent on its way already. But if it goes to Cat five before that, and has a big eastern flank pushing waves north, then we'll get tons of surf. We need to check the Navy charts again. Dean can run away all he wants now. The swell is there, and that won't change.'

I suddenly realised this was the first time Marc had used a pronoun for Dean. 'Dean can run away all he wants'.

Some of the waves we planned to ride had been made almost a week ago, and were almost here. It gave me a sense of foreboding – Dean was no longer our responsibility (and it had been stupid to imagine he ever was). He had matured, gratified us, but was now flying the nest – going off to make his own way in the wide world. I hoped that by wishing for this storm to deepen, though, we hadn't become party to creating a monster.

Surf-wise, 'monster' certainly was the right word.

There are two measurements by which you can judge a swell. The first is wave height – a simple one to understand. This is how much the Navy's data-gathering buoys are rising and falling with each wave. But the second measurement, and the one which is actually the more important, is 'wave period' – the time between waves. The greater the period, the more powerful the swell. For example, 4 feet of swell at three seconds would be no good – there'd be no gap between waves and no clearly defined faces – little organisation and no power. By the time you saw a swell with that reading break on a beach it would be a little over knee high. However, 4 feet at *ten* seconds would be a very different proposition. At a nicely exposed surf spot, these conditions would produce beautifully lined up waves that were well over head height.

The current reading (for the conditions in which we'd surfed Sandy Hook that Saturday afternoon) was 3.5 feet at five seconds – a locally produced bit of wind swell in essence – nothing special on the North Atlantic's wide scale. The forecasts for the next few days were very interesting, though. Long Island was to see a drop in conditions to virtually flat for tomorrow, Saturday, before things would begin to change drastically on Sunday – clearly, according to Marc, the first day of Hurricane Dean's swell.

'On Sunday we're getting three feet at *thirteen seconds*,' he choked, excitedly. This was a huge increase in power. 'And that's just the start. Monday's showing five-point-five feet at fourteen, before another three days during which the waves are pushing towards eight at fifteen!' He paused, and then added, 'Fifteen fuckin' seconds! This is a *serious* swell!'

I turned on our motel room's television. Consumer demand must have been high for it, because it took less than a minute to find something about the storm.

A CBS reporter was live in Galveston, Texas. 'Hey guys,' she called back to the studio, against a backdrop of what looked like summer in full swing. 'Well you'd never think it right now, looking at the glorious day around me, but I'm standing in what Americans fear could be the unluckiest state this year – for weather, that is.' She went on to talk about how this could be the 'calm before the storm' again. It was wonderfully sensational, and the excitement made me sit up on the motel bed.

'Heatwaves and rains,' the reporter continued, 'meant that the state got flooded when Tropical Storm Erin moved ashore here earlier in the week. And this means the ground is not going to be able to cope with the phenomenal amount of further rain a major hurricane would dump on it. Places like Freeport and Corpus Christi just won't cope. It's that simple...'

'Thanks Melissa,' said the anchor man, from the air-conditioned comfort of a studio. (I thought Melissa sounded like a great tropical storm name if we got to 'M' this year.) 'And isn't it correct that we're hearing Hurricane Dean may have actually made it up to Category five?'

'That's correct, Daniel. The storm is currently passing over Jamaica, with winds of one hundred and fifty-five miles an hour plus, and experts say ocean temperatures could make this the most powerful storm on record! Right now, we're all praying this doesn't happen over Texas. After a bad year, the last thing the United States needs is a landfalling Category 5 hurricane – something that hasn't happened in almost twenty years.'

Then came the inevitable question, delivered with dramatic intonation and a cosmetically whitened grin (I suppose it would have been worth Daniel's job's if he didn't pop it):

'And what of rumours this storm could be set for New Orleans? Is that still a possibility?' Before Melissa had a chance to reply though, Marc changed the channel.

'Why d'you do that?' I groaned.

'Coz they're talking bollocks, son.'

He carried on hopping through the various programmes, until he found CNN. After barely time to pour myself a glass of warm, fluoride-heavy water from the tap, their rolling news service had come around to the story too. CNN went a few better than CBS, showing pictures of the building winds and rain over the Caribbean. Although branded 'live', the shots were clearly on a twenty-second loop, but their impact sent a chill up my back. That quintessential image of the land-falling hurricane; a set of usually idyllic palm trees bent almost to the ground, their branches billowing like hair under a dryer, coconuts tearing away to become natural cannonballs. You couldn't tell if it was night or day, and frequent lightning tore across the island skylines.

CNN's other exclusive was news of building gale-force winds in the Midwest too, and speculation that residents of Chicago and Detroit were considering boarding up windows as a separate inland system made its way towards the Great Lakes and Quebec. Linking reporters on the beaches of both Michigan City and Texas's South Padre Island must have seemed a nice touch to the editor. It was as if the country was preparing for a grand, sporting showdown with Mother Nature.

'Is this the new face of American weather?' asked their newsreader, balancing the matter-of-fact with the sensationalist only slightly more smoothly than CBS had.

'There's probably waves back by your old girl's house in the next few days too, then,' noted Marc, with a grin. 'Lake Ontario's got a massive western fetch. But it's not gonna be anything like what we're in store for.'

It had taken days of speculation and uncertainty to get here, but as Hurricane Dean bore down on the Caribbean, and then the Gulf of Mexico, we finally knew what he would send to the north-east of the US: a very powerful swell, driven from the south-south-west, and due to arrive in about twenty-four hours' time – to the unbridled delight of surfers from Jersey all the way to Nova Scotia.

With one last day to wait, we took the train into Manhattan to see Central Park, the UN, Wall Street, the Empire State and all the other places that had always been prominent in so many Western minds, but never at the top of Welsh surfers' must-see lists.

But first to a Starbucks coffee house off Broadway and 42nd.

Marc had fought that suggestion at first, but minutes after our visit to the Quiksilver shop I had succeeded in getting him to abandon an ideal he'd held on to for years: he had entered a Starbucks. The reason he gave was that the ten minutes we'd just spent walking around Times Square had been so intense he needed to get indoors at any cost.

'Desperate times, desperate measures, son,' he cursed.

Over a two-hundred calorie latte I asked him what the problem was with places like this – as with McDonalds. I quite liked digging myself in and defending these sorts of establishments – especially when it provided a chance to wind Marc up.

'It's so bland,' he spat. 'So cultureless. There's a Starbucks in every town on earth now, just about.'

'Yeah, but we're in New York,' I pointed out, in case he'd forgotten. 'It's the done thing.'

'Really? Even if Starbucks is from Seattle?'

'Same difference. And, anyway, I asked what's wrong with it, not whether you knew more about its origin than me.' I winked at him. 'Didn't realise you were such a fan...'

'I suppose I just don't want to help it to spread,' he replied, thoughfully.

'It?'

'I dunno. American influences?' Marc didn't sound as sure as usual. Maybe this not-going-into-Starbucks thing was something he simply did out of habit, for original reasons since forgotten. He tried to elaborate: 'I just don't like the idea of a franchise or chain. I mean, these places are everywhere in Cardiff. There's like ten of the buggers.'

'I bet you'd be delighted if we saw a Welsh pub on Broadway though. Imagine that – a dragon and a Brains SA logo opposite the Flatiron Building!'

'I wouldn't actually. I'm happy to keep Wales in Wales.'

'Bollocks. You've backed yourself into a corner and you know it.'

Marc paused, and then sipped at his paper cup of Earl Grey.

'Come on,' he said, 'let's move on.' He hadn't cornered himself at all. He knew I was trying to wind him up but was avoiding taking the bait. Since we first knew each other, it had always been said that nobody could rile Marc better than me – and vice-versa. Over the years it had almost been a game to us – as if we were happier disagreeing than sharing a consensus on something. However, these days I'd started getting the feeling that Marc was growing out of this little game. Of course, he remained one of the most opinionated people I knew but when it came to attempts to get him on edge he had lately evolved some sort of radar that steered him away.

'Nice tea, eh? My coffee's great.'

He smiled and agreed.

We walked up a couple of blocks to the edge of Central Park and sat on a boulder finishing our drinks, before finding a bin and then deciding what to do. Marc wanted to go to the UN – that was his number one priority. If I wouldn't agree to it, then he was going to go anyway. Besides that, he thought an open-top bus ride would be the best way to go about the rest of the afternoon.

'You're mad,' I told him. 'An open-top bus ride? With the tourists?'

'*We're* tourists, you tit!'

'Yeah, but...'

'Look. I've tried it in a few cities now. It's wicked. Whenever I'm on a conference somewhere like this I do it. Brussels was the last one – saw the European Parliament. That's why I want to go to the UN. I'm into that stuff. It means something, you know, the *United Nations*.'

'Well, it doesn't matter what perks you list, it's not going to get me to come along on a tourist bus. You go. I'll do something else.'

'OK,' he said. 'Let's meet up later.'

And so it was agreed. True to his word, Marc walked off, back towards Broadway, where the bus tours climbed over each other to take your business. 'We'll meet in two hours at Grand Central,' he told me. 'The train station. Just stand in that main bit – the one you always see in films. You've got my "cell" number anyway. Then we'll go to the UN.'

In the spare time I decided to walk around, observing what was around me and trying to fight off a feeling that Marc might actually be in for the better experience. Surely a few hours in New York was whatever you made of it.

My first thought was whether I knew anyone here. The immediate answer: no. Although a friend from home lived upstate – or at least had done the last time I'd heard. He even used to surf when we were kids, too.

A couple of blocks south-east of Central Park was the Apple Store, inside which crowds were poring over rows of iPhones connected up to the internet and free to try out. I hated new technology, but had a go anyway to login to my hotmail account, where I found the address for Lee – the guy I thought might be living in New York State. Once logged in, the keypad irritated me so much that I settled for just an instant message which read:

GUESS WHAT... IN NYC NOW! AROUND FOR A FEW DAYS MAYBE. DEPENDS ON SWELL. PROB GO LONG ISLAND WHAT D'YOU RECKON?

As I walked back out into the daylight, a guy with a backwards cap was trying to pose for his girlfriend to take a photo – his palm outstretched and mouth open, trying to line up the giant crystal Apple sculpture in the background so it looked like he was taking a bite out of it.

Everything was perpetually moving – a TV camera crew stood recording some kind of game show on the pavement, taxis were dropping off preppy-looking young men in polo shirts and pleats, off to strut their stuff in the city for a day, while more people seemed to be taking photos than not – and at anything you could think of.

I sat at the edge of a small fountain on a patio area in front of the glass apple. It was breezy and the sun was weaker than I had expected. Glad of jeans, I took off my sunglasses and wondered where to go next. I stood up, on the thick rim of the fountain, and noted the usual spread of corroding coins on the bottom, clustered like little galaxies, and then got tapped gently on the shoulder by a security guard.

'Sorry sir, could you not stand at the edge of the fountain.'

'Er, uh, no problem,' I replied, thinking it was a bit of an odd thing to ask.

'People fall in, and then try to sue, sir,' he added, beaming. 'I'm sorry. If it were up to me people could swim in the fuckin' thing. I don't care. Just doin' my job. I'm sure you know the feeling.'

'Of course.'

'Where are you from – that's not a British accent?'

'Wales.'

'Oh, cool. I'm Welsh. Third generation. Didn't mean to call you British there.'

'Actually, I am British. You mean *English* – that's what you mustn't call the Welsh.'

'Oh yeah, English. Well, have a nice day.'

'I will,' I replied.

As soon as he walked off, a young couple with a camera mounted the same fountain to take a picture. 'Er – you can't stand up there,' I told them immediately – to a blank response. They didn't understand – wrong language, probably. I gestured downward to the floor and repeated myself, louder. They stepped off, nodding. The security guard waved, and called out, 'You can always trust the Welsh! Thanks, man!'

From there I walked south-west down Fifth Avenue, passing Trump Tower where another tourist was having his picture taken next to the entrance sign. This guy was throwing a middle-finger salute to his mate behind the lens. That seemed about right to me – all I knew of Trump was from an article in *USA Today* about how he tried to build record-breaking skyscrapers. Apparently a reclusive and much younger Irish entrepreneur had planned an even taller one in Chicago, though, which Trump had complained looked like a giant penis. That had been when I stopped reading and flicked on.

I picked up a giant pretzel from a street vendor, which tasted so good I almost made it two, before carrying on south along the same road and then crossing over a few blocks eastward. One of the intersecting roads, running from north to south, was so long you could see for about a mile each way. There was less traffic than I had imagined but plenty of yellow cabs. Everything was lit with bright summer colours, and that steam rising out of drains was disappointingly absent. This was a quieter part of downtown – sheltered from the wind. The buildings immediately around me were so tall that I couldn't gaze across at any landmarks. The Empire State could have been a block away, and still I'd have not been able to see even its spire for the sheer vertical height of the offices and apartments that engulfed every street. If you paused to take them in, the enormity of what mankind had built made me feel light on my feet – and each window, wall or facade glistened like cars in a front-lit showroom. Washing windows here must have been a never-ending task.

As relaxed, perfectly dressed people wandered in and out of airy fashion shops, I tried to get my bearings. Business districts joined onto dining and drinking areas, shopping streets or square clearings with no obvious pattern or sequence. Then, another two or three blocks down, everything began to look older – dirtier, and more used. An east-to-west road intersected, rising under an industrial-looking, cast-iron bridge. To my knowledge, there were no major highways going through the middle of Manhattan, which meant this was probably where the main railway lines crossed over: Grand Central Station.

By walking this route slowly for an hour or so I had inadvertently arrived at the *point de rencontre* with Marc, who was probably atop of a bus now learning new facts from the tour guide. He would probably ask tough questions at the end, too.

Moments later, I was in a pub – The Oyster. The atmosphere alone was enough to tell me it was the correct decision. The barman laid out a plate of nuts, poured me an Irish whiskey with heaps of ice, and proceeded to talk. He was from Baltimore and had a masters in politics, but had worked minimum-wage jobs for twenty years, raising a family, kids in college – and now had no desire whatsoever to change career, as the people he met here 'were the best in the world'.

The Oyster had a discreet entrance, but once inside it spread out into a wide floor with a long bar and a ceiling of half-arches and domes overlooking the dining tables. You had to descend a few steps to reach the bar stools, where the place began to feel really intimate.

The only other customer, Caribbean looking with glasses, was a PhD student called Jack, studying African-American History. We barely had time to introduce ourselves before he was talking about New Orleans.

'You know, it made me embarrassed to be an American,' he explained, calmly. 'The whole thing was a fuckin' disaster – including the television coverage. And that corruption stuff about the US Army Corps of Engineers.' He meant the conspiracy theory that a government agency had won the right to build the levees despite putting in the weakest design proposal.

'You mean corruption?' I asked him to clarify.

'Yeah, the claim that it was just the rich white men taking all the cash and giving it to their buddies to build shitty levees. It ain't true. That scam involved black mayors too – so it wasn't just a colour thing. And the people who claimed even more bullshit like the levees being blown or sabotaged didn't help their own cause either. I mean, what reason can any sane person think of to do that?'

I had heard that theory before; that deliberately flooding the poor neighbourhood would divert water away from the rich ones. But he was right; it did seem far-fetched. Jack explained how he thought people claiming conspiracy had made the rest of the nation less sympathetic to their cause. 'We're a real uncompassionate country when we want to be,' he stated, tilting his glass at me. 'It's almost as if we get angry at the unfortunate for having forced us to have to see disturbing images on TV.' I thought about insensitive comments I'd heard some people make about the destitute of New Orleans being responsible for their own plights.

Then I told Jack what I was doing in the US, and braced myself.

'Cool,' was all he had to say though. And then, 'Hurricane Dean, right? How's that one workin' out for ya?'

'Er, it's sending loads of swell,' I explained.

'Swell?'

'Waves.'

'Oh, OK.'

'Yeah, but at the moment I think the storm itself might make landfall. Which to tell the truth I'm a bit worried about.'

'Fuck it, dude. No one else is. Unless it hits Texas, and then it'll be like a big-time national disaster.' I couldn't believe he knew so much about it all.

'Last I heard it was near Jamaica,' I said, reaching for some nuts from the second complimentary dish that had just arrived in front of us.

'I wouldn't worry about Jamaica,' Jack replied. '*Mexico* is the place that can't handle getting hit one more time. You know, I'm glad you've been following that one. At least someone's been showing a bit of sensitivity. The shit you've been seeing about New Orleans or Texas being in the path is typical of the dumb-ass media coverage I'm talking about. Everyone's crapping their pants going "please don't hit Texas", as if the storm missing Texas will send it off the face of the earth without harming anyone else. You know, we Americans have what I call a lazy intellect problem – we *can* think, but only about what suits us. I mean, you see those fuckin' hippies that put "Save Mother Earth" stickers on the bumpers of their cars, right? You know, like right next to the damn exhaust pipe – and they still can't see the irony. Fuck it. I hope that storm *does* hit Texas – that'll be the best possible outcome for some of the poorest people on earth at least.'

I raised an eyebrow. Who did he mean?

'Mexico, Belize, Honduras, Nicaragua. *Latin* America ain't *American* America, dude. Those places are like in the frickin' stone ages still. They won't cope at all with a storm like that.'

At this point the barman cut in. 'D'you know where they really couldn't handle getting hit though? In the US?' He'd been wiping a few glasses down, but now seemed to feel it his duty to come and converse with the customers for a moment – especially since there were only two of us. Everything about this place was already spotless, and I presumed there wasn't a great deal else to do.

'Matter of fact I do,' was my smug reply. This suddenly felt like a pub quiz back home. 'Tampa, Miami or here – New York.' Without him here, I could get away without crediting Marc for the knowledge.

'That's right, man,' the barman nodded, amiably. 'If a major hurricane came to this place it'd be total carnage. We're like below sea-level here or something. And so over populated it's unreal.'

'Tell me about it, dude,' Jack exclaimed. 'And we got no way of getting everyone out either – 9/11 showed us that slight itsy-bitsy problem that no one had thought of: it made the authorities realise that they needed an evacuation plan for Manhattan Island. Coz they never had one. This place is like the oldest city in America.'

'After New Orleans,' added the barman. 'And maybe Boston.'

'Yeah,' Jack carried on. 'And so billions of dollars later, and after shit-loads of panic, which we Americans are very good at by the way, guess what their big plan was? The *Subway system* – which you may know failed last week.'

'Really?'

The barman nodded. 'Yeah, it did,' he confirmed, raising his posture authoritatively and leaning forward with both hands facing flat on the counter in front of him. 'We had fifteen inches of rain last... er, Tuesday, I think, and it flooded like ninety per cent of the underground rail system.'

Jack laughed: 'Yeah, so the number one threat to Manhattan – a flood or storm surge – is the only way of taking out their big-time evacuation plan. I love it. That's what we paid Cheney all those millions in bribes to do.'

'Don't forget terror though,' added the barman. 'Someone setting off a bomb on a train, like these guys experienced in London.' He gestured towards me. 'That would have the same effect. You wanna evacuate the city on a train just after one's blown up? Yeah, right!'

Time had passed quickly here, so I wasn't particularly surprised when the next person to walk through the door was Marc.

'T-W-A-T,' he said slowly, gathering his breath. 'I've been waiting half an hour in that bloody train station.'

'Well you must have been early then,' I said, hopefully.

'Bollocks! You know the time. So, er, were you going to come down there eventually then?'

'Yeah. I was just leaving now to come and find you.'

'We're gonna be lucky to get in the UN now,' he moaned.

'The UN?' The barman came to the rescue. 'Oh, that's open for another two hours at least,' he said, looking at his wristwatch.

I introduced Marc, who began talking about research specialties with Jack, before ordering everyone except me another round of drinks. The barman poured mine anyway, and himself one too, raising the glass. 'To Hurricane Dean,' he suggested. Marc looked confused.

It was with a much better attitude that I agreed to walk the few blocks east to the concave tower that housed the UN's administrative offices. This was mainly because the two we'd just met, when I asked them, had endorsed it as a perfectly legitimate and worthwhile New York thing to do. Marc was right, it did seem kind of cool. We were asked for ID by a uniformed and armed officer at a gate, frisked for metal objects and then told that this was neutral territory. American law had no power here. I wondered whether proper international fugitives could come here and demand amnesty – like the dictator Noriega had once done in the Vatican Embassy of Panama City, while US bombs rained on targets all around him. Somehow that didn't seem so likely here.

Once we got inside the ground-floor court, I found myself really liking what the whole thing stood for – all the decorations were about peace, global citizenship and international co-operation. Paintings by children the world over projected the innocents' thoughts on pollution and arms – and the future of a planet they would one day inherit. It felt like all the most emotionally advanced ideas of the human civilisation were being celebrated, and fostered.

In a thoroughfare room full of sculptures and ornaments, labels told you which items were gifts from state dignitaries, or which were the results of UNICEF or UNESCO initiatives. Oil paintings of former secretary generals ran down one wall, each framed against the backdrop of a sky blue UN flag.

The layout of the interior meant you had to pass by all of these displays before getting to the kiosks. From there you could book a tour of the next few floors – in the language of *any* member state, as long as you had time to wait for a translator to come down.

'Oh, hello,' said Marc, to the woman selling tickets, his voice smarmy and worryingly warm in tone. 'Two tours of the Security Council and General Assembly please. *In Welsh.*'

I looked at the floor.

'Sorry sir, we don't do tours in Welsh – except on St David's Day,' came the reply, an Indian accent in flawless English. I looked back up. Tours in Welsh on our national day? That sounded fair. Not to Marc though.

'And why only on March 1?'

'Because Wales isn't a member state, sir.'

'It should be. It's a colony.'

The woman smiled, confident of being correct. 'In your opinion it may be, sir, but the UN awards colony status only to countries democratically recognised as being under the *unnecessary* rule of another. Usually we allow the people of that country to make our minds up. For example, if you look at Western Sahara, you'll see that an electorate majority do feel they would be better off *without*

Moroccan rule. This is why that country is recognised under our ongoing decolonisation process – and is on our list of non-self-governing territories. In Wales, the last referendum was only for regional and partially devolved power, I believe.'

Marc nodded, gulping.

'So,' she concluded, 'as it is effectively self-governing, Wales, *at present*, is neither a colony, nor a member state. It is a part of the United Kingdom – which certainly is a member state – and in fact one of the five permanent nations on the Security Council, and I'll book you a tour in English. The next one leaves in five minutes. That's seven dollars each.'

Total silence reigned all around, as Marc handed over a twenty and awaited change. Even the woman behind us in the queue was ashen-faced.

As we walked away to where four other people were waiting by an immaculately dressed guide, I inhaled, as if to speak.

'Shut up,' Marc snapped immediately. 'Load of bollocks, I reckon.'

'I wasn't going to say anything.'

'Well... good. Don't.'

During the next hour we were shown all about the UN's charter: reasons for its existence and the work it did these days preserving cultural heritage worldwide, keeping the peace and defusing land mines. Marc claimed that he'd always planned to one day do a voluntary stint as a UN blue beret, perhaps on his next sabbatical, which he reckoned was due in four years' time.

'One of the profs in the maths department did it, see. Surfer, he was, from Oregon. You'd like him. Anyway, he said they sent him to Sierra Leone, to this tiny little village right on a perfect right-hand point break. He surfed every single day of his posting, and never had to even fire a shot. Although knowing my luck I'd get sent somewhere shit like Afghanistan, or North Korea.'

'Hey, don't knock North Korea,' I warned him. 'It's got sick waves – haven't you seen that James Bond flick? Pierce Brosnan surfs his way to shore to go and blow up this nuke facility.'

'Are you sure that wasn't actually Sandy Hook?' asked Marc. 'Riding waves up into a nuke silo and all that? Oh no, I forgot. They've moved those to the Midwest now, eh? I should ask this guide what the UN has to say about that nonsense.'

'Bet they're not keen on it,' I suggested.

'Aye. Bloody right they aren't.'

After the tour was done, we wandered out into the cooling evening, stopping for a drink in another bar along East 42nd, before I suggested catching the subway back out to the motel in New Bergen. With the swell due tomorrow, I figured getting sloshed wouldn't help the mission. New York's night-time face could wait for another visit. But Marc had completely the opposite idea.

'We might never come here again. Some of the streets round here have like the best nightlife in the world.'

'Since when have you been interested in the best nightlife in the world?' I demanded.

'Since... always. What d'you take me for?'

'You know what I mean. Tomorrow is the first day of this swell we've been waiting pretty much all of the last two weeks for. You want to get mangled the *night before* we start surfing?'

'We could just have a couple. You know. Mingle a bit. Come on, man, when will you and me ever be in New York again?'

'When will we ever be about to surf waves from a Cat five hurricane again?'

Marc claimed the swell was going to last days, and that we could still make it to the coast tomorrow, even if we went out in the city tonight. That wasn't the point though, and he knew it.

'There's another reason you want to go out, Marc. What is it?'

'I dunno. You know, it would be kind of nice to, well, meet people innit.'

'What people?'

'You know. Birds.'

'What? Like that chick in the Quiksilver shop? Bloody hell, you wooed her all right.'

'Yeah, so. There's loads more people here. Interesting people too.'

'There are interesting people everywhere,' I said. 'In fact, you'll probably meet the least interesting people bopping on the dance floor of a sweaty nightclub. A girl who's a match for Marc Rhys wouldn't go to places like that. And anyway, what's with the rush?'

'You know, we should be meeting more people. That's all. I just think we should be talking to more members of the opposite sex too. I'm getting fed up with your company all the time. I want to meet some people who see things differently to us. That's what's good about girls. They have another point of view.'

'Well Elaine's one girl who certainly saw things differently to us,' I spat, immediately knowing I'd crossed a line. Marc pushed his empty glass away and stood up.

'Fuck you. Fuck off.'

I paused, awkward. 'Sorry, man.'

'Nah, fuck you.' He looked determined. 'Get fucked. I'm going for a walk. You piss off back. Leave me to it.'

I tried to calm him down as we walked together to the subway station, insisting that if he wanted to start talking about chasing after girls it was only fair we talked about Elaine. But he didn't want to know. Far from changing his mood, I'd merely strengthened his resolve. As with the bus tour, he was going out tonight with or without me.

On the subway back, as the train rocked its way between stations, I looked at the few forlorn faces elsewhere in the carriage. Everyone was alone, and it didn't look to me as if anyone was heading out. Bored, tired, worn down – they all looked as if they'd been out of their homes for too long already that day.

I remembered when I first went to visit my mother in Toronto with my younger brother. He kept saying he wanted to go out at night to see 'the real Toronto'. I tried to tell him that the real Toronto was more likely to be by day, or by going around the outskirts meeting ordinary people. To me, nightlife was nightlife – it was homogenous in most cities (perhaps with the exception of Jacksonville, on this trip). We could cane it all we wanted once the waves dried up again.

The motel was dead quiet, although the roads around were flowing with cars. My raised feet were aching and filthy as I flicked on the telly, moving automatically to the Weather Channel again. It was my turn to hide in weather trivia. It had become strangely comforting to sit and hear about Dean. Almost as if it wasn't real so far – just an animated sprite in a game we'd been playing.

While we'd been out for the day the storm had run just past Jamaica, pouring heavy rain on to Kingston's brittle roads and washing away buildings. A couple of people had been reported missing, too. Despite that, the Weather Channel carried images of tourists in bikinis, frolicking and hollering on the wind- and water-swept beaches. They looked as stoked as any surfers. Fair enough, I thought. That was probably what I'd be doing too. Going out into the storm and wandering on the sand – like John back on Hatteras.

The reports moved to airports around the Caribbean, filled with cross, anxious and panicked people – all wanting to get the hell out of Dean's predicted path, which was still aiming for somewhere around the Texas-Mexico border. Whether the US would see a landfall was still anyone's guess, much to the anchor's delight as it meant they still had a big story.

'Hurricane alerts are being issued across the Gulf and Caribbean right now, and into the US,' he smiled from behind a glowing, metallic red desk. 'Even Cancun is seeing some evacuations, as Dean making it to the mainland at Category five becomes increasingly more likely.'

I opened Marc's laptop. It didn't need you to type a key to get it running. Lee, our Welsh friend living upstate had replied to the instant message I sent him from the Apple shop. Only he'd taken the time to write properly to my hotmail:

Tom and Marc!

No way – didn't know you plonkers were heading this way. You should have said earlier! We are about 5hrs north-west of NYC living now.

Hurricane Dean looks like a full on grinder. It's a pity it wasn't going to send much lined up surf to the south – you'd have loved the outer banks if they'd done it for you. Montauk'll be pretty good mind over the next few days. Watch out though, it's all really expensive. Marc Rhys'll hate it!

If you are heading back north and over to Canada again though you could go past Rhode Island which I used to surf all the time. Point judith and around Naragansett can get epic and probably will with swell from Dean. Try Matunuck. An A-frame peak from heaven, There is a ferry from montauk to newport RI I think.

Even more important – Terry Perry is now also living in the states in Portland Maine. He'd LOVE to see you boys if you went that way. Email him as I don't have his number but he'll take good care of you once you've had a surf.

If you need any thing else let me know. I'm proper jealous of you bastards.

All the best (iechyd da) Lee.

This cemented my idea that partying could wait. Terry Perry was another friend I hadn't seen for years, and he'd have got to know people pretty quickly, wherever he was. Marc would be stoked to know we had someone to call in on further north, if he was in the right mood when I told him.

Lee's advice on what to do with the swell looked good too.

I lay in limbo for an hour or so, not quite asleep, but unable to get up and turn the screen off either. The Weather Channel had a good formula – it was nearly a forty-minute loop before the same report repeated itself.

I started thinking about home – Porthcawl, the town where I'd grown up and learned to surf. Here in New York I was able to find people who came from the same place as me – people who knew how I worked, who saw the world the same as me. Coming from a small town full of strong characters who all know each other, it did allow me to feel strangely self-assured. The scale of America, the speed with which it could simply leave you behind, the ease of anonymity seemed all the more bearable when I remembered that, in a far and unique corner of the planet, there existed a weird town with a pier and a promenade in which I was *at home*. A place where I knew every street, every dog-walker and surfer, every nook and cranny of coast and every tide. These were roots that Marc and I would forever have in common, whatever either of us tried to do to shake it off.

A few hours of on-and-off sleep lapsed before I heard him come in. I pretended not to wake as he switched off the TV and went straight to sleep. He must have had a few beers because he didn't climb into his bed, opting instead to lie straight over the bags he'd chucked on it that morning.

I wondered where we should go first tomorrow. It had to be Montauk. Lee's advice could be relied on for sure. Montauk was the very eastern end of Long Island, and would pick up the most swell tomorrow anyway. It had a good reputation for powerful beach breaks – especially in a hurricane swell. And getting there ought to only take a couple of hours.

I hoped Marc wouldn't mind an early wake-up call. I wasn't going to miss any more waves. Not for anyone or anything. Dean was waiting.

CHAPTER FIFTEEN

OCEAN AVENUE: THE SWELL BUILDS

I arose with a real sense of energy. By tonight we could have ridden some of the best waves we'd ever seen in the Atlantic Ocean.

'What time is it?' Marc mumbled.

'Six. We're already late, I reckon. Come on, what's the matter with you? Today's the day.'

To my surprise, he didn't moan at all.

'OK, let's do this.' Marc seemed as focussed as me.

There was no mention of what I'd said to him yesterday as we pinched a few bagels from the breakfast room. I poured two lukewarm coffees from a creaky container into a pair of dusty, Styrofoam cups, and we were done. On the road by quarter past.

Today's the day. The words ran around my head, as we pulled out into the already thickening inner-city traffic.

Before any of the new swell's promises could become reality, we needed to get the Betty Ford across Manhattan. At the Lincoln Tunnel we had to queue for a quarter of an hour simply to get a lane. From there, crossing downtown went smoothly. Marc was on the ball with his directions, and through a back street we circled the Times Square area before dropping onto Broadway, southbound, with little stress. Of course, a few yellow cabbies honked and one even cut me up, but that was welcome. It seemed to set the mood.

As we passed the Flatiron building approaching the Wall Street and World Trade Center blocks, directions appeared for Brooklyn and Long Island. So far, so good. The pressure to pick out the right turn had been the only real hazard.

'This often happens,' said Marc. 'I crossed Central London once in a car. Piss easy. Once you make it into the congestion zone, it's really smooth – everyone else thinks it's gonna be a mission so no one ends up driving it and all you get is taxis and buses. I went up past the bloody Houses of Parliament, Big Ben, the lot. Threw a middle finger at the MI6 building, and was in Gatwick Airport for tea and strumpets. Sweet.'

'Well, don't jinx us yet,' I warned.

No matter who you are and where you may have been, travellers always experience a euphoria in passing classic, instantly recognisable and iconic landmarks, and riding out onto Brooklyn Bridge made me feel like I was in a movie. The grand stone turrets stood larger than in my imagination, their instantly familiar archways and supporting cables drooping down to a strip of street lanterns. Across Upper New York Bay to my right I could see the mouth of the Hudson River and Lady Liberty – motionless, as she had been yesterday, last week and fifty years ago. The city skyline began to appear neatly laid out and to postcard scale by the time we were halfway over. I hadn't expected there to be so much iron – steel supports overhead made the road appear suspended in a tunnel or cage. My mind ran through which songs might best accompany the moment of New York City getting left behind (if life were being set to video, that is). It couldn't be one of total happiness and accomplishment, as milestones also meant you were that little bit closer to the end, too. I imagined a wide-angle shot of the car leaving the city – perhaps taken from the air – provided you could get clearance to fly a chopper over here these days.

It didn't last long enough. A few hundred yards on, the neighbourhood that engulfed us could have been almost anywhere in the country. And after that, we probably took a wrong turn. According to the map, Interstate 495 was meant to appear as quick and easy to find as the freeway out of Manhattan. But it didn't.

Against the plan, we were heading towards Rockaway Beach – which would probably have surf, but nowhere near as much as the eastern shores. As the waves were coming from the south, logic suggested the further you went up Long Island the more exposed it would be to swell – as the blocking effect from New Jersey below was reduced, and the edge of the continental shelf got closer. And also, we fancied clean water. My eyes had started to feel sore and I was convinced responsibility belonged to Sandy Hook, the Army Corps of Engineers, the UN, Wall Street and whoever else had pumped gallons of crap into Raritan Bay. All cities tended to have polluted beaches, but Jersey had been something else altogether.

Around Brooklyn the roads were actually slower than going down Broadway itself.

'We will definitely need the 495 if we're gonna get anywhere today,' Marc insisted. 'It'll take hours this way.'

Using spatial instinct alone, I decided to turn back north at the next main intersection. Ten tedious, stop-start, Achilles-tightening miles later we found the 495. Two minutes of driving off course had taken half an hour to correct. But from there it was a straight line, and time to start thinking of surfing.

'Now, the waves could be all-time out here today,' Marc explained. 'It's been flat for so long that the beaches will be really steep. Normally, calm oceans allow really good sandbanks to form.'

Rain had started falling again, albeit lightly and only briefly.

'I wonder where the term "rain check" comes from?' I mused aloud. No noise from Marc indicated he probably didn't know the answer.

We turned off at a small town called Riverhead. This was the start of the Hamptons – The wealthiest place in all of the US, and certainly not somewhere you'd automatically dream of one day surfing. Mind you, it wasn't only the boot full of boards that made us unusual as far as visitors to the Hamptons went. Our method of arrival – by car – was already far from the done thing. Most people opted for the traffic-busting private jet charter instead – one of which we could see descending on to an airstrip a few miles further up the coast.

Along with Miami's waterfront, or the hills between Hollywood and Thousand Oaks, this was some of the most exclusive real-estate in the known universe. Hamptons wealth was off the scale as far as most of humankind was concerned. Even the smallest mansion here could set you back over twenty million dollars.

This was the hangout of the world's uber-rich: Paul McCartney, Steven Spielberg, supermodels like Christy Turlington, household names of American TV and film such as Seinfeld, Renée Zellweger and Sarah Jessica Parker – as well as the shamelessly self-renamed rapper 'P. Diddy'. Every other road here was off-limits.

The silly rich might wish to boast their fortunes, building vast mansions that would tower over the sea- or mountain-views they had (sometimes) worked hard to enjoy. The sickeningly rich, however, hid their estates away – and it was this core of sickeningly rich inhabitants that descended annually on second, third or fourth homes in the Hamptons. The most excessive of the palaces would be marked by little more than a gate between high hedges and a sign saying 'Private Road: No Entry'.

To make it in this neighbourhood you needed to cruise the streets in top-of-the-range sports cars. Clothing pretty much set its own trends and, according to the tabloid media, the gossip centred not only around who was shagging who, but in which movie set or exotic presidential suite the shag had taken place.

The entertainment business may have been the more obvious route to a Hamptons plot, but this kind of money often couldn't even be attained that way. A lot of land here belonged to 'old money' families, the descendants of post-depression business boomers, or fashion and jewellery pioneers. The hottest of all the properties on this part of the Long Island coast would be owned by people with surnames that contained hyphens and began with connectives like 'von' or 'de'. And then there were always the Kennedys – one of America's most famous power-broking families – who themselves owned property here, including a pad in East Hampton which was probably walking distance from good surf.

The modern legacy of this region dated back to the early twentieth century, when America's money really started to outgrow its cities. Ogling the mansions that remained visible from a car window, you couldn't but recall the world of F. Scott Fitzgerald's Great Gatsby – a place where the new neighbour could come from any background provided they were able to demonstrate their power and money through laying on functions or polo games. The Hamptons still has a big polo scene – with companies like Mercedes-Benz queuing up to sponsor glitzy summer tournaments.

As the New World was first finding its feet, the freshly born bourgeoisie began settling here as a lavish, natural alternative to

Brooklyn and Manhattan. The poet Walt Whitman eulogised the virtues of heading eastward from the city towards these luscious landscapes that attracted artists, socialites, businessmen and their families. The unspoiled beaches and pure sunlight became legendary to those still stuck in the New York and Boston rat races, and by the 1880s and 1890s, leisure and holiday home settlements were thriving in Southampton and East Hampton. From there, it was the place's destiny to become the grand, rolling playground Marc and I were now driving through.

That pure, electrifying sunlight of early Hamptons legend, which had once magnetised Whitman and company out of the urban in search of the sublime was nowhere to be seen today. The air was salty and humid with no clear sky visible anywhere, although we didn't care. After days of waiting, all that was on our minds was swell and where we could go to get a first glimpse of the lines that were throbbing towards the shores of eastern Long Island.

We carried on east, past an autumn back-to-school fete, rows of parked cars, a fruit farm and some gift shops, through Bridgehampton towards the easternmost town of Montauk. Here the buildings began to drop away again. Mist drifted off the ocean, rising up the cliffs and hills onto which the two-lane highway feebly clung.

The off season was moving in. A couple of campsites just off the winding road were emptying out their last RVs. As the Betty Ford climbed another incline, we were given our first good glimpse of the ocean spread out below us. The moment of truth...

The Atlantic had finally undergone the transformation we'd been craving. The ocean now had a rhythm – a pulse. Thinly concealed through the fog and the apparent calmness of the sea's surface, horizontal lines were marching from sea to shore. The swell was here.

Through the cloudy and chilly air I saw, quite clearly, a growing triangle of bubbling white water, as a wave broke both right and left. There was a perfect peak peeling right here, down the hill from where we were parked up. Straining my eyes, I made out the patched surface residue from the wave before, rising and crumbling as another slightly smaller set broke behind. There was no one out.

Our first, instinctive thought was how to get down there. The steep incline to the beach was protected by fences and hedgerows – private property.

Apart from the ocean, it was ghostly quiet. Another car hadn't passed for miles, and there were no other signs of recent human activity. The lack of any surfers was eerie. Usually that would add to the perfection, but this place was known for good beach breaks, and right now a row of stickered-up surf wagons would have been re-assuring – it would have shown we were on the right track.

I got out of the car and sat on the bonnet. We had to remember the rulebook. Driving away from good surf never yielded a result. Everyone knew that. If surfing had Ten Commandments it would have been top of the list. If you got presented with waves good enough to make your heart beat that little faster, then it was your duty to get in there as quickly as you could.

Another wave rolled through, again breaking mechanically to both the right and left. Masked from view by fog, its sounds seemed emphasised. Behind it, the second, third, fourth and fifth peaks of the set all walled up with beautiful symmetry.

'It's fucking pumping,' I whispered to Marc.

'I know.'

'What are we gonna do? How do we get down there?'

'No idea. Leave the car here and run through this guy's garden?'

It was tempting.

We were not quite desperate enough, so I drove us on into the town of Montauk itself. Rule broken – or was it just bent slightly? We were going to surf the same stretch of sand anyway. Two miles further along the shore, among plenty of other surfers, we parked up in a place we knew was kosher and began waxing up.

Almost everyone else had wetsuits now – the dream of surfing in shorts had passed. But this time we had swell; throbbing, thunderous swell. Nerves made slipping into my overly-dry wetsuit even harder. I just wanted to be in the water, paddling out.

As my feet crunched across the gravelly sand, I could feel the energy from Dean fizzing through the water. Mist was thick here too, all around, and you could hear the surface foam crackling as it released its air. I pushed through the shore break, and flicked the cooling water out of my hair. It was moving with power, so I dropped my shoulders and started paddling hard, not really knowing if I'd started in the right part of the beach. Sometimes rip currents can exist that help you get 'out back' – but we didn't take the time to work any of that stuff out. All that mattered was taking the shortest, straightest route to the take-off zone.

Halfway through the inside section a set filled the horizon, way overhead, and washed through the whole line-up. It bashed both Marc and me back towards the sand, locking us into a duel of duck-dives. I pushed and pushed against walls of wave, before eventually one relented and released me into the calmer waters behind. A couple of other surfers were taking a breather before the next thumping set appeared.

'Hey, how's it going?' I asked them.

'Good, dude.'

'Couple of waves, eh?'

'Yeah, man. It's firing. Where's that accent from? Australia?'

'Wales.'

'Oh, cool! My bro' went to Wales once. Stayed in Queensland. Sick waves. Warm too.'

He obviously meant New South Wales. It was OK, though. Marc was still scratching through the last of the white water and hadn't heard. I grinned back, and had just enough time to catch my breath before the horizon began to rise again. A macking set of waves was about to break way outside us all.

'Stay alert, man,' one of the other surfers smiled at me. 'There's often a reform section on these ones.' This meant that you could catch the white water of a broken wave – because it would then back off and start breaking all over again as new.

The waves here rolled through a fairly wide take-off area, so I spun around as one such row of white water pushed through the line-up. The guy was right. I could feel this one was going to move back through deeper water again, and paddled for it. A surge smashed me forward and I clung to my board, lying prone. I jumped to my feet and wove an s-turn across the half-broken face, waiting for the section to strip itself back – and for that reform to happen. It did, and for the first time on the Right Coast I was flying across a serious wave face – with no need to think about speed preservation at all. I angled downwards and engaged with the flats, hooking into a bottom turn. It was my first moment of being 'on-rail' during a hurricane swell. All the weak, hard-to-get-going waves I'd ridden in the last weeks of waiting were eclipsed in one driving turn off the top. As I dropped down into the pocket again I saw Marc out on the shoulder hooting from the base of his lungs. A pitching end-section lined up in front of me, and I just caught the lip in time to float over, landing yards from the shoreline where I'd begun. The session was on.

Dean liked me. I could tell.

Surf-stoke filled my frame, and this time my shoulders tore through the white water, back to the line-up, frothing for the chance to catch another one. Just before I got out again, Marc went left into a dredging close-out, and I saw him pop up the other side shaking water out of his eyes as trapped air exploded from the back of the wave.

I'd always had a thing about riding the first wave of a swell properly – falling in tune with the ocean at the first attempt – and here it felt like I'd managed to do just that. But then again, I'd been trying to tune into what Dean was doing for a week. I'd come to this meeting prepared.

Marc was just as pleased with himself too.

'I got fuckin' creamed by that one,' he laughed. 'It pinned me to the bottom like a crab or something. It was awesome. That was paying my dues for staying out last night. But my next one's gonna be a bomb. I can feel it.'

It couldn't have been dues, because moments later the same was happening to me. Any false sense of security from my first wave was bashed out of me when I tumbled down the face of the next one, trying to get an edge on a backhand drop. It rolled me over, filling my sinuses with water and sand, before letting me up just in time to see Marc and two others ride almost over my head.

Marc's second wave was indeed a screamer, and he had a grin welded to his face by the time we were both sitting out back again. I made a note to myself to ask him about where he went last night when I got the chance, but then another wall of white water pushed towards us, threatening to reform into another perfect peak.

As the tide rose further, these 'cloudbreak' waves got less frequent. But that simply meant that with no dissipation of power out the back, the whole of Dean's energy was now being unloaded on the sandbank we were surfing. The waves were getting more powerful with each set, and closing out with greater ferocity too.

We had to bob and weave around the line-up trying to find where and when a good one would break. Sometimes you'd get one which would annihilate you, and then the next would set up perfectly. You could do turns, try to get tubed – anything. Things went on like this for another hour, before the top of the tide took the edge off it. As the rest of the pack made for the beach, and hard-earned food, we sat waiting for one last one to cap off the session.

'So, have fun last night?' I asked Marc.

'All right like. Bit shit really. But all right. Lovin' this though, eh?'

'Yeah, worth waiting for wasn't it?'

Marc nodded, and slipped off his board, diving downwards. He came up face first so his hair washed out of his eyes.

We sat still and quiet for ten minutes. Sets had slowed right down. Eventually we both caught fat, backwashing waves towards the beach and the buzzing car park. This was, right now, probably the best place to be surfing in all of the USA. One session into Dean's swell and we'd scored a direct hit of our own.

'I bet that peak by the cliffs was even sicker, though,' said Marc. 'And nobody out. Wonder what would have happened if we'd gone there.'

I didn't care. As far as I wanted to believe, we'd done everything right. I'd be quite happy to let Dean make all our decisions if it meant we got surf like that every day from now on.

On land, I felt much less love for Montauk. A loaf of bread and a chunk of cheese was too much to ask, it seemed. You either had to eat out (for a price that not even selling the Betty Ford could raise), or get out. We did find a small convenience store, but it had nothing in it that I felt like eating. So I bought a packet of doughnuts. Not the ones with the rings in them, proper doughnuts – like you got back home. Jam doughnuts, I hoped. Marc had pretzels.

'There's a lighthouse at the top of Long Island,' I said to Marc. 'Let's drive up there. Apparently a point break sometimes works behind it.'

Between gulps from his packet of pretzels, Marc nodded. We got back in the car and waited to pull out into the queue of other vehicles, all far superior to ours.

On our left a load of art stalls had been set up. I wondered whether these people had got caught in a cruel time warp – although Marc could rule out the science of that (especially since the Bermuda Triangle was nowhere near us any more). Gold-skinned women in their seventies, dressed like they were going to Wimbledon or a 1920s beach party, argued and haggled over paintings, while men of similar age gazed beyond them, looking back at the Bentley or Aston Martin convertibles they'd left on the roadside. I felt like scratching one, or doing something even more petulant and useless – maybe throwing Marc's pretzels through the open tops into the seats. Part of it was certainly down to hunger, and I tried to deny that this feeling could also rooted in any kind of jealousy. I wouldn't want a car like that, ever – would I?

I remembered Katherine in North Carolina saying so matter-of-fact to me that if you grew up in Jacksonville, you went into the army. Perhaps if you grew up in Montauk or the Hamptons you were expected to drive wasteful cars, passing your time bored and thinking of ways to spend your money. It didn't seem fair. If that were me I'd have spent my life doing something useful – like surfing all day.

We left the town behind to our west and drove the couple of miles out to the very end of the Long Island peninsular. We pulled into the lighthouse parking lots, surrounded by cliffs and rocks from where you could see boats making their way towards the New England shores of Connecticut, Rhode Island and Massachusetts. The ocean out here was wild – dark, dense and in total command. Through the clouds, the afternoon was warming, getting sticky. I took my T-shirt off and sat on the car bonnet. It was time to open the doughnuts.

'Aw, give me one of them,' Marc pleaded.

'Go on then.' There were three in the pack.

One bite was all we needed, though, to know they weren't what we wanted. Jam doughnuts they may have looked like, but they were actually just lumps of tasteless jelly surrounded by a skin of sugar and crust. No substance at all, and sickly sweet – making you feel even hungrier by being so unsatisfying. Furious, I threw mine at the car – it splatted across the headlight, as if we'd hit a big insect or bird on the way up here. Marc just laughed.

Over a hot dog and fries in a little diner near the lighthouse cabin, we came up with a plan.

The point break was going to turn on as the tide dropped, said a girl working in the kitchen. She was going to go out herself once work finished. Immediately, this interested Marc.

'You from Montauk?' he asked.

'No way, sir. I could never afford to live here. Us workers are all out in Amagansett. It's a town back down the road. Although even that's expensive, too. I'm thinking once the season's done I'm gonna head off somewhere. You know Nicaragua, Panama. Somewhere warm and cheap.'

'Sounds good,' said Marc. 'I'll come with you!'

The girl smiled and went back to the kitchen. He was still a little direct, and for that reason I knew he couldn't have got far in New York last night.

As we ate, Marc admitted that surfing a point with a hundred other people just to try and talk to a girl wasn't worthwhile. Which is why we got right into this other idea.

'Let's go back into the heart of the Hamptons,' he said. 'And prowl.'

'Prowl? What the fuck has got into you?'

'No. I mean prowl for surf.'

Marc's idea was that in such rarely pumping conditions, somewhere along the Hamptons beaches would have to have epic waves. And access may be hard, therefore no one else would be out. Unless the people who lived there wanted to surf, of course – but they'd surely be kooks; clueless and with no real sense of what it meant to live life from wave to wave.

'It's impossible to be a stockbroker or movie star and rip,' Marc explained. 'Can you think of a single one? No... Of course not. My point exactly.'

We'd had good surf already – so now we could afford to gamble a little. There was time to kill as high tide would be around for a while longer and being back in the Hamptons would leave us well placed to go anywhere we wanted tomorrow, such as Rhode Island.

'So are we keen then?' said Marc, wiping his hands and chucking the polystyrene tray in the bin.

I nodded, picked up my sandals and stood up.

'Good,' he added. 'That hot dog was awesome. Now let's hit the fuckin' road. We're on a mission. I'm going to surf again today and it will be in the Hamptons.'

Running the Betty Ford back through slowing traffic in Amagansett, the one thing the place certainly didn't remind me of was a 'worker town'. I remembered seeing the inland village of Villareal once in Costa Rica – the run-down shacks in which the local bar staff, waiters and cleaners lived when they weren't servicing the hotels, restaurants and surf schools of Tamarindo. Amagansett wasn't anything like that. The Bentleys and Aston Martins may have been rarer here, but our car still looked like a skip on wheels – and property was sure to come at a nasty premium.

Traffic began to let me accelerate a little, before all the unnamed lanes and private roads resumed on our sides. We were re-entering the Hamptons.

'Let's just try one,' I said. 'Any road will do.'

'OK. Which one?'

'I dunno. You pick.'

'OK. The next one... Here.'

I flicked on the indicator and made a left, into a little southbound lane. It was about half a mile before we saw any buildings between the two-storey hedges that rose around us. The first was a twenty-plus-bedroom mansion with a gravel driveway looping up past the front steps and out through a different gate. It had three cars parked out front. The lawns were flattened like a Premier League football pitch – you'd feel guilty walking on them – and sculpted hedges enclosed about twenty acres of land.

'They've got fuckin' tennis courts,' said Marc. 'That's when you know someone's taking the piss. I've seen swimming pools in the valleys at home, but when someone's got a tennis court – well, it's like the next level.'

'Does it get cold here in winter?' I asked him.

'I think so. Worse than Wales actually. That's a summer home, man, look at it. Probably empty all the rest of the year.'

It was already late enough in the season for a few of the other pads to be out of use. The afternoon had begun darkening – the mists dropping right over the whole coast again, so thick you could feel the cold droplets in the air. Closer to a mile down the road – during which we'd seen another four huge homes – Marc reckoned we weren't headed towards the beach.

'I've got my compass in the glove box now... wait there... no – I knew it. We're going north-east.'

As he said that, the main highway reappeared in front of us. We'd done a gradual loop.

Frustrated, I turned back towards Amagansett again. Marc looked like he was about to disagree, but a few junctions up we plunged back into the nameless roads. This one went straight for almost a mile with nothing but three overgrown driveways going off it. Then it bent to the right, whereupon a lorry was blocking the way. The driver gestured aggressively to us to reverse, which we did. Using one of the driveways, we let it pass. It was big – a proper long-distance artic – and its box trailer was as tall as you could imagine for it to be legally driveable. It must have been torture trying to manoeuvre that thing through these lanes.

'Luxury Car Delivery Service,' read the flank. It was dropping off a new motor to someone.

Once the lorry passed, we continued up the lane. After winding a few times each way the lane eventually joined onto a two-lane highway, well maintained, but with no cars. It was running parallel to the ocean, which I could sense was only a stone's throw to our left. Hedges and mansions then gave way to a long field of reeds and what looked like corn plants, before we saw an access road which ended right on the sand.

There were two other cars parked up, but nobody else. A fortnight ago this beach was probably filled with celebrities and rich New Yorkers, but now there was hardly a soul present to see Dean's goods unfolding onto the hard-packed, gravel and shingle shoreline.

We walked out towards the water's edge. With the tide still up everything looked too deep. Waves were coming in through the full water without even feathering, before crashing onto the dry sand – a shore break that could swallow anything and anyone. Over to our left we could see one wave breaking far out to sea – but crumbling. It was huge, yet running tamely over a deep-water bank. Not what you chased a hurricane swell to ride – and a bit of a let-down. The other direction looked better. To the right after about another mile I spotted a series of groynes. These, or any other man-made object like a pier, would hopefully harness some swell and force it into a breaking peak. The trouble would be working out how to get there. Finding your way over there would depend largely on who owned the land between.

'This shore break is almost rideable,' I pointed out. 'You'd get creamed, but some of them are breaking far enough from the shoreline to get onto.'

'Yeah, but what would you do with one?' Marc asked. 'Just pull in and then get worked.' (Waves that break too close to dry-land are often dangerous to ride, as you don't want to hit the bottom.)

I looked at him, shrugged my shoulders and then tried to follow the next wave's movement with my hand – mapping it out to see if it might be rideable.

'Nah,' said Marc, noticing my gesture. 'It'd be hard work. Let's try and get to those groynes. There's a better chance of them shaping the waves into something more useful.'

'Will we be able to get to the beach there?'

It was Marc's turn to shrug. 'If we can't, we'll come back here and see if it gets better on the dropping tide.'

'Deal.'

We wandered back to the Betty Ford, enjoying the bite of cold in the air – whatever humankind had done to the surroundings, this place still made you feel alive. Sand had blown over onto the asphalt, and the white lines were faded. A fence was falling slowly into the ground and I hadn't seen a beach rules signpost or parking regulation anywhere.

There were two guys and a girl standing about, who looked around eighteen. A white sports car and a green pick-up purred behind them, one playing pop-rock loudly. As we approached, the tallest of the trio, a handsome blonde boy in a loose, part-unbuttoned white shirt smiled at Marc.

'Yo, man. Whatsup. Seth. I saw you guys at Kelly's last night, huh?'

He offered Marc a high-five. Marc left him hanging. 'I don't think so, mate. You got the wrong person.'

'Oh, really? Ah, no problem, dude. You goin' surfin' then?' Seth was utterly unphased and took a deep, draining drag on a joint. As I got downwind of him I noticed he smelled drunk too.

'You want some smoke?' he offered. 'There's a sick little wave down past those boulders you were looking at, dude. But it's like private property now. I used to surf there all the time but now I can only surf this side. You can park here though. They just give you a ticket. Forty dollars – that's all. I got some awesome tubes this morning and yesterday.' He plugged the joint between his teeth and made a 'pig-dog' shape – the position a surfer would go into to ride a tube if they had their back to the wave.

'Yeah, dude. It went shitty though,' he continued, standing up again, and draining another deep puff out of the blackening paper. He nodded back towards where we'd been looking. 'It's called Georgica – the bunch of houses down there. There's gonna be good surf down that way now, most probably.'

I started walking away – convinced Seth was a bullshitter. Marc stayed and talked while I waited in the car, falling further out of love with this place by the second.

Marc got in a few minutes later and Seth and the others promptly left, turning away from the field opposite to where we came in and presumably home to mom and pop's summer residence. His white sports car swerved around the bend with a skid, only just staying on the wet road. When rich kids decided to go off the rails, they did it literally and with total commitment.

'So – is he for real?' I asked Marc.

'Probably not, but I like the sound of that Georgica spot. He reckons we could try running through a footpath to the beach. There's access apparently. Says we could surf for hours before the security noticed us.'

'Hours? There's barely ninety minutes left before dark!'

'So? It's worth a go. The tide's not going anywhere in a hurry here.'

'Did he tell you how we get there?'

'Yeah – we go back to the proper main highway, then take a left by a big Starbucks. It's down Ocean Avenue apparently. Although it's not labelled. He reckons it'll take twenty minutes.'

'And you believe him?'

'Dunno. Let's try anyway.'

I remembered our journey over to the Gulf Coast. It had been me trying to persuade Marc to give it a go there – even if it meant renting longboards; my desire to give it a go somewhere new, while Marc had been reluctant and unsure. Now it was he who appeared keener to surf.

I was worrying about the time. With mists like this, it felt as if sunset had passed already. But then I decided I'd better get with the programme.

'Come on then. Let's go.' I fired up the engine with a splutter of smelly petrol, and put the car into drive.

En route back to the main Hamptons highway, I was keeping a close eye out for other motorists like Seth; intoxicated, carefree brats with too much engine power under their hoods. Waiting for a chance to turn out into the traffic flow, I rubbed the salt on my eyebrows – reminding myself that only hours ago we'd been riding great waves. There was no rush any more, I thought. If Dean wants us to score again today, Dean will let us score.

At the Starbucks junction there were two roads bearing left. Marc was sure it was the first.

It was a test of patience, winding down what we hoped was Ocean Avenue. More mansions taunted us from the sidelines, as constant changes in direction made me keep doubting that we'd hit the correct side of the fork. Eventually, I couldn't take it any more and stopped to ask a woman who'd emerged from one of the homes closer to the road.

'Is this Ocean Avenue?'

'I don't know. What's your business here?' She looked at us over dark glasses – presumably because looking through them in this light was nigh-on impossible. She had a grey running suit and trainers on – but didn't seem to be going jogging.

'Never you mind!' Marc shouted, leaning over. 'And perhaps you should learn your own address.'

I winced.

'Who are you? This is a private road,' the woman replied.

To prevent Marc from launching into a tirade, I pulled quickly away. These people were bored, I decided. I'd have been thrilled to see someone with a foreign accent asking directions outside my house – it would have been something different to the usual – and would have tried my best to help. Getting in the water had to be our answer to such curt treatment – it had come to mean more than just a surf now. This was us against the Hamptons. And we had to win.

Many, many times in my life I'd felt an incredible relief at the sight of the ocean – but never quite as I did ten minutes later when, through a gap between some homes and a little freshwater inlet, we saw breaking waves. It was straight ahead of us. Through the piece of private land Seth had mentioned, via the footpath. Maybe he wasn't so full of shit.

We passed the 'No Trespassing – Security Guard On Patrol' sign and parked up to partially block the pathway. Marc jumped out and ran towards the beach. He only got halfway before running back towards me making a tube shape with his hand.

'It's fuckin' pumping!' he cried. 'It's total death, but let's give it a go.'

'Is it heavy?'

'Yeah – it's thumping. Hell barrels!'

Usually I'd approach something like this with apprehension. But we had to beat the Hamptons. We had to surf.

'Shall I use my old board?' I asked Marc. It wouldn't matter if that thing broke.

'Good idea. Can I use it too?'

'What?'

'Let's share it. The waves are breaking like five yards out to sea. Let's catch two each at a time, like we did in the Gulf. I'm not wearing a wetsuit either. What if someone comes while we're changing? Come on. Let's do it.'

He pulled his T-shirt off over his head and flicked his sandals into the boot.

'Come on! What are you waiting for?'

I got ready as he reached for my old, battered 6'2". I was already shivering just from stripping to my boardshorts. There was a biting wind, and you could feel that the grey evening would soon slip into night. I tied the car key to a string inside my pocket and we ran across the footpath, sprinting to keep warm. My spare board had no leg rope, so once we got to the water's edge Marc kept going, running head-on into a macking lump of vicious shore break. He threw the board sideways as a lifeguard would throw their float out before diving under. It just cleared the wave, and with only a few strokes both he and his watercraft were floating back out. His skin had gone slap-red with cold.

The waves were thick, and breaking in only a few inches of water. I wondered if Marc would get one at all and, if he did get one, whether he'd live to tell the tale.

After a minute of paddling around to keep loose, a set loomed. The first one didn't peel at all and shut down across the length of the beach, exploding twice as high as it had broken. You'd be risking more than just your board going on something like that. The second looked for a moment to have a flattening shoulder, so that was the one Marc went on.

Everything went wrong. He got hung up at the top of the wave on take-off, and then had to jump, freefalling into the pit. I saw him kicking his legs as he plummeted six feet to the bottom. The board was blown into the air by the foam-bounce, which sent it spinning like a piece of confetti. It rushed up the sand, as the water turned brown with silt. Marc came up feet-first and spluttering. By the time he'd recovered his senses, the wave had spat him back onto dry land like Jonah.

I laughed so hard my sides ached, while he hooted. The sound filled the empty beach, before another breaking wave drowned it out.

'I'm going again!' he yelled, as fired-up as I'd ever seen him. He grabbed the board and ran straight for the water.

He managed to get down his second wave, stroking like a madman to get over the ledge. After a wobbly drop, he drove a turn, trying to squeeze under the breaking lip for a close-out tube. He just about made it, and disappeared from sight – only to re-emerge coughing on the sand again. This time I just clapped. Marc was trailblazing here. Not only for himself, but for me too. These waves were suicide – but here we were. Now I had to ride one too.

He handed me the board, checking the fins were all still secure.

'Just pick one and go for it,' he advised. 'They change shape anyway, so it's all guesswork.'

I ran at the ocean. Only by jumping straight in could I bear the cold. Diving through an oncoming wave, all I could do was yelp. The air rushed out of my lungs as my body contracted and constricted. My neck and back were tingling, and the side of my head tensed. It was freezing.

Like Marc, once out back I kept paddling in circles to stay warm. My teeth were already chattering by the time a wave lined up that looked good enough to surf. It was going to peel right, if anywhere, so I could go for it on my front side.

As I paddled for it, I became less sure. In front of me I could see a slab of sand, grey like freshly mixed concrete, which I knew the wave wanted to pound me into. I pulled back, giddy, only just avoiding getting sucked over the falls. I looked at Marc on the sand. He was jumping, hopping mad at me for wimping out.

'You *fuckin' PIKER!*' he yelled. I knew he was right. The mood he was in, he'd have gone on that one.

I knew I'd played my one and only joker now. The next wave that came I would have to go for, whatever it looked like.

I sat up on the board and called to Marc: 'I'm on it. Don't worry!'

Another set started to wall up. The first wave looked nice and clean – as accessible as any other. It was going to break to the left though – my backhand. It had been a long time since I'd gone for a left-hander as sucky as this. I dug my arms deep around the board, and paddled furiously – it was all about getting over the edge early enough. *Tuck your neck in*, I muttered, *otherwise you'll never fit the tube*. The wave surged forward, twisting, plunging at the sand. I jumped to my feet and grabbed the outside rail of the board, side-slipping down it. I heard the outside world cut off, as the vortex noise surrounded me. The lip came down between me and the shoreline, like a tinted glass curtain, while I was still slipping sideways towards the beach. I looked up. A cavity of water twenty yards long lay ahead, dark and angry. There came a moment of total peace in which I forgot the cold, the danger, the money matters, and then I got slammed face-first onto the seabed.

As I was ground into the loose sand, I felt the water rushing over me, and my board went flying. I came to a halt sitting on the sloping beach, with Marc screaming for joy just in front of me.

'That was a fuckin' peach, son! You got pole-axed! Come on. Do it again. I went twice!'

I don't know how long the guy had been watching for. If it had been the whole time, then I wonder whether he'd been intrigued to see what we planned to do, because I'm sure he'd have never let us continue out of generosity. Maybe he thought the ocean would do his job anyway, like Keanu Reeves at the end of *Point Break* when he lets Patrick Swayze go out one last time. Perhaps he hadn't thought we'd make it in again.

I was halfway through my second go with the board when I noticed he'd approached Marc. It was going to be the last wave anyway. It was too cold to carry on much longer without ripping myself limb from limb with stiffness. Marc looked like he was chatting to the guy so I kept waiting for a set, floating dead still this time. It didn't matter how cold I got now. We were going to dry off in a minute.

The wave was a less successful repeat of my first one; a no-hope fall into a dredging pit that tried to batter me in half. Staggering up the beach, sand in my hair and everywhere else, I noticed the bloke had gone again.

I was grinning, planning to offer Marc a high-five for one of the most memorable sessions I'd had, when I saw the look of concern.

'That was fun, eh?'

'Yep.'

'Who was that?'

'Son, we need to go. We need to get the fuck out of here, now.'

'Really? OK. We're going now anyway.'

'No. I mean quickly. Like *immediately*.'

'Why?'

'That guy was some kind of security guard. German, I think. He said his clients were very concerned by our breach and have asked him to deal with us.'

'So. That's fine. We'll be off any minute now.'

'No, son, he had a gun.'

I thought I'd heard him wrong at first. But I hadn't.

'A gun?'

'Yeah. He said it wasn't loaded. But then he said, totally calm like, that he's going to go and load it. And if we're still here when he gets back then we're never going to leave. If you know what I mean.'

'What?'

'Yeah, man. He seemed really serious too.'

'Fuck off. He can't do that?'

'Can't he? Is there anyone else around here? Are we even allowed to be on this beach?'

Marc didn't often lend himself to rash emotion – and panic rarely made it into his repertoire. I looked at him for a moment more, before realising the situation. We had to run.

I tore ahead of him, chucking my old board against the fence by the Betty Ford, desperately curling frozen fingers around the key, trying to release it from my wet pocket. Marc stood, helpless. He grabbed the board, ready to fling it into the rear as soon as I could open up. The central locking had broken years ago, so I needed to open all three doors. Salty and sandy, the key ground its way through the locks, needing to be coaxed into turning. I held the boot open – no time for the mole wrench – as Marc ploughed the board through our belongings. We jumped into the front. In my haste I didn't hold the ignition long enough and the car failed to start first time. I'd always thought that if in desperate need to run away in a car I'd make sure it started first time – and now here I was fucking it up like you'd always fear. The second attempt lasted a whirring, juddering couple of seconds, before the spark kicked in and the engine rattled in to life.

Among the hedges I heard the voice, unmistakably from northern Europe, as Marc had said – gurgling and nasal, harsh, aggressive.

'Riiight you fucks...'

The engine noise meant he knew exactly where we were. I revved and then slid into drive. The handbrake dropped and I added more gas. There would only be one chance to do this. Pulling away in an automatic car is usually something you'd do with your eyes closed, but now it seemed a complicated process of hard-to-coordinate skills. A searing sound of burning metal accompanied our sloppy jolt forward. I was over-accelerating. The gravel and sand underneath us trembled before the tyres bit the road again and we tore free. The voice dropped away, still cursing just behind the hedge, as I skidded around the first corner, feeling more and more secure as the distance between us and the security guy grew.

'Oh my God,' Marc bellowed. 'That was sooo fuckin' sketchy. We could have been killed. *We could have been killed!* Do you realise?'

'I know!' My voice wavered. We were doing seventy now, through a narrow lane.

I remembered the frustration I'd felt seeing Seth blaze through these roads in that sports car, drunk and stoned – that irritatingly grown-up sense of responsibility. Now, though, as we tore through bends ourselves, dizzy with fear and adrenaline, the double standard seemed fine. This was survival, after all.

It must have been about a mile before I began to go easy on the driving – and then only for a moment – before the thought occurred to me that we could be followed. That wasn't the only worry, either. Earlier these roads had sent us on a loop. With each bend we rounded I half-expected to run into a car blocking the way. He'd be sitting on the front, waiting patiently, looking at us along the barrel of that gun.

Only when Marc started laughing did the chances of anything bad happening seem to be getting slimmer. I saw a chubby man with a tatty white T-shirt and spectacles walking a red setter at the side of the road, slowing to about five miles an hour to let him pass, and finally realised we had got away with it.

I waved at the guy, who could have been anyone. He tapped a salute back to me, and winked, like anyone would. I wondered who he was to be living around here and whether he knew that a few miles down the road security guards threatened to shoot people.

'That shit was your fault,' I blurted to Marc. 'Imagine we'd not got away then? I reckon we could well have got shot! Over some freezing close-out barrels!'

'I know. Your mum would have been *so* angry with me!' he laughed back. 'Worth it, though. And we won't tell her anyway, eh?'

★   ★   ★

For the second time that afternoon, Highway 27 represented salvation. The Hamptons lanes didn't like us, and we knew it. Outside Starbucks, we finally changed out of our wet boardies – under the light of a streetlamp at the side of the road.

I pulled socks over my numbing feet. The cold made it feel as if my life-force had retreated deep into the very core of my body (so maybe a bullet would have missed it anyway). Wrapped in a thick hoodie, I felt that nucleus of warmth slowly spreading back through me, along with a tremendous sense of achievement. The air was filling my lungs to the diaphragm. I felt like drinking something strong – if I'd had the money to.

'We're not done yet in there,' Marc said with resolve, nodding back towards the coastal lanes and the gated homes. 'We're going to sleep somewhere around here tonight.'

A few miles back towards New York, but still in the heart of the Hamptons, we turned again into the narrow, hedge-lined roads. By night they were even more desolate and unwelcoming. Marc kept looking to the sides until he saw a gap in some of the bushes.

'Stop the car,' he ordered.

I did as he said. He got out and walked through the undergrowth – gone about twenty seconds. When he came out again he was nodding.

'Done this before in Switzerland,' he said. 'I got sucked off with a conference once and went away for two days. You can drive cars through big hedges and then kip in them.'

I wasn't sure what he meant. Did he want me to punch the car through the bushes and out of sight?

'Just drive straight in,' he insisted. 'We can kip in the car. I'll set an alarm for five in the morning. We'll be on the ferry to Connecticut before any of these lazy fuckers even stir.'

I didn't know what to say.

'Come on, I'll guide you in.' He jumped out again.

I was sure someone was going to come around the corner at any moment. I pictured blue lights flashing, visas revoked, sitting out the rest of Dean's glory week in a Long Island jail cell. I heard branches scratching against the car's sides as I reversed back further into a tiny gap in the hedge, until the front bumper was out of view. Then Marc opened the door again, pushing the hedgerow aside to climb back in.

'Sorted.' He rubbed his hands together. 'Seats are a bit wet but we'll get a few hours.'

It was pushing ten o'clock. I lay back on my makeshift bed, pillows over the automatic gear stick. What had Dr Rhys been thinking, skipping that conference and driving around Switzerland alone, sleeping in a car? Did he make a habit of that kind of thing?

It reminded me how close below his civilised, haughty surface there lurked the old Marc. I thought about how torturous it must be for him to hide that side of him from so many people and for such periods of time – especially from Elaine. How had he coped? The answer was that he hadn't.

I'd often had a recurring dream about a perfect A-frame peak – always hollow, always breaking exactly how I'd want it to, but below a cliff or around a corner. In the dream I'd try and try, but never reach the water's edge. Either I'd fail to find a way down the cliff, or while running towards the shoreline my legs would go to jelly (as my body remembered I was actually asleep). In the dream, the arrival of nightfall would always end the quest, incomplete, usually after a gorgeous, reddening sunset during which the waves would glass off to sickening perfection.

Today it felt as if parts of that dream had been waiting for me out here on Long Island. As if Dean had wanted me to face that challenge – to battle some personal demons: my fear of not being allowed to surf, of not being able to surf – and ultimately of not being *alive* to surf.

Whether they'd been beaten was not so clear. The glee at pulling off an illicit session with nobody else in the water had been replaced by a depression – a come-down from the buzz of being chased away. I felt strangely flat, and this feeling was getting in the way of sleep.

I wondered whether Marc also had similar tribulations and rites of his own to deal with, and if Dean would allow him to live out his dream – whatever it was. He'd never talk about that stuff anyway – wouldn't give it enough time in his head. Sometimes I questioned if Marc actually knew himself that well. When he hit his stride it was as if this unthinking energy could lead him; a spontaneity that would give his rational mind a real run for its money.

Before we'd had a few hours sleep he was going to wake us and want the journey to go on – leaving this place behind before it had a chance to affect him any more. He was on the run, I realised – that was Marc in essence. A fugitive.

I wanted him to get caught though. He needed it.

We needed it.

NEW ENGLAND

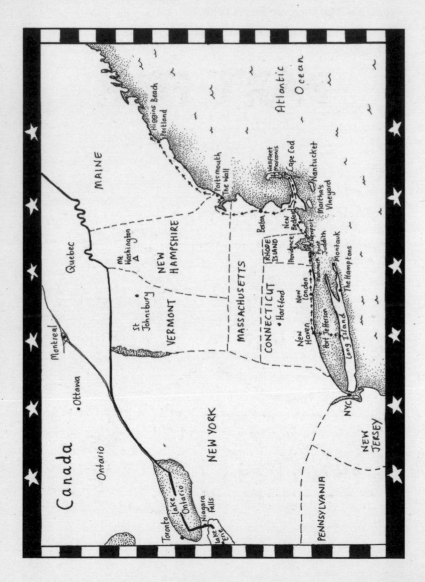

PART FOUR

CHAPTER SIXTEEN

HURRICANE DEAN

It seemed a fair deal in the end – surviving that run-in with an armed guard in return for getting truly shafted filling the car with fuel. Compared to some of the other ways the Hamptons could have caught us out, this was getting off lightly, really.

It was my fault – I'd stopped looking at the price-boards weeks ago. It never cost anything for a full tank in the States – pretty much a quarter of what you'd pay in Wales. But I hadn't reckoned on a pump in this area costing nearly five dollars a gallon more than usual (arsehole tax, perhaps). Suddenly, without realising, I'd filled up the Betty Ford for a price that, on my budget, was crippling. It may have been quarter to six in the morning, but there was no excuse.

Apart from the petrol, I'd managed to spend nothing in the Hamptons. That was Marc's influence – the most expensive place in the entire US, and we'd slept in a hedge, with no evening meal. It had come at a cost though – besides being groggy from too little sleep, I was so hungry my stomach was beginning to cramp. We were still set on trying to catch the earliest ferry from Port

Jefferson over to Bridgeport, Connecticut, but both desperately needed something to eat. Driving would be impossible without it.

'They got bagels, son,' Marc called over to me from the doorway to the kiosk, 'except it's fuckin' shut.'

There was a guy working a nightshift at the pump, though, and it was he who came to our rescue: 'Ah, man, I can open for ya.'

'Can you?'

The guy had an inviting demeanour. He was black and wore braided hair and glasses, stood about six-foot-five tall and had a songlike accent that reminded me of some of the New Orleans locals. He smiled a lot for this time of day.

'For sure, bro. Can't deny a man a bagel at this time of day. I mean, it's sunrise, so that equals breakfast time. I can turn the coffee machine on too, if you want.'

The New York Bakery bagels were Marc's favourite brand, and the garage had cream cheese too. As we waited for the coffees to warm and pour, conversation came around to our surfboards and, surprisingly, a mutual 'acquaintance':

'So you guys are surfers, huh? You bin up to Montauk?'

'Yeah,' Marc replied, wiping bleary eyes.

'I know somewhere that's got huge surf right now, man. My hometown – Kingston, Jamaica. There's rivers in the streets there today. Water everywhere. You'd love it!'

Hurricane Dean had walloped the place. I didn't know what to say back.

'Yeah, Jamaica's got a storm all right,' he went on.

As Marc counted up his spare change to see if it would cover breakfast and coffee, I asked the guy how long he'd lived in the New York area.

'Twenty-two months. Got family in Texas, though. I'm an American. Been here seventeen years.'

I wasn't sure if that meant he still had the right to make flippant remarks about a Category 5 hurricane in Jamaica – but it wasn't as if we had any moral high ground on that one either. I was trying to feel comfortable with what we'd been doing, but each time I heard more news on the storm it knocked me back. I had hoped Dean would wind down now he was done making surf, but knew that in the Caribbean or Gulf of Mexico, without land or cold water to intercept, it was wishful thinking. Odds were somewhere else was going to get a big hit soon enough.

Marc had finished counting his change, and it wasn't nearly enough. It didn't matter, though, early and with nobody else around, we were allowed the coffees as a freebie. The first and last break anyone around here would give us.

I thanked the Jamaican-Texan-New Yorker with a handshake and drove away northbound, looking for the 495 again. Meanwhile, Marc served up the bagels and cheese. I was so drained by the thrashings I'd had from the sea last night – the cold water stuck in my sinuses, and serious lack of sleep made my jaw ache when eating breakfast. The coffee was still too hot to drink, although its smell was starting to stir my senses. Feeling grumpy, I came back to worrying about the runaway storm that was governing our trip. While we'd pranced over Long Island yesterday, it had been easy to forget that Dean was very much alive and doing whatever he wanted a few thousand miles away. Jamaica had narrowly escaped a devastating landfall and some people would be waking up to demolished homes this morning – while we simply looked to Rhode Island and hopefully more perfect surf.

I didn't even need to ask Marc to know that he'd say Dean wasn't our responsibility, but still, you couldn't help thinking it.

Back off the 495 and heading for Long Island's north coast, cheaper housing began to line the road. Schools with ramshackle US football pitches and spectator stands ran into wide shopping malls and retail parks, factories and wholesalers. The coffee was starting to work, and I felt more alert – emerging from our bizarre experiences in the Hamptons' microcosm. I was trying to work out which bits of it had really happened.

The crisp reality of Port Jefferson, its blustery, grey air and swirling ocean scent was beautiful. It was like waking from a coma. I could have been in the British Isles. Seagulls bleated overhead, and the corroded metal railings looked like Porthcawl harbour back home. The colourful walls, with bubbles in paint caused by years of sea salt and wind were so familiar to me I felt melancholy as the Betty Ford moved out of daylight, into the ferry's hold. I knew the rest of New England was going to give me similar moments of *déjà vu*, and felt a surge of excitement as the deep rumble of the boat's motors shook us from below.

If you have the sea in your soul, then boat rides can become a spiritual experience. You feel like an antenna for the ocean's mood and pulse. On land a keen surfer can read what the water may be planning to do, but on boats those senses are sharp and acute. If the sea is sad, angry, calm or unpredictable, you feel it too. The flat waters of Long Island Sound were closer to New York City than the Hamptons had been, and I detected weariness in the waves. But somewhere in the distance, calling out to me, was the swell – its hollers getting more and more distinguishable the closer we got to New England.

The conditions were tempestuous by the time the Connecticut shoreline was coming into sight. The ferry was rocking from side to side as Dean's swell lines bombarded us. We were almost travelling sideways to keep an even keel against the rises and drops, and all around us the other drivers were vomiting.

I felt one particularly violent swing and then a smashing noise. A load of plates in the kitchen slid off their shelf, just too quickly for a chef, unsteady on his feet, to intercept. One person screamed while others whispered to each other, nervous and nauseous.

We decided to walk up to the top deck. A squall of rain was passing, and we found a spot behind the horn that remained dry. The shores ahead were built-up, packed with industry and shipping. We were going to blaze through Connecticut as quick as we could – Rhode Island was where you'd find the best waves in New England.

'It's gonna pump today,' I told Marc.

'I know – d'you get butterflies when you're waiting on surf like this?'

Who didn't? The anticipation was difficult to deal with. If I didn't keep the excitement down though, the first task of finding our way to the surf could be really difficult. It needed rational thought, and yet more patience.

The sea calmed again just before we moved to dock. Harbours are always in protected waters, but I wanted to believe this renegade swell had chosen to stay away from Bridgeport of its own accord, that Dean was saying to me, 'I'll head on to Rhode Island. Meet you at Point Judith in a few hours!'

For the past hour the coastline ahead had sat on the horizon, unchanging in size and scale. Now it was moving past us at touching distance as we slid in for the boat to moor up. Already, without even putting my foot on terra firma, I could feel a different atmosphere to that on Long Island. We were moving on now. A more mature swell, and a different seascape in which to harvest it.

A lot of the waves in southern New England were point and reef breaks. Of course, it got a lot colder here than down south, and the poor light often dissuaded surf mags from giving the place a lot of photo coverage. But anyone who'd read up on the Right Coast would know that from Rhode Island to Maine there was a host of world class waves, and a wide, deep water swell window that could pick up some seriously big surf.

The information we had to go on was from a combination of articles and surf guides, as well as word of mouth. Lee's email mentioned Matunuck, which was one place I'd heard of before. A basic village on the beach, it was meant to have a set-up of several points and reefs all close to each other, and would handle a bit of swell.

Back on Interstate 95 and making good headway to the north-east, we were almost bouncing in our seats. Marc was happy. We hadn't just got waves yesterday – we had a story, an experience. This was how Marc was going to be poached back to the life of a hard-core surf traveller – he had to be shown the thrill of the quest.

'Yeah, I've been getting a bit sucked off with work lately, see, son,' he explained to me as we passed a sign for Yale University. The urban sprawls of Bridgeport and New Haven were growing thinner, their hold on the countryside weakening with every mile the Betty Ford covered. 'That conference bollocks in Miami. It sucked – the whole thing. I mean, the paper I got to write was pretty cool, but these days I'm over that stuff. I only agreed to that one coz I knew there was a chance of a free trip over here.'

'Are they really gonna pay for you to fly home from wherever we end up?' I asked.

'Probably. That's what I told them to do if they wanted Dr Rhys at their gig.'

'Isn't that amazing? Think about it – FREE travel, man!'

'Not really. Coz it just makes more work for me to do.'

This wasn't the same Marc that had held himself back from surfing so he could further his career. Not even the same person who'd baulked at spending five days on the Outer Banks with nothing to do.

'Yeah, this year I'm more inclined to try and cut back on going to conferences and that stuff,' he added. 'You know, just lecture some simple undergrad modules, keep my head down, do my research and avoid talking to anyone who might rope me into being chair of some fuckin' committee.'

I wondered what his superiors would think, hearing the golden child of *Computational Geophysics and Markov Chain Theoretics* talking like this. Like a good honest surf bum with a healthy desire to question the purpose of anything not immediately related to riding waves.

'I moved offices in the spring,' he explained. 'During all that rain we had. I've even got a route planned now through the building to my desk that avoids bumping into any fucker who can ask me something – let alone the Dean.'

I laughed. Dean.

Marc smiled too. 'Son, they may share the same name, but *my* Dean is much less interesting a character than *our* Dean.' The way he rotated his finger in a circle as he said this was as if he thought our Dean might be all around us, affecting everything we did.

Outside of the open windows, city had turned into country. Pine trees and other thicker, non-tropical species swayed in the cool air. Sporadic patches of hazy sunlight shone through watery clouds. The sea was near again.

At East Lyme the I-95 forked, and we took the southern option – the coastal road. We crossed the mouth of the Thames River in New London, over a pair of grand, eccentric bridges – the kind that looked like they'd been designed with aesthetics in mind, instead of cost and efficiency.

These were some of the oldest places in the USA. The freeway kept offering us the chance to stop to look at somewhere of historical interest. Geographically, southern New England was less uniform than the rest of the East Coast. It was filled with rocky outcrops, cliffs, and winding shorelines that looked windswept and wave-battered. The towns we saw seemed not to conform so much to the grid shape, and had quaint churches, lighthouses and thick, stone homes with slate roofs.

After crossing the next big waterway by the port at Mystic, Marc directed us off the I-95 towards Matunuck, where we hoped to score some surf.

It didn't take long from there. Straight, flat roads ran through farm fields and forests before the lanes thinned and the Atlantic came into view – a dark, greying-green and thoroughly foreboding.

There were more people living in caravans in Matunuck than in houses. On our right a large plot of scrubland catered for a grid of mobile homes. None of the lawyer or stockholder homes you saw in the Outer Banks and Jersey. A few quiet streets wound off the oceanfront road, leading to other discreet dwellings. Only a few buildings were on the beach side of the road – the most prominent of these being a pub.

We got a few glimpses of the waves before driving into a small, dusty car park with a wooden walkway leading from it to the sand. It was obvious there was a ton of swell – although the wind was up. The only big truck parked in the Matunuck beach lot was old – ten years at least. It wore surf stickers proudly, and had thick, knuckly tyres. A few smaller and equally aged cars had clothes and board bags inside them, so we knew surfers were around. The Betty Ford would be in good company left here while we paddled out.

We ran over the brow of the small dune and surveyed what was on offer. A churning right-breaking, semi-close-out reef break to our east looked dangerous, and wasn't liking the wind. There was only one guy surfing it, and it would have been wrong to gatecrash that solo-session. To our far right I could see a peak with a few longboards on it, but the best was out front. A-frame peaks were rolling playfully through, well overhead in size, with both fast-breaking and slower, mushy sections. It was perfect for high-performance surfing. The right-handers were taking on a bowl shape, the shoulder folding inwards, while the lefts were running further into deep water, but with bigger sections to hit. In California, or even Florida, a wave like this would have at least fifty people on it. Here there weren't more than ten.

Ecstatic, we ran back to the car to begin suiting up. The wind whipping around us made me feel at home. I didn't care that the sub-tropical waters of the south were gone for good. Wearing wetsuits was what I'd grown up doing, and New England was my kind of place.

When we got down to the water's edge there was a surfer making his way back in.

'How is it?' I asked him.

'It's going off, dude! This is like the best I've seen this place all summer. Man I'm fricken exhausted.'

Just like I planned to be in a few hours time, I thought.

You had to perform a careful rock dance to wade out here. The boulders under the surface were sharp and covered in barnacles that tried to break off in your feet. I saw Marc wincing a few times as he used his floating board for support. It was impossible to go slow enough – we were just too excited.

Once paddling, I felt my shoulders fill with energy again. There wasn't one wave breaking out here that you wouldn't want to ride, and the dark, thick water gave them an added power. My feet were stinging with cold as I reached the line-up, where I noticed everyone else was wearing booties.

Before I could say hello to anyone, I'd spotted a wave.

'Go on, son!' Marc yelled as I paddled. The wave drew into a thick trough in front of me, and I slid over the ledge and straight into a speedy bottom-turn. I was quite far behind the section and had to take a high line to make it around. This left me flying for the shoulder with loads of speed to burn off. Already my mind had found a state of total concentration, so I spread my arms wide, felt for the water behind me with the trailing hand and threw the board onto its outside edge. All of my speed was poured into a cutback, which I was able to draw out, taking aim at the white water behind. I snapped back off the foam ball and found myself at the bottom of a long wall of green water, breaking almost sideways to the beach. I put two more turns in before the wave shut down. The sensation of motion and oceanic flow made me want to scream with joy.

Out the back where we sat waiting for waves away from the noise and froth of the impact zone the local crew were all friendly and stoked to see people in the line-up from Europe. Between sets of pumping waves, I got chatting to a guy called Rich from Connecticut. There could be even better waves out towards Point Judith today, he said – but we'd probably missed the right stage of tide to get over there now.

'This swell's gonna hold up for days anyway, man,' he explained. 'I tried to work it out. The hurricane had at least six days out in the Atlantic – so that's like almost a week of waves before it drops off again. Even more if you wanted to follow it up north. Maine and New Hampshire oughta get an extra day, too – coz they're further away. You guys are really lucky. It's early in the season, you know. Normally I don't remember good hurricane surf coming along before late September early October.'

Rich was riding a purple hybrid, with a wide, fanged tail and two wood-carved fins. It meant he had to keep a really low centre of gravity on such chunky waves, but the speeds he could get to were astonishing.

Halfway through the session though, I already knew this was Marc's day and nobody else's. The grin welded to his face had begun to form even before he got his first few waves. When we were younger I remembered Marc being a good surfer, but it had been so long since he'd been in the water with any regularity that he had let his abilities slide. I used to tell youngsters at home that Marc could rip, but they'd never believe me. He had faded photographs of himself charging cavernous waves in Indonesia, but he kept them in a drawer somewhere. On top of that, when surfing at home he would rarely go in the water with the right equipment; he was so reluctant to spend money that his boards all belonged to a time when he was much more agile.

During our time in the US, though, Marc had spent more energy thinking about surfing than he had in years. He'd had a chance to ride different waves, in warm water and more regularly. And now, as if from inherited memory, perhaps from a long-forgotten past life, his surfing skills were returning to him. He was making clever decisions about his positioning on waves, quickly and spontaneously adjusting his line and boldly jousting with even the heaviest of pitching lips.

After an hour or so I saw him puff and pant his way into one of the bigger sets of the day, barely getting into the wave and from a ridiculously late position. I knew right away that he was going to do something special. A week ago I'd have been smiling with the knowledge he was about to get crucified, but now I smiled at the prospect of his induction back into our world – the world of his youth. Marc got to his feet and drove hard and fast for the channel. The section in front began to fold and he ducked, letting it pour over him. I saw a splash within the tube, and then the dark of his wetsuit, still upright, still in there. As the wave moved to the shore, I got to see right into it. A chandelier of water broke through the barrel to reveal Marc, perfectly tucked a yard back from daylight. The wave opened again, and my friend came racing towards freedom, fingers leading the way. He emerged from the shadow of the lip, careering for the shoulder with even more speed than I had done earlier. He kept going, running over the back and into deep water still standing. Then he went cardboard-stiff and dropped into the sea, gargling water as he hooted below the surface. It was the best tube he'd had in a decade.

I yelled my approval, as did Rich from Connecticut. Marc burned past us paddling back out, going for another one. He was in dreamland.

As others in the line-up came and went, Marc, Rich and I surfed for another two or three hours, before heading in to eat some bananas we'd picked up back on the ferry. We waited in our wetsuits, sharing the flask-coffee Rich had brought with him, before going out for another session.

An hour into the second go-out, I could see the suncream on Marc's face cracking from too much shrieking and laughing. And his best wave was still to come. Every quarter of an hour or so, a bigger set of much more powerful waves would come through. Rich reckoned these were from the very epicentre of Dean. They'd often catch us unprepared and wash through the take-off zone, but Marc managed to scrape his way out in time to get one. He got down the thing easily, and smashed a hole out of the lip twice with a couple of enormously ambitious manoeuvres. I saw his fins releasing as he dropped back into the pit on the second turn. Now a thick end-section was walling-up in front of him, and he took aim. I saw determination in his eyes – so intense a glare that I felt sorry for the wave. Marc angled his board up at the section and then released his speed through the tail pad. I saw him twist as his knees sucked up the pressure, and then he was gone in an explosion of white water. I wrote off his chances of making it straight away. The wave bubbled and puffed, beginning its final run on the sharp Matunuck rocks. And then, nonchalant and cocky, I saw Marc rise from the soup, standing, shrugging his shoulders. He'd stuck three turns so intense I felt like giving up.

To toast a mammoth day of surfing, we persuaded Rich to join us in the beachfront pub for dinner.

'I gotta drive back to Connecticut, dude, so I need to go easy,' he warned. 'Got one month of work left before they pay me off and I get the hell out.'

'Get out? Of where?'

'Here, dude! I'm gonna get the hell outta *here*.'

In a two-car convoy, Rich led us back up the road to where you could park outside the pub. He had an old GMC station wagon, which had been in the space next to us while we surfed.

I asked him again what he meant about getting the hell outta here.

He explained that he'd been repping for a plastics company for the past two years, but had had enough and wanted to go away – for the long-term.

'Been saving and surfing. Gonna bail somewhere warm. My bro lives in Guatemala so I might go there. Otherwise maybe Mexico. It's too cold here in the north-east and California's full of jerks.'

Rich was born and raised in New England. His family actually owned a bit of land on Block Island – way out in the ocean between here and the tip of Montauk. He and his brothers had surfed empty, perfect hurricane waves there as teenagers because nobody else could access the place. These days he rarely boated the 30-mile round trip though, more due to laziness than anything else.

'I've kinda fallen into a groove here lately, man,' he moaned. 'Sure, I love surfing, and get as stoked as ever, but I need a change of scenery. New horizons.'

Rich was well connected in the Rhode Island surfing scene. He'd lived at Matunuck for a year and also knew a few of the

Point Judith and Narragansett crew. He was back living with his folks again to save money for his trip, but was still on first-name terms with both the barman and waitress here.

We settled into watching a baseball game, as a plate of nachos arrived. The Boston Red Sox were in action. Rich wasn't cheering them on though.

'Man, I don't care about the Sox. I got no feelings for Boston. That place is like a frat party that grew old.' He would, however, be cheering for the Patriots as the American football season began, but that was because they represented all of New England, instead of just its biggest city.

The waitress came back to take our orders, and Rich introduced her.

'Hey guys, this is Lauren, from upstate New York. She's been workin' the summer. Hey Lauren, these guys are from *Wales*. That's Wales Wales, not Wales England.'

I laughed. Marc would have scowled normally, but Lauren was cute, and I could shortly imagine him embarrassing himself trying to come on to her – something he was making a habit of lately.

'Chick's hot, huh?' Rich winked to us, as she walked back to the kitchen.

'Aye, all right,' Marc mumbled, adding that he was going to try and shout mine and Rich's food on the faculty card. I felt like changing my order to something more expensive.

As we ate club burgers and fries, we passed on tales of our trip to date – New Orleans, the Carolinas and New York. Rich knew a lot about the places, and the storms by which they were known. Isabel, the monster that rearranged the geography of the Outer Banks, had been exceptionally generous to New England surfers, giving some of the best waves ever seen at Point Judith and Ruggles (a point break nearby). Charlie was another who had been good to the northern states too – in fact, we learned that any of the ones to lay into Florida tended to send a good pulse of south swell up this way.

'You didn't get surf from Katrina though, did you?' I asked.

'Sure we did. It pumped. That storm spun super-hard in the Atlantic before it went anywhere near the Gulf. The lighthouse at Point Judith was going off.'

Rich told us how the storms that came really far north (enough to make New Yorkers panic) had the potential to create never-before-seen surf spots in unthinkable locations. If a powerful hurricane passed by a sheltered area, you could get waves in harbours, inlets – all sorts of places. Even in Connecticut – a state supposedly protected by Long Island Sound, but dotted with sea walls and other constructions that could make great surf spots once the swell got in.

'It's the same everywhere, huh. Man-made objects always make frickin' awesome waves.'

I asked about beach breaks in Rhode Island – it seemed as if everything here centred around reefs and points. He said that there were a few peaks to be found in Narragansett, but for proper grinding beach breaks a good shout was heading out to Cape Cod, or up to New Hampshire.

'How is Cape Cod for surf?' I asked.

'Sick – the place pumps. But you gotta find the right sandbanks, you know. And watch out too – it breaks boards. I'd look it up maybe a bit later in the week. There's wind tomorrow so best place is either gonna be here, or at the Lighthouse.'

'Lighthouse?'

'Yeah – Point Judith. You go inland a bit then round the point to get there. It's easy.'

We had a few more beers, before Lauren joined us at the end of her shift. She looked a different person now – her brown hair, now loose, had been straightened and was running over a long pair of earrings. She wore a gypsy-style skirt almost to her ankles, and a purple fitted T-shirt with 'art matters' written across the front in white lower-case type. I recognised the slogan – it was from 'AGO' – the art gallery in Toronto. I told her my mother lived there.

'Cool. I *love* Ontario,' she said. 'I live kinda near Buffalo, so I can cross in through Niagara all the time. God, you're making me homesick already!'

The kitchen had closed for the night as it was the end of the season, but the bar was still going to stay open for a while, so Marc ordered her a drink immediately.

'Thanks, Marc,' she smiled – remembering his name already. 'I'd love one. How about a beer – you know – like a *beer* beer? The ones you guys drink in Wales?'

The barman looked awkward. 'We don't got no Guinness here, Lauren,' he said, as if it made his job somehow inferior.

Instead he ran through a list of weird ale names – mostly from New England. Marc and Lauren agreed on one and he ordered a pitcher. So-called 'real ale' in a pitcher seemed a very American compromise, but it was one Marc made without fuss.

In the last few years, I don't think Marc had spoken to any girls in this sort of environment. Elaine's stranglehold had been tight, and after that he'd only really bothered with his work. I wanted to interrupt wherever I could to protect him from the inevitability of looking like a tit, remembering times when he'd manage to find a girl he liked, only to succeed in coming out with a blunderous comment of some kind. He had a knack for that stuff, unfortunately. Once he even pulled Jim Carrey's legendary *Dumb and Dumber* line on an Austrian girl, deliberately mistaking countries for what he thought was a sure-fire giggle: 'G'day mate! Let's chuck another shrimp on the barbie!' (Like in the film, she too turned away, thoroughly unimpressed.)

Perhaps it was the cross-cultural differences that saved his blushes, but Lauren didn't even notice Marc's early, cumbersome way of getting to know someone. Before anything awkward had been said, she had him at ease and being himself. I tried to think about whether I'd ever seen him like that with a girl – not even the ones we went to school with. And certainly not Elaine.

I turned back to Rich, feeling a little drunk, and told him all about Marc's tribulations with the fairer sex.

'Dude, he's got no chance there, then,' Rich chuckled. 'The boys have been trying all summer. Nobody's going there. I think she may have a boyfriend or something, you know, that nobody else knows. It's the only explanation.'

Lauren was going to leave Matunuck shortly. The seasonal work had run out and she planned to go home to New York State. In a few weeks she was set to start her last year of a masters degree in archaeology – which I thought was about as far away from *Computational Geophysics and Markov Chain Theoretics* as you could get (apart from studying literature, obviously).

Lauren, like Rich, was pretty clued up about her geography. She could locate Wales on a map of the world, and knew about Princess Diana being Welsh (technically not the case, but good enough for Marc right now). That was only the start – as if rehearsed, she reeled off a comprehensive list of our famous compatriots: Tom Jones, Catherine Zeta-Jones, Anthony Hopkins. The girl had clearly thought about the existence of our homeland prior to meeting us. Best of all, she knew that Joe Calzaghe was Welsh. This thrilled Marc – especially once he checked that all this info had been acquired and committed to memory *without yet going to Wales*. Lauren had even watched Calzaghe's last fight, and talked about how she had always thought the guy's main challenge would be knowing when to retire.

'He wanted to go out unbeaten,' she said, 'but as long as he kept winning it was gonna be tempting to keep lining up another opponent.'

She had never heard of rugby, though, which couldn't have impressed Marc much at all, but still, it was going OK. Perhaps more important than loving a game played with an egg-shaped ball, she shared his quirky passion for facts.

'Did you know Rhode Island has the highest percentage of deficient bridges in all of the USA?' she said, when Marc told her about our crossing of Chesapeake Bay. 'Ain't that an awesome claim to be able to make? Rhode Island's a crappy little state most of the time, so they need to brag about anything they can. Yeah, almost a quarter of the bridges here aren't safe. I read about it in *Time* magazine. Kinda scary when you think how the entire state's highway system is basically water crossings.'

'Sick!' said Rich 'How about Connecticut?'

'Yeah, Connecticut's up there somewhere too. And out of all America's major roads, the I-95 had the worse record. The risk, huh! Bet you guys won't wanna drive anywhere again now.' She rolled her eyes. 'I mean, not on the 95 in Rhode Island, at least – as that road is, like, *so dangerous*. Did you see it on the way in? They got some lethal tractors out there, man.'

'Wow,' said Marc. 'Did you just use sarcasm?'

'Sarcasm? What's that?' He and Lauren stared at each other for a moment, then they both laughed. I looked at the floor.

Since it seemed a topic of mutual interest, I started talking about the world's longest bridge in New Orleans. This led us to discuss Brooklyn Bridge too, and then our day in New York. Marc was only too happy to repeat everything he'd learned in the UN, as well as his open-top bus-ride, but his conversation got hijacked by a much more interesting piece of information.

We discovered that, without knowing each other, both Lauren and Rich had been to the UN headquarters together a few years ago as part of a bigger group planning the peace marches preceding the Iraq War. The planned route went right past the building, but on the day itself the NYPD saw to it that nobody was allowed anywhere near.

'That decision sucked,' said Lauren, 'As if half a million peace activists were gonna damage, or I dunno, bomb, the frickin' UN. It wasn't them who'd planned the goddamn war anyway. The UN didn't want any of it to happen. It was our government, flying solo again. Jeez, flying solo is what American life is all about anyway. You do realise this, don't you?'

As if afraid to take note of her earrings, clothes, deep green eyes or anything else, Marc decided to compliment her on her foreign policy and political beliefs.

'Thanks,' she said. 'I like yours, too.' He'd marched in London himself that week – during his more typically student days.

As he told her about our night in Jacksonville with troops from the Marine Corps, I turned to Rich again and asked about surf. I had a feeling it would do Marc good to chat to Lauren on his own for a while, and besides, this was a chance to probe someone in the know about where to get the best waves.

'So, when d'you last go to Cape Cod, Rich?'

'I ain't been this year – but I can tell ya that the best sandbanks are almost always around the Marconi Beach area. That's where the National Seashore is the most stable – I mean, there's a *helluva* lot of water moving around there. It's wrecked more ships than the Outer Banks. The ocean's cold too. And I mean *cold*. Not like here. Cape Cod's a frickin' frontier, man. The place is wild.'

I wanted to know whether he'd been up as far as Maine and Nova Scotia before. He'd been to Maine a few times and had scored some classic surf there, but Nova Scotia remained merely a target on the hit list for now.

'Problem is, when you come from somewhere cold, you kinda want to go places warm when you travel, you know?'

'Yeah,' I said. 'I do know. Only too well, unfortunately.'

We shared our collective experiences of winter for a while. Rich told me how he'd walked through waist-deep snow once to surf waves the height of a lamp post with two others in the water. It got a lot colder than Wales here but, then again, they got much better surf, too.

Even though I detested winter there was a small comfort to be found in thinking about the cold. As I looked out of the windows into the northern darkness it felt like we were closer to home, and to habit. Our wetsuits, even though they chaffed, stank and soaked everything around you, were a way of life to Welsh surfers, and it was nice to meet people on another continent with whom to share a bit of solidarity.

In a break in conversation I looked over to Marc and Lauren. They too were reminiscing about life in the more extreme parts of the globe.

'I went to Newfoundland last year,' said Lauren. 'My gosh, it was just the most beautiful place I've ever been. But then I've always loved the cold. But you kind of have to, coming from near the Canadian border.'

I asked her what she'd been doing in Newfoundland.

'I was on a dig there. It was awesome.'

'You mean an archaeological dig?'

'Yeah. What other kinds of dig do you know about? Unless you've worked for a CSI team and aren't telling us?'

Marc laughed, swaying on his stool. For a moment I wanted him to fall back off it.

She explained to me that Newfoundland was an incredible place to excavate if you didn't mind the cold. 'Sure, it ain't Mexico or Peru or Rome, but people have been there since like ten thousand years ago. I was up there looking at Viking stuff, which was only one thousand years old. But hey, that's not gonna interest you. Guys from Europe don't come to North America for history lessons! Marc was telling me about your trip. Sounds awesome.'

'Yeah. It's been an eye-opener,' I said.

Marc didn't agree with Lauren's comment about history. 'America's got plenty of history,' he protested, 'and it's all quite interesting. Especially around here – Boston, the whaling ports. There's loads of stuff to see in the US.'

'New Orleans too,' I added, getting in on the act.

Lauren thought we were just trying to placate her but, when I thought about it, I realised part of the United States's appeal was the fact its history was still being written around you, today. The first European settlers had made their landing hardly any time ago on the grand scale of things. In the case of one of the biggest colonies, the Puritans, the birth of the New World had happened only just down the road from where we were now.

'There's a spot on Cape Cod called First Encounter Beach,' Lauren told us. 'That whole place is wild. Rich is right – you guys have gotta go there. That's where loads of the ships arrived when this area was first civilising.'

Civilising didn't quite seem the right word to me – and I reckoned Marc would think the same too, but he was being nice. I could tell.

'How easy is it to find waves on the Cape?' I asked.

'Easy,' Rich said, authoritatively. 'Like I said, just remember to look for Marconis. It's near Wellfleet. By the drive-in movie theatre.'

'Drive-in movies? They still exist?'

'Of course, man. You can't miss the theatre if you're driving up the Cape. A big place on your right, that looks kinda like, er, I dunno, a movie theatre.'

He thought we'd stand a good chance of being able to chase the tail-end of Hurricane Dean's swell northwards later in the week. Once Cape Cod and Rhode Island ran out of swell, we could catch the same waves all over again by heading north to New Hampshire.

Rich had started drinking coffee now. He needed to drive soon – back to Guilford, Connecticut – which he reckoned would take over an hour.

'Gotta stay awake,' he grinned. 'Then I'll be fine. I've only had two beers.'

I wasn't counting myself. My drinks had come from the jug, which Marc had now refilled at least twice. Matunuck was definitely the end of the road for tonight – the car becoming bed yet again. And I didn't get the feeling any of the place's residents were going to mind that much, let alone threaten to shoot us over it.

What I hadn't reckoned on, though, was having the Betty Ford to myself. I stepped out into the darkness and said goodbye to Rich, who drove away, back towards the I-95. Through the ocean breeze, I didn't hear Marc and Lauren making arrangements just behind me. As I walked to the car, Marc called out.

'Son, I'm gonna crash at Lauren's place.'

'Cool,' I said, assuming the invite was for us both. I was about to go and get pillows from the car, when I realised this wasn't the case.

'Ah... I see. And what's the plan in the morning then? Does she live around here?'

'I think so,' he said, walking towards me. 'I can't see a car anywhere.'

'OK.' I looked back at Lauren, returning the friendly wave she was giving me. 'Well, I'm gonna crash right there, then.' I pointed at the car – at the obvious.

'Take my mobile,' Marc added. 'Then I'll come and find you tomorrow. How's that for a plan?'

'Er... OK.' I didn't really have a choice.

Marc came over with me to collect a surfboard from the car.

'If you get up early and want to go surf without me then I can find you tomorrow.'

'OK, yeah, well Rich said the lighthouse over the bay could be the spot tomorrow morning.'

'Cool. Well, I'll either see you here or over at the lighthouse then,' Marc grinned. And then they walked off towards the caravans, leaving me alone in the windy night.

However cool you try to act, there's no way around the fact that this kind of situation is hard. Being around people who are hooking up is awkward at the best of times, but here I didn't really know what to say. Was I jealous? Not directly. I mean, it didn't bother me that Lauren liked him – and he deserved a break in that sense. But there was something frustrating me, something I don't think even the most emotionally intelligent of people could pin down for sure. Perhaps I envied the adrenaline, the excitement I knew he must be feeling at meeting someone new and interesting, who liked him back. And then there was being alone. Did I mind that?

I tried to remind myself that I'd bought flights for this trip before I even asked Marc about coming, and that being alone was great. But I still felt kind of embarrassed that I'd first thought Lauren's offer was simply for us both to crash indoors overnight.

I moved things around in the car, locked myself in and then lay there, looking up at the ceiling and the slightly open window – through which I could feel the sea breeze pulling in and out of the car. I felt numb from the beer, and my mouth was dry. I rolled around a few times until I found a position I hoped could get me to sleep.

This wind might mess up the waves in the morning, I thought – if it does go on to blow all night. This was the same kind of Atlantic we were used to at home – an ocean that blew where and when it wanted. No trade winds, no morning offshores. The wind was the wind; all governing, shaping land and legend before it. Maybe I could go straight to Cape Cod tomorrow. Perhaps Marc had wanted a few days space anyway. He had a board, so I wouldn't be completely leaving him in the lurch.

The thoughts swirled around my head. I kept trying to switch off to it – *just sleep, and decide in the morning*! That moment seemed so far away though.

I wound the gap in the window closed. Immediately it seemed more serene and private inside the car. The wind was outside now – *outdoors*.

Sleep came, but only until first light, when the cold and the anticipation of more waves left me sitting upright, stiff-legged but amping to get back in the ocean. That was the one place where I did know what to do.

I sat a while staring straight ahead. It was an overcast day, and dawn hadn't so much broken through in splendour as meekly moved itself into place. I needed to get up and about, even if for the minute it seemed easier to stay still. Marc wasn't going to come back in a hurry, I knew that – and if roles were reversed he'd never wait around here for me.

About an hour after waking, certain there was no chance of getting back to sleep, I decided to check the surf. The Betty Ford's driver seat yanked back up with a shearing sound of greased metal, and her engine shook to life. At the car park there were no other vehicles anywhere, which couldn't be a good sign. The wind was really up too.

I walked to the sand, and was greeted by the sight of waves much bigger than yesterday, and ravaged by gales. The peak we'd been surfing with Rich, where Marc had got the waves of his life, was hardly discernable among big lumps of foaming water – while to my left the reef break would have been useful only to surfers with a genuine death wish. It was obvious why nobody was giving it a go.

I went back to the car and spent a little while looking at maps and wondering what to do. I tried to deny hoping Marc would show, but kept looking up each time a motor seemed to be heading this way. A few cars pulled in and out of the lot, but only to turn around, and none of them were being driven by Marc or Lauren.

My knowledge of the jagged coastlines at home told me that big waves and wind could lead to great surf in a place like this. Rhode Island's shore wound its way around coves and inlets of all kinds, so somewhere there would be a point, reef or beach break perfectly positioned to get the best of it. Miles to my east, across the turbulent, mist-covered sea, the lighthouse's flash seemed to be winking at me.

To get over to Point Judith, you needed to head back inland a few miles, around an inlet of water – known as the 'Pond' despite being the size of a large lake. A few hundred yards inland the mist diminished. From the glimpses I got, the west side of the Pond was showing white caps, while nearer the other side the surface was much calmer. The wind was coming off the Atlantic itself – blowing across Cape Cod, Nantucket and Massachusetts after forming over the deep, cold recesses of ocean beyond. Land to the east could provide shelter from it, which was exactly the case at Point Judith.

I pulled into a parking lot, now empty of tourists and families but busy with surfer activity. A boarded-up beach complex also hinted at the one-time presence of holidaymakers, who had now retreated until next summer. A building with fish-scale tiles was also locked, and on its rusted garage door a sign read, 'Sorry, no restrooms'. The 'No Parking – Tow Away Zone' warnings that would have been so pristine in Montauk, East Hampton, Jersey or Florida were salt-corroded and decaying, and there were surf stickers dotted all over the 'No Fires, Dogs or Alcohol' notices. At last a beach community that gave these constant rules and regulations the attention they deserved. Pillars intended to surround the parking area were sinking into the ground. Unassuming yet interesting; I liked this place immediately.

The main wave was supposed to be a right-hander that broke around the back of the lighthouse, but today the wind was tearing it to pieces. Instead the action was on the other side of the headland, where waves were neatly peeling left into a bay of partly submerged rocks and a shoreline of shingle pebbles. Protected from the brunt of the wind, here the faces were being groomed only by a light side-shore breeze.

As a squall of cold, salty rain lashed across the car park, I pulled my soaking wetsuit out of the reusable IKEA bag it was being kept in. This was a surfing experience I knew all too well: hard core and challenging even before you got to the water's edge.

The ocean was freezing once more. Planting my feet on a slab of slippery rocks, I jumped over the shore break and began paddling out against a persistent rip current. The crowd of surfers in the water kept the line-up marked out. Surfing a wave like this alone would be really difficult. The water moving sideways through the take-off zone meant you had to paddle continuously just to stay in one place on a watery treadmill.

The surfers out at Point Judith all responded when I said 'hi' and 'how's it going?', one or two even asking about my accent, about being from Wales and what it was like surfing in Europe. But beyond that, the constant movement and waves grinding down the point kept conversation brief. The focus required to get a good one out here was intense. In this kind of mood, the ocean was company enough for anyone, and nobody really felt the need to talk to anyone else.

The left-hander here was a powerful wave, but with sections that backed off enough for you to carve and s-turn, before running into the next reform. Occasionally a gust of wind got around the point, and you'd see patches of surface water being scratched. This was probably what the sea looked like inside Dean's eye over a thousand miles south – albeit on a far, far greater scale. I wondered where the hurricane itself had got to now. Then another torrent of rain set in, followed by a series of well lined-up, foreboding set-waves that raised heart rates and anticipation.

I surfed for nearly two hours before it occurred to me that I'd had nothing to eat since last night. Immediately I felt drained of energy, my concentration waning. I looked to shore, and to the lighthouse with its immaculately mowed lawns, neat fences and service buildings. It made dry land seem so inviting. I was reminded of trips to Scotland, or out to the western fringes of Wales – when you'd surf unfamiliar spots in stern weather conditions, before feeling a new appreciation for the warmth and stability of being back home and indoors. For me though, the nearest place to here that had any hint of home was Toronto, probably two days' drive away.

I rode a wave halfway down the point, then straightened out and aimed for the pebble beach. In the frigid rain I got changed quickly and jumped into the car, leaving my stuff outside on the tarmac.

For twenty minutes I saw surfers come and go from behind the hypnotic rubber of the wiper blades, and studied their individual reactions to the waves on offer. Day three of the swell was showing a very different character to the others so far. This was an unsettled, angry sea – in need of finding itself. I had faith though. Faith the conditions would settle again, that we would get plenty more out of Dean in the days to come.

It was nearly two o'clock, and Marc's mobile phone hadn't rung or received a message while I was in the water. He'd be awake by now, so it was obvious he was in no hurry to get back in touch. I really hadn't liked the thought of being alone this morning, but after the surf it was bothering me less. I could get to know the waves and my surroundings better this way.

Turning my back on the two places where Marc would try to find me, I threw my board and wetsuit into the boot, and drove out of the parking lot – away from the lighthouse, Point Judith, Matunuck, and back towards the bigger towns and cities of Rhode Island. Something was telling me to carry on the trip as planned. If I wanted to go to Cape Cod, I should just do it. Waiting for other people wasn't going to get me anywhere.

A salt pond passed by on my left, surrounded by reeds and looked over by a lone, red-painted, wooden house with a US flag on the weather vane. A hanging basket of fresh flowers adorned the mailbox, the 'got mail' lever was raised. People around here obviously saw tending flowers as being of greater importance than checking for post. After Pilgrim Avenue and signs for Galilee, I looked around for places to eat. Iggy's Doughboys and Chowder House appeared, along with another place that had algae-covered lobster pots surrounding its porch, but I pressed on. Just the other side of Narragansett I crossed more suburbia and saw kids selling lemonade from the front garden of their home. After that everything thinned out and I was in the countryside again.

For a moment I was worried that I had made a mistake by not stopping, and that lunch was going to be miles away. But then I saw a gas station and a Tim Hortons – the Canadian coffee chain my mother loved going to. In my current state of mind it was a fitting discovery, so I pulled in for a sandwich and some 'Timbits' – a box of cut-offs supposedly made from doughnut holes.

In the queue I saw a row of newspapers. I leaned over to see the headlines, and was suddenly reminded of the powers that were governing this trip. At the bottom of the page, after the two main stories concerning a shooting and a trawler getting into trouble, I saw the story:

HURRICANE DEAN HITS MEXICO

I couldn't concentrate easily on reading it. I was hungry and the aroma of food was all around. The writing was turgid, too, and hard to get any facts from – probably a bastardised press release from the National Hurricane Center. The storm had ploughed into the Yucatan Peninsula yesterday morning – still at Category 5 status and with gusts of up to 200 miles an hour. The town of Chetumal was flooded and no longer fit for habitation. But worse than this, Dean had survived the trip over the Yucatan and was back over the warm waters of the Gulf – regaining power and bearing down on the Mexican mainland port of Veracruz. I couldn't get any information about fatalities or whether there was a response being prepared. It seemed unfair – I hadn't wished for this in any way. And again I missed Marc, because I knew he'd have something philosophical and matter-of-fact to say about the situation.

Instead I had to make do with the charms of the Rhode Island locals.

'Oh, I'm sorry, did I just cut in?' an old lady asked as I stepped back into the queue.

'No – don't be silly,' I replied. 'I stopped to look at the newspaper.'

'Are you sure? Coz you were ahead of me...'

'Of course. It's fine.'

'What would you be looking for in that paper that's so interesting, then?'

'Er, sorry?'

'Well – you're from England, and you're reading the *Providence Journal*. People from Providence don't even read the *Providence Journal*.'

'Oh – no, er, I was reading about the hurricane.'

'In Texas?'

'No, Mexico.'

'Wasn't it in Texas?'

'No.' I paused for a moment. 'I'm a surfer, see, and I've just been riding waves from the same storm. Today – this morning.'

'At Narragansett? Isn't it raining?'

'I was at Point Judith – and it was lovely. I didn't mind the rain. Surfers never do.'

'Oh, how fabulous! Surfers must enjoy Rhode Island. I do hope you feel welcome and enjoy your stay.' She turned her back to me with a smile, and looked up at the menu board.

Enjoying Rhode Island was next on my list of things to do, although it would have to be done the same way as most of the other places so far – from the window of the Betty Ford. Approaching through rural Connecticut and then sticking to the coast at Matunuck and Point Judith, I hadn't yet seen the sheer beauty of the state's more extreme meetings with the Atlantic. There may not have been surf this far up the bay, but as I neared the city of Newport I slowed down in awe. You could see why car licence plates here had 'The Ocean State' written on them. The state's centre was a vast inner network of seawater – ten per cent of its area – surrounded by rugged cliffs and hills, and dotted with islands and crags of rock – some of which had houses clinging to their sides. At first the bridges seemed to dance across the inlets and bays, until you got close enough to comprehend the sheer scale of the constructions.

The relatively new Pell Bridge carried Highway 138 over Narragansett Bay, from Jamestown and Conanicut Island into Newport, and gave me a bird's eye view of the boats running below. I realised with complete clarity the differences between New England and 'Old England' – or the British Isles as Marc would probably rather call it. The greenery and rolling landscapes here could have easily belonged to the UK, but for one contrast: in *New* England ocean and rock were much less of an obstacle. If you wanted to get from Cardiff to Avonmouth back home, you had to go right up the channel to Bristol first. If there had been a New Cardiff and a New Avonmouth in this part of the world though, I was certain a zippy, smooth-to-drive freeway would have been pillared or suspended between the two (probably leaving no need for a New Bristol).

Age and history were proudly present in Rhode Island though. This was the first state to declare independence, and Newport had a maturity and dignity that some of the newer, grid-plan cities could never earn. The streets were quiet, and leafy, running quickly into residential areas. Newport was situated on the original Rhode Island itself, with the rest of the state having originally gone by the name Providence Plantations.

I thought about how far I'd come since passing Fort Lauderdale in prickling humidity weeks ago, and marvelled the diversity of the USA as a nation. It felt as if I'd been steadily driving back through time – especially since Cape Cod was next on my horizons.

I stopped in a parking space just on the way out of Newport to think again about my situation. Nothing had changed – Marc was still conspicuous by his absence, and I had no reason to wait for him. If he really wanted to find me, he could.

A guy was emptying the pavement meters, and as he arrived at my car he tapped the window.

'Hey, if you wanna park here I can set her at two hours for ya,' he grinned. 'I knock off in thirty minutes, and I'm feelin' kind.'

It seemed an invitation to take a walk.

On foot, Newport seemed busier. Its traffic was noisy, even before a pair of fire trucks blazed past. I covered three or four blocks, before getting bored, fed up with the sounds and smells of cars and concrete and feeling the need to retreat to the humble coastal scenes. I wanted to be somewhere like the Outer Banks, Sebastian Inlet or Point Judith again.

If I left now, I figured I'd get to Cape Cod in two hours. Tomorrow I could wake, alone, at the very frontier of US life. The edge of this great civilisation's earliest colonies would be revealed to me at sunrise – and hopefully complemented by the sight of more hurricane perfection.

Back at the car I looked at the phone again. It had no messages, and almost no battery. I switched it off and turned the ignition key.

The car started smoothly. Two hours, I thought. That's nothing in this land.

CHAPTER SEVENTEEN

THE RIGHT COAST

The edge of the New World was a fairly understated place. Fog had rolled in overnight, so by dawn the next day I couldn't even see the water's edge at Nauset Heights. I'd parked up and slept in the car again, after stocking up on muffins from a roadside Dairy Queen near Hyannis. Hardly the breakfast of champions, but it would be enough to see me through a morning surf – once I found where to go.

I flicked through the notes I'd made on this place over a month ago, and remembered Rich's advice to look for Marconi Beach. 'Just after the drive-in movie theatre,' I remembered him saying.

That was a few miles north, so without even trying to check the surf here at Nauset Heights I drove back to the main road, and turned to head up the peninsula.

Just before flying out to Toronto from Wales, reading anything prolonged had been hard – especially books or articles about the places I was going. If you've got a big surf trip to look forward to your concentration usually can't hack much, and the excitement is hard to suppress – but Cape Cod was one of the places that had still held my attention. A two-pronged peninsula of sand reaching right out to the east, boldly into the Atlantic, isolated from the rest of the continent. Even from an atlas the place looked wild.

In the early half-light of another autumn day I sped along the two-lane highway, both sides flanked by tall forests, looking to surf the coast that had inspired many of America's early writers. So near to Boston for this current, motor-owning generation, I remembered how Thoreau had once hitched his way here from the city in the 1850s, arriving just in time to see corpses washing ashore from a European shipwreck. It moved him to imagine what it must have been like for the victims to get so close to the New World, maybe even seeing the flash of a lighthouse, only to die there and then in the freezing Atlantic. The cause of the wreck had been a storm. Not a hurricane – just a local tempest. He wondered what the last thoughts must have been before the once hopeful emigrants transcended this 'new' world for another one, even newer – one that we would all eventually experience. Morbid stuff.

Now at Cape Cod it was almost instinctive to think about the people who had set sail for America during the country's beginnings. It seemed to me as if humankind's attitude to the sea had become more timid as science progressed. We had the National Hurricane Center with its hourly updates and spy planes, but in the nineteenth century people used literally to wave goodbye to their family in places like Liverpool and throw themselves to the mercy of the unknown deep. The sea defied understanding, and crossing it merited a rebirth. If you made it to the other side, if the hurricanes and other perils spared you, then Ellis Island would await – where you'd get a new life, and sometimes even a new name. All too often, though, the journey ended prematurely at Cape Cod, drowning off this coastline of cliff-like, uniform dunes – miles of towering, hard-packed sand that appeared near vertical, like the walls of a fortress. Never to see Liberty on her plinth, never to learn your new identity, never to feel the ecstasy of laying eyes on the New York skyline – a place we had found such euphoria in leaving just a few days ago.

Another invention the modern water user could benefit from was the red flag – one of which was now flying proudly over Marconi Beach, warning us that today the sea was in one of those historically famous foul moods. Once upon a time today could have led to the death of a thousand immigrants, but now, through modern technologies, the ships knew to be careful, and the swimmers couldn't risk it for fear of arrest. That wasn't all, either. Courtesy of satellites monitoring the oceans' every move we also knew that the entity responsible for these latest high seas was called Dean, that he was safely away from the US Coast and pounding Mexico instead, and that these distant effects of his temper were due to last for the next few days before petering out harmlessly.

None of this took away from the reality of a very powerful and menacing swell. The dunes here were higher, and the mist had begun lifting. Below I could see a couple of surfers trying to negotiate another deadly shore break while around me others, sleepy and reluctant, hugged themselves in coats and watched, eyes searching the length of the seashore for something they might want to ride.

I knew that I had to give it a go. The waves were shifting, and dirty – far from what you'd call perfect – but it was one of the most humbling pieces of land on the planet, and I'd made my way here as a surfer. In a few days I'd be gone (and so would Dean), but in the meantime it felt like my duty to paddle out. That was why I was here.

As I changed into my soaking and unwelcoming wetsuit, I wondered whether the swell would be different to yesterday.

At Point Judith I'd met an angry swell, disorganised and unsure of itself. A swell that wasn't sure if it wanted to gratify or harm. Would it still be the case twenty-four hours later?

More mist rolled in before I'd waxed up and locked the car. Again Thoreau's descriptions of the place came to mind: a damp, desolate frontier beyond which only the imagination could travel; a place where 'man could put all of America behind him'. Knowing what I had to do, I walked over the brow of the steep, commanding wall of dunes. The beach felt wild, battered, haggard and strewn with driftwood half buried in cold, expansive sand.

One of the surfers making his way back stopped to say hi.

'Hey, how're the waves?' I asked.

'Oh, dude, the waves are great. It's pumpin'. Kinda scary, but some awesome sets coming. Getting bigger too. Real heavy. You gotta watch out for the mung though.'

'Mung?'

'Red tide. Yeah, it's like some weird sea life type thing. Hundreds of 'em. Dunno the real name. You'll see it – all dark on the water surface and kinda itchy. You learn to hate the mung when you live here – always washes in when we get a big autumn swell.'

This was sounding better by the minute. Usually in a place like this the sensible part of me would be urging caution, but I was buzzing at the idea of a challenge. The decision to surf had been made and I was sticking by it.

There were five others out. I watched them for a minute, trying to warm up a bit with a few stretches. The whole sea was moving with the swell, so predicting how each wave would break was mostly guesswork. Whether or not there was water pushing up the sandbank made a difference, and I could tell there was a bit of a rip from south to north as well. The guys already in had figured it out a bit, showing where to sit and which ones to go for, but nothing could be taken for granted. I could see the mung now too.

It was a mass of claret-coloured fur; shredded plant life. Some was washing ashore, and when I started paddling it was as if the ocean's surface was a swamp of the stuff. I could feel it every time I pushed my hands through the water, and it would stick in my hair with each duck-dive. It also made the waves look dark, and eerie.

The cold water was dense, heavy, and the first wave I caught bounced me terribly. The shore break from the previous set had backwashed through it, making me flip head first, feeling awkward and stiff. I hadn't slept properly for days, and I knew these times in the water were my best chance of feeling fresh. Undeterred, I wanted to get another one. It was just the sort of session from which the best wave of the trip so far would unexpectedly appear.

There was determination in my mindset as I paddled for the second one. It was probably due to being alone – surfing for myself and no one else. The wave sneaked over the first part of the sandbar, pushed me in close to the shore break, and peaked cleanly. Another surfer was set up for the left, so I dropped in right and tried to accelerate across the face. Immediately it began to dredge sand and thick, blood-coloured mung up its face. I knew it was going to throw out. Inside me the internal voice, calm and firm in its tone, ordered me to stay put, and keep my line. The wave lurched over my head, casting blackness all around, before I saw the side of it bending in towards me. For a moment I was inside a thick cavern of water, peaceful and private, a black hole surrounded by belligerent energy, suspended in time. The curtain had fallen, cutting off the outside world, and was pouring down inches from my head. As things darkened I heard the noise of the vortex, the sound of a breaking wave echoing from within. Then my board began to lose its grip and I felt myself being grabbed by the foam from below.

The battering didn't matter. That wave was a sensation of purest bliss while it lasted – something so profound you could easily be persuaded to spend the rest of your life searching for it over again. Already I'd had a moment with this place that would last forever.

I knew no other wave like it would come my way again that day and also that if Marc had been there everything about it would have been different. I thought about everything that had happened to get me here, at this point in time, and realised that given the chance to do it again I'd change nothing. I felt fate all around. This was what surfers lived for: the absorption of mind, body and soul into powers so much greater, and the helpless yet heart-warming knowledge that you counted for nothing on the bigger scale. It was a feeling that Cape Cod had shared with its visitors since it was first discovered. A feeling its faithful followers had spent centuries trying to define, and still couldn't. It was the ocean.

Teeth chattering, I waged war against the rip for another hour before getting one to shore. Sun breaking through the mist did nothing for the sea temperature, and a stiff onshore breeze began pulling in.

Even the sand was reluctant to warm up in the momentary sunshine – perhaps fearing false hope and the arrival of more fog. At the top of the dune I looked back at the sea, a royal blue with packed corduroy swell lines heading for shore. From the high vantage point you could make the curvature of the horizon out, merging with the watery skyline.

The wind coming over the dunes was strong, shaking patches of sand over to the parking lot. The Betty Ford stood alone in the furthest row. I opened the door and put the keys in the ignition. Local radio was playing a Clash song, 'The Card Cheat', as I changed in the mild air. The sun felt flat, weak, on the wane. Florida was probably still too hot to move, but here the season had clearly shifted.

I lay a towel out on the tarmac behind the car, where there was a tiny sun trap, and looked up at the sky. Wisps of cloud, pure white, were drifting inland towards the cities of New England, casting shadows on and off. The sound of wind pulling through dead trees, waves rolling over the shore and the swaying dune-grass cleared other thoughts away. I looked at the sun, then closed my eyes and watched its shape change on the back of my eyelids. The noises moved with it, swirling around my ears and then entering my head.

Enough time passed for me to sleep a little. When I stirred again it was from a dream, of which I couldn't remember a single detail – not even at the moment I awoke. My face was warm now, and I was hungry.

Thinking about lunch, I got back into the car, dazed but content, and started to make my way towards Wellfleet, the main town along this part of the Cape. Joggers passed on their way to the beach, and near the road I saw a family flying a kite off a lone dune. The forest engulfed me again, and then I was at the junction with Highway 6. It took no time at all to find the town centre – it flanked the main road.

Here I found a plaza of shops surrounded by more swaying trees. The Betty Ford parked up next to an F-150 Triton V8 with a customised grill depicting skull and crossbones, and a pirate sticker on its side door. The quieter the place, the louder the characters, I thought. There was a shop called Maurice's Market & Package Store from which I bought a crab sandwich and some fizzy peach-flavoured water, and a surf shop next to it – good for getting some advice on the swell, and where to surf.

Of all the attendants I'd spoken to in US surf shops, the guy behind the counter was by far the friendliest. As soon as he heard my accent I was made welcome. He told me about the contests they ran, the trips he'd taken to the Outer Banks storm chasing, and of course the Cape's own tales of hurricane perfection. Like so many other people along this trip so far, he was also suggesting I kept moving, onwards up the I-95, chasing the tail of Dean's swell to make it last as long as possible.

'Dude, we got great banks at the moment,' he grinned. 'But if I were you, I'd be outta here by tomorrow and heading up to New Hampshire. The Wall's gonna fire, and so might Rye Rocks. If you get either of them on a good swell...' He paused.

'Good spots, eh?'

'Oh yeah. The Wall is like the best beach break in New England – pound for pound, you know. Sure we get barrels here, but it's all kinda tidal. And anyway, you saw that other storm going over the Midwest, huh?'

'Er, I think so. You mean the one that was in Chicago?'

'Yeah – you saw that. It was insane, huh! Well, it's kinda weaker now, but it's gonna come over Vermont and into New England over the next two days. Gonna pull an awkward wind over the Cape here, but it's lookin' like New Hampshire's gonna blow offshore the whole time. I know my stuff, dude, and I tell ya, either the Wall or Rye Rocks are gonna be the best score of the whole swell.'

'Really?'

'Yeah, really.'

This tall, goofy guy with a short mop of receding brown hair, sitting here in his place of work with no shoes on, didn't have to dish out information like this. It was simply out of kindness. He just wanted a visiting surfer to score – a sentiment that had grown rarer and rarer in the surfing world these days.

'You gotta love Dean,' he grinned at me. 'The thing's so far away you don't have to worry about it swinging about or changing direction. That's what usually happens, you know. One day you're gonna get swell, the next you're not, and then hours later it's time to hide indoors from killer winds.'

'This far up?'

He frowned. 'Yeah, sure, we rarely get the real bad stuff, but hurricane season can blow out from time to time here. But a swell like this with an offshore? Worth driving anywhere for, man! It's gonna barrel all day.'

Given the winds I'd already seen in New England, the idea of a spot that would stay offshore throughout the day was definitely a lure northwards. He showed me a print-off outlining the forecast. With such cold water, any heating of land would usually bring in a sea breeze, but this one seemed to be a dead cert; New Hampshire was going to get a light offshore for the rest of Dean's swell.

I thanked him for the info, bought a few bars of wax and walked out to the car. Mid afternoon had made it almost feel like summer. I wondered what to do tonight. Should I go north now – or stay on the Cape until tomorrow? I figured that moving on too quickly was going to speed the trip up, as from there I could only really go to my friend Terry Perry's in Maine (if I could get hold of him), and then home to my mother's place in Toronto. It would be over after that, and I didn't want it to be.

If I was going to stay here though, it had to be in a bed. Four nights in the car along with surfing and eating from roadside places had left me with a headache, a sore back, burnt face and a new level of road weariness. They'd had local copies of *RoomSaver* in the store, so I flicked through looking for Cape Cod coupons. The prices had been slashed because of the season's end. I started driving back towards Wellfleet again – past several quirky-looking places. The Captain's Quarters sounded cool – like it might have a bit of character, nostalgia or adventure behind its doors. The Blue Dolphin Inn reminded me straight away of its namesake in *A Wild Sheep Chase* – the mysterious bed and breakfast in which the anonymous narrator meets the mad bovine professor. Worth a closer look for sure.

I was just thinking about turning around yet again when a small gold-coloured car flew past in the opposite direction, honking its horn. Dropping away was the sound of a voice calling 'Tom!' A voice I could recognise anywhere as being that of Dr Marc Rhys.

At first I decided I was hearing things, but then common sense took over and I realised it probably was him. He knew I'd come here, and when you thought about it the world of a storm-chasing surfer in New England wasn't that wide a place to search. But whose car was he in?

I pulled into a wide gravel driveway – the entrance to another motel – and waited to see if the car would come back. For a minute the road was clear in both directions, before a trio of vehicles appeared. Each swooshed by, their drivers gazing ahead expressionless, oblivious to me. And then there was another pause before the gold car, an old-ish Honda Accord pulled out about two hundred yards away, its lights flashing at me in what looked like a drunken Morse code. As it got nearer the horn honked four or five times and I saw who was driving. It was Lauren, and Marc was in the passenger seat.

'All right, son!' he beamed at me, leaning out the window. They passed at about ten miles an hour, before doing a u-turn just up the road and pulling up alongside the Betty Ford.

'How's it going?' I replied, and then nodded to Lauren. 'Hi Lauren. How's things?'

'Awesome man,' she smiled, leaning across Marc. 'Your boy said you'd probably be out here somewhere. We've been in New Bedford.'

'New Bedford?'

'Aye!' said Marc. 'Lauren's sister has an apartment there. Nice place, son, you'd love it. *Moby Dick* starts off there. They had a whaling museum and, best of all, you could go to the church and see the pulpit shaped like a ship's bough from the film. And it's got Herman Melville's pew in there too.'

'Cool. You been in the water?' I asked, noticing his board in the back seat. I realised how little I had to say of interest. Marc had never read *Moby Dick* – I remembered him telling me.

'Nah, haven't been in the water again yet,' he said. 'Still frothing over those waves we got in Matunuck to be honest. Has it been any good here?'

I didn't know what to say. Calling it great would sound like I was bitter at him, and calling it crap would make me seem grumpy. I settled for 'Yeah – good fun'.

He nodded over-enthusiastically behind his sunglasses and then there came a silence, which I broke by starting to tell them about Point Judith. Lauren interrupted, though.

'Hey, we should park up somewhere else, or all get in one car together. We're like blocking someone here.'

I agreed, and so we went in convoy back to the parking lot by the surf shop. Lauren left to look for takeaway coffee straight away, leaving Marc and me sitting on the bonnet of her car.

'Whadd'you reckon then?' He nudged me, and winked in Lauren's direction.

'Reckon about what?'

'Her! She's fuckin' lush isn't she! Super-cool too. I know the waves have probably been pumping, but I tell you what, son, I haven't come across someone like her in yonks.'

'Cool.'

I felt happy for Marc – he deserved a girl he could get on with, and seemed to have completely unwound since New York and Long Island. But I had concerns too. If he was to take this any further than a fling he'd have to really abandon 'Dr Rhys'. He'd need to keep this frame of mind for good, and past experience had taught me this was unlikely. It was great to see my friend in such high spirits, but my fear was it couldn't last.

It also threw me a horrible dilemma. I was here to go surfing, and was going to drive up to New Hampshire on the trail of Dean's swell. That decision had been made. But should I ask Marc to go with me? For some reason I didn't fancy Lauren coming along, and I felt kind of cheated that we'd spent all this time waiting for hurricane surf, only for Marc to then go and miss it.

As if reading my mind, he started asking me about the waves again.

'So has it been good? You're not gonna believe this, but in the last two days, what with going to meet her sister and all that jazz, I haven't followed the swell at all. It seems windy. We haven't even been to the beach yet. Only left New Bedford an hour ago. She drives fast considering her car's even shitter than ours.'

I laughed. The sunburn on my face stretched, and I realised I'd been frowning.

Various ways to give him the information drifted around my head. I started working him through the story of how I'd surfed Point Judith, and then Marconi's, but he didn't seem to be listening. Then Lauren returned, and conversation went back to the trivial.

To buy time, I suggested going to check the surf. With a sun- and wind-baked face and keen to get indoors, it wasn't what I would have done next myself, but still it was a plan they both liked. This brought us up to Marconi's again, where we walked out to the edge of the dune together.

Another legion of fog was pouring off the ocean, and you could just make out seagulls gliding in the wind vents rising off the tall dunes. From the top you could only hear the surf, but Lauren wanted to go down. She ran ahead excited, sand flicking off her sandals. Halfway down the dune's flank she leant down to remove them, and dropped barefoot to the beach below. We followed, sliding sideways between steps, pulling sand with us.

323

The waves were pounding onto the shore without any room to surf. It was the shore break from the Hamptons several times over – powerful and sinister. The sandbank I'd surfed that morning had disappeared, either washed away or concealed by the rising tide. Saline spray was flying onto us from the exploding white water, as it tossed mung into the air and up the beach. Cape Cod was telling me to leave, I could feel it.

Marc walked on to where Lauren was allowing the edges of the waves to touch her feet. I stayed back and let the two of them be. I could have turned and gone then, but still wasn't sure if Marc would want to come.

Back at the foot of the dune I found a big piece of driftwood and sat down, watching them. Was it rational of me to want her not to come for this last, best surf? I remembered them getting on famously from the moment Rich introduced us back in Matunuck, how nervous I'd been hoping she would have time for him and then how odd and awkward it was when they went home together, leaving me in the car.

I concentrated on feeling the wind in my hair, and looked at my hands. They were tanned and cold. I didn't have a watch, but tried to guess the time. There was an oddly pure light coming through the fog, but I would never be able to pin down the position of the sun beyond. It had to be late afternoon – time to get on the road if I was going to get a warm-up surf in New Hampshire that evening.

Marc and Lauren were walking towards me now. As they got near I saw them both laugh, but hers was the one that carried through the wind. She looked at him as if she'd known him for years and flicked sand playfully at him with her toe. As they got nearer I could hear she was ribbing him for not wanting to go in the water.

I came out with it straight: 'So anyway, as you can see, this place isn't really doing it now, but it looks as though these winds are turning around over New Hampshire. I've got a tip for somewhere that's going to be offshore all day tomorrow. Barrelling beach breaks, and the swell will still be around...' I paused. 'How about we all go, now?'

The response threw me completely. Lauren laughed, nudged him, then nodded and said 'You go, Marc. It sounds fun.'

Marc looked lost. He mumbled 'Er...'

'I can't go up to New Hampshire today – but go, man. You can call me.' She bumped him with her shoulder, hands in pockets. Her face was flushed from the wind and her eyes wide and honest.

He looked back out at the ocean, now covered again by more thick Cape Cod mist.

'What d'you mean?'

'It sounds fun, man. You've been saying about surfing while the hurricane waves are still around. Go with Tom, man. He'll look after ya.' She flicked another bit of sand at me. 'You guys gotta do it. You got my cell. I'm gonna be in New Bedford all week.'

I stepped away from them a bit, edging back up the dune.

'Do what you want, Marc.'

I'd said many things to Marc Rhys over the years, but reminding him to do what he wanted had never been one of them. He'd been the master of that as long as we'd been friends.

It was then that I realised he didn't know what to do, and that this wasn't his decision at all. It was one Lauren and I could make for him.

None of us talked as we trudged back to the cars. Lauren, I realised, understood the situation at least as well as me. This could be big for Marc. If she was genuine, she'd answer his call once we were done with surfing and he'd see her again.

Then another thought hit me. Who was I kidding thinking Lauren and I could tell Marc what to do? It wasn't us who possessed that power at all. And it wasn't him either.

'It's two or three hours from here to the New Hampshire coast, Marc,' I said. 'And dark at nine. D'you know what time it is now?'

'No.'

'Nor me. So what's the plan, then?'

★ ★ ★

The Boston skyline behind us had just started to glint as the sun dropped into the thickest edges of the atmosphere. The top windows of the towering buildings flashed dark yellows and oranges back at the cloudless sky. Back in the real USA, away from the absorbing mists of Cape Cod, urban life was moving at the usual, constant pace.

'Touch wood the traffic's been OK for us so far,' I noted.

'I know. Wicked isn't it! All we gotta do is find our way back on to the 95 and we're in business,' said Marc. 'Our bloody map's too small again though. The AAA are useless.'

'AAA?'

'American Automobile Association. Like their version of the AA. Only being the most powerful country on earth they get to have three "A"s instead of two.'

'I see.'

Marc, now back in the passenger seat of the Betty Ford, had found himself. We were only a few miles past that alluringly titled First Encounter Beach – not even off the Cape – when he'd let out the first hoot. It may have been almost a century since Ellis Island's heyday, but that hadn't stopped this continent from helping Marc Rhys become a new man.

With the appetite for life this guy now had, it was no wonder the freeways through one of the planet's busiest cities had simply opened up before us. Lanes on the temporary I-90 through central

Boston had been switched to avoid rush-hour, and yet the queues in the opposite direction were almost heartbreaking.

'Serves them right for working in a city,' Marc yelled. 'We're going to the beach – and look at the road ahead of us! There's the 95 coming up in... three miles. We're gonna get plenty of time to surf!'

The changes in him had been rapid, and sweeping. It had begun somewhere on Long Island, with the start of the swell, and from then he'd come on immeasurably. I wondered if it wasn't too late to try and redo the whole trip with this new Marc; New Orleans, Alabama, Hatteras, Sandy Hook. Everything up to Long Island, when Marc had transformed into this madman.

With his exuberance, the trip up into New Hampshire flew by, and before the sunset had really began in force we'd passed the welcome sign with its motto 'Live Free or Die', and rolled onto the oceanfront road at Hampton Beach in search of The Wall – this beach break so renowned for its tubes and the place where tomorrow, along with offshore winds from the Midwest, we hoped to meet the Category 5 part of Dean's package.

The Wall was living up to its name. High tide was allowing the chunky swell to bash against the man-made sea defences, sending backwash through the wave faces. The tube-fest that had been forecast for tomorrow hadn't started yet.

It wouldn't put us off though. We were suiting up by instinct, waxing and jumping around, getting ready to throw off some of the energy around us. As with everywhere else in New England, the water made me gasp for cold, but then I raced towards the line-up, paddling out in sync with another lump of backwash. Marc was alongside me.

The evening surf was hard work. The swell was big, shifty and rocking with the impact of the tide along the wall. This spot was a wide stretch of beach fronted by rows of rustic New England-style homes – wooden sidings painted with soothing colours, pastel roofs with dormers springing neatly out and windows and shutters that looked like they'd been glued on. It was all so dainty that it needed to be protected from the encroaching ocean by a foundation of concrete and a man-made promenade. At the north end I could see a point, beyond which was the reef break of Rye Rocks and a whole wealth of other spots.

As the tail-end of the day ebbed away, the air of anticipation in the line-up was electric. I could hear the conversations all around. People were arriving to get ready for tomorrow – the day of days. I kept making out the name 'Dean'. It was on everyone's lips. Like us, these people had been watching the storm from earliest conception, waiting and hoping that it would send swell. And now it had – at the same time as another system inland which at some point during the night was going to pass over and shape these waves into world-class barrels. In surfing nothing is ever certain, but that night, as darkness fell on The Wall, there wasn't a hint of doubt in anyone's minds that we would all be going to bed awaiting the best waves in years.

With time edging on, Marc whipped out the faculty card for us to check in to the seediest motel I'd ever seen. It didn't matter though – the place was a stone's throw from the shoreline.

A row of tiny rooms opened onto an overgrown garden, and a reception which doubled up as bedroom, TV lounge and smoking room for the elderly lady who ran the place. She wore her dressing gown to take us through a simple check-in, during which we kept having to repeat ourselves in order to be heard over the TV, which was blaring with the sounds of a horrid game show.

The room we got was next door to an arguing couple who we quickly realised were drunk beyond sense, and inside it only one light was working. Marc stuffed his computer under a bed, and set about looking for The Weather Channel. 'For the last time,' he claimed.

Sure enough, Dean had grabbed the headlines again. As well as a place in the record books.

The storm's landfall in Mexico's Yucatan Peninsula had been at Category 5. Storms usually weakened a bit immediately before hitting land – but Dean had become the third most powerful landfall ever recorded. At the centre, its eye had dropped to 905 millibars, with winds of 175 miles per hour. The last storm to run aground still at Cat 5 was Hurricane Andrew fifteen years before. The only reason it had done less damage than Andrew was because the Yucatan was a sparsely populated area. However, the storm had then run back into the Gulf of Mexico and over yet more warm water. Dean had re-strengthened yesterday and was now expected to hit Veracruz on the mainland coast within hours. At exactly the same time as we were planning to surf.

Even in Marc's state of mind, it was a heavy thought. This, I'd learned by now, was the condition of the East Coast surfer. Praying for hurricanes to come along, but all too aware you were feeding from a source capable of such immense harm elsewhere. Here, in a land where everything was geared towards comfort, freedom and personal choice, it was almost impossible to put yourself in the parts of the world where these storms meant life and death. I remembered the communities along Florida's Gulf Coast – perhaps the most in harm's way of any Americans – and yet constantly willing huge, spiralling depressions to form over the deadly Loop Current. Our storm, Dean, would be sending them waves tomorrow as well. It was a way of life.

The main angle of tonight's news story was a second near miss for Texas. The state had been put on blanket alert again when Dean found water a second time – and only now was the country breathing a sigh of relief that the storm had gone elsewhere.

'It's bullshit,' Marc mumbled, allowing himself a few sombre moments. 'But I bet the BBC would cover it better... you know, the Mexican version of events, like...' He thought about what he'd just said. 'Well... BBC World, at least.'

He continued philosophising the coin-flip manner of nature, like I'd heard him do so often before – trying to argue it was ok to enjoy the surf tomorrow.

'Put it this way – you're not gonna find many others who are worrying about it tomorrow,' he said. 'The storm was always going to go wherever it wanted. Dean's been good to us, so be grateful and learn the lesson. We've got lucky lives, son. So let's live them.'

Marc turned the TV off, and pulled a blanket over his head. 'Get some shut-eye,' he suggested. 'We've got waves to catch tomorrow.'

The morning, crisp and clear, came around quick and with it one big moment of truth. Through the dishevelled grounds of our motel my eyes searched for anything that would let me know what the wind was doing. There was nothing visible – no flags or trees – so I walked to the edge of the road and raised my hand.

It was offshore. The leftovers from the Midwest had come in, over the northern Appalachian Mountains to blow straight out to sea. This was going to happen. Exactly as everyone had predicted.

It was still high tide first thing, and with the wind set to stay like it all day we ran the car down to Hampton Beach again to get muffins and coffee. We then drove back up to The Wall to eat breakfast watching the surf.

Waves were breaking in the head-high range, but in deep water and through that high-tide backwash. But this time it was perfectly lined-up, the offshore wind grooming the swell smoothly. Last night's missing catalyst.

'In an hour or so,' said Marc, 'that is going to be absolutely firing. The deep water means it's probably showing only half its real size right now.'

'I know,' I nodded. 'This is it!'

As we waited I got Marc to message Terry Perry, and tell him we were in New England and looking to call by soon. It showed how much had gone on in Marc's life lately that he'd forgotten all about calling in on a friend once surfing was done.

'Shit – how could I not remember to ask you about that?' he said, bewildered.

'You obviously had more important things on your mind.'

It was then that he realised his laptop was still under the bed in the motel.

'Oh my God! What's happening to me?'

'Dunno,' I laughed. 'But you'd better be quick getting it. That tide won't wait for you.'

You can try to wait for a tide to drop or rise a million times. But on every occasion, if you're a surfer with any dedication, you'll end up in your suit too early. Today was no different. As soon as Marc got back, out of breath from running to the motel and back, I decided it was time.

As the day warmed around us, I shook the sand and mung from Cape Cod out of my wetsuit by banging it against the floor. Then, methodically, systematically, I began waxing, turning the suit through and taking off my shoes and socks – all the while watching the waves out front.

Minutes later I was applying sunscreen and locking up the car. Both of us were ready to get in the water.

We paddled out with the horizon blueing up around us. Mid morning brought the first few properly shaped sets through the line-up, and then, as if someone had switched a button, the Wall turned on.

A set of right-handers began to queue behind the sandbar, the first breaking with a crumbling lip. The one behind it lined-up mechanically, but bigger. A middle-aged guy on a mini-mal made the easy take-off, and bottom turned around to face the next section, which suddenly held up and pitched. If the guy had been expecting it he could have got barrelled standing tall.

Another wave immediately rolled through the line-up, also folding over, and then the one after that turned inside out and spat. It had taken four waves for the surf to suddenly become mouth-wateringly hollow.

I looked back at the beach, and saw sand finally starting to emerge between the sea wall and shoreline. The tide had slipped into place, and all the while we were still getting waves off this extraordinary set. A fifth, sixth and seventh poured through, each of them caught by surfers who'd waited all summer for their chance to get barrelled beyond sense. The eighth wave gave a young girl a warping, frothing tube ride which made everyone else start whistling and hooting. And still they came.

Like a conveyor belt, surfers were arriving in position and promptly turning around to drop into flawless, throaty peaks. The set lasted minutes and cleared the line-up. Everyone who wanted one got one. The last few waves were getting caught by the same people who'd been on the first. And then there came a lull.

I sat, feeling the sunshine warming the back of my wetsuit, dipped my face in the water, flicked my hair away and looked for Marc. He was a bit further up the beach, towards Rye Rocks. I called over to him.

'Have you ever seen anything like that?'

He grinned back and splashed water. 'I know. Mental, eh! There'll be another set now. Watch.'

He was right. Just in time to prevent the full crowd from arriving back in position, another row of waves appeared. Again each one drained its way across the bank, rolling blue and barrelling, drawing patches of disturbed sand up the face. Over on the next peak, I saw Marc take-off on one, dropping in to the right – travelling away from me. He jammed his arm in the face and stalled, waiting for the lip to pour over him. A few seconds later I saw him pop out the back, treading water.

With a soft sand bottom, this was a forgiving place to really experiment with the tube. All around us surfers of all abilities were pulling into any wave they wanted. You could look around the inside, change body shape, pump, stall, yell – anything. And each time your arms started to feel tired, there would be a break in the sets. This was the kind of session which made you forget about anything other than the pleasure of surfing perfect waves. Hunger, wetsuit rashes, sunburn – it could all wait.

'Fill your boots, son,' said Marc. 'This is it.'

As the tide dropped lower, the waves became even more hollow. The lefts peeling towards me were bending so rapidly I saw surfers getting hung up and flipped over. A guy on a purple hybrid board paddled sideways into one, and slouched through two sections of tube on his backhand, before the floor opened up. He dropped off the wave-face, still in the tube, and ran out of speed, getting swallowed by the downward movement of the foam ball. When he popped up his eyes were wild with adrenaline.

Marc and I started trying to count the number of consecutive waves on which we'd been barrelled, before the tide dropped below its original bank, setting up a grinding close-out almost the length of the beach.

By now we'd been surfing for over three hours and others were getting out, but still we kept going. I went to renew the Betty Ford's parking meter and put more sunscreen on, while Marc just surfed through. In the lulls we'd sit and giggle about whatever had happened on the last wave, and think we were ready to call it a day, before another set would come and draw you back into the thick of a marathon session. The tide began to rise again, and with it the waves sharpened, shifting back into clean, peeling peaks, starting the session all over again. Movement was only possible because of adrenaline, surf-stoke and the knowledge that this was a one-off. Anything beyond this session bore no significance at all to us. Our sole purpose was to keep riding waves until it was no longer possible.

Everyone knew where the swell had come from; thousands of miles south, off the tropics. It was hard to imagine that a gargantuan mass of oceanic rage was responsible for something as beautiful as the tubes folding over these sandbanks.

Duck-diving, I peered down a breaking wave, through the pitching barrel. I felt the vortex and the pull of the lip wanting to drag me back, and then heard the noise, a moving, echoing torque. It was the most enthralling sound on earth; the acoustics of water. A sound that, for a few fleeting hours that afternoon, was available to you every time you stroked into a wave.

When the session was done – when tide, wind and energy levels had finally all abandoned us – we left the car open and sat on the wall, legs dangling down. I took my t-shirt off and slung it over my shoulder, feeling the sun on my back. Neither of us said anything for a while. I watched the waves fatten with each set, as the shoreline crept towards high water again, ready to mask beyond recognition the perfection that had been breaking here today.

Quietly, along the seafront other surfers were all doing the same as us. Wistfully watching, gazing out to sea, no need to say anything to anyone.

I knew what the silence meant. It meant we had found what we'd come here for.

★ ★ ★

When you're on the road, with the waves good and plans flexible, things just seem to work out. I'd announced last-minute arrivals to old friends many times before – with mixed results. Sometimes they'd berate you for not calling sooner, other times coincidence would put them only a street away and ready to do anything.

Terry Perry – a guy Marc and I used to go to watch rugby and football matches with back home – had been living in the States for four years now and, apart from the odd email, I'd barely heard anything from him. If I hadn't wandered into that Apple shop in New York and contacted Lee, that would have still been the case.

But once we were quite sure that the Wall had given us our fill – that it was physically impossible to paddle for any more of the mind-bending waves on offer – the text message that awaited us was gold:

IN MAINE? NO WAY! Party, my house tonight, and you are invited. Bring the missus. 872 Gillespie Drv, Portland. 1st jn off the 295 and you're there.

Marc laughed. 'Bring the missus!' It was a quote from *Twin Town*, one of Terry's favourite films.

'I take it we've got a place to stay then?' I said.

'Well, you'd imagine that to be the case, eh?' Marc grinned. 'Let's go. I can't surf any more for at least the rest of the day. My arms are finished.' He grabbed his shoulder and rotated it backward, wincing.

'Mine are too. Fine by me.' I looked out at the wobbly waves left behind as the tide pushed rapidly back in, filling the whole beach with turbulent water. 'Yeah, let's go to Portland.'

We started to drive north along the coastal road. It was a slide show of reefs and beach breaks that you just knew had been firing all day. Surfers were at the roadside by every turning, towelling off, laughing, joking, reliving their sessions with each other.

After rounding a harbour we turned away from the coast and through an area of bush and marshland, into a network of streets. This led to two-lane highways and then the centre of Portsmouth, one of New Hampshire's biggest cities, although it was nothing compared to Boston. Small-town America in character. A short run through a few sets of traffic lights before we crossed the border and returned to the I-95,which was now the Maine Turnpike – meaning we would have to drop coins in to a tollbooth somewhere between here and Portland.

Finding Terry Perry's house wasn't hard. Interstate 95 forked into the 295, and he was three sets of lights away from a ramp that plunged us off the freeway and straight into suburbia. After needing to plan days of driving at a time, everything in New England suddenly seemed so close together: smaller streets, little villages, rapid roads, quick driving times.

'Shit, man. Terry Perry could surf the Wall every day after work if he wanted,' Marc noted.

'So what? You can surf Rest Bay or Coney Beach every day after work,' I pointed out.

'Yeah, but it's not the same,' he scoffed. 'I've had enough of home.'

'Whatever you say. Haven't we all?' I didn't want to push him on the issue – didn't want to break the mood by inviting him to talk about anything too serious.

You could have spotted Terry Perry's house a mile off. An enormous pair of flags hung directly down from the upstairs windows of a two-bedroom, wood-exterior detached home, in a street shaded by pine trees. One was a Stars and Stripes, the other *Y Ddraig Goch* – the Welsh Dragon.

We parked up and got out. Standing tall, I stretched my back and yawned, walking towards the door at the side of the house. There were three cars in the drive – including an old Volvo 850 with another Welsh flag stuck to the bumper – and voices in the garden.

'So, do we need to knock?'

'Nah! Not here.' Marc opened the gate and yelled, 'Terry!'

'What?' bellowed a voice from around the corner.

'It's Marc! What's happening?'

With a shriek, our friend came charging towards us, grabbing me in an embrace and repeating 'I can't believe it!' and 'No way!' with a loud, elongated 'o'. A minute later I had a beer in my hand.

I'd met Terry Perry through Marc originally. They'd played football together, before Terry decided he wanted to try surfing. That was when they'd called me. One summer we pushed him into a few waves and got on famously from there, even though he didn't stick with it – claiming the sea was for fish and sharks, not people. ('What you do in that water is wrong,' he famously said.)

Terry was from Porth in the Rhondda Valley, so once he had made his mind up there was no swaying it – even if he made you laugh in the process. Surfing wasn't his thing, but field sports certainly were. We used to watch Wales play football in Cardiff together, along with a few other friends. Terry was always the driving force of the group, the one who knew where to get tickets and who was who in the ever-changing, ever failing team. He then went away for a year to Australia (without even surfing once, of course), and met an American girl, Anna, who had brought him to live in Maine with her. Although it had been years, I knew life had treated him well because he looked no different to before – the same spiky brown hair, facetious grin and T-shirt with slogan. I did wonder whether his teeth were a little whiter when he grinned, but didn't know if it was good etiquette to accuse him of anything as un-Welsh as getting a dental makeover.

As he introduced us to his American friends I saw they'd all taken on his mannerisms and humour. Rhondda Valley phrases were all around us as they barbecued and drank. Everywhere I looked or listened there were hints of home.

'Where's Anna?' I asked.

'Oh, she's gone to see her folks for the week – awesome eh! Means we can have a hell of a bash tonight. I've got like thirty people coming round. All coz of you boys!'

It wasn't all because of us. He'd only known we were in New England a few hours ago, but still, that was Terry. He put you at ease straight away.

'So, did you bring some snags?'

'You what?'

'*Selsigs*. Sausages. For the Barbie, like.'

'Er.'

'Ah. Don't matter anyway, we've got loads. What d'you want? How about another beer?'

The evening still had the drawn-out feel of summer, and we all sat around in Terry's garden way beyond sunset. Still cold from the sea myself, I stood by the hot coals for a while, before things moved indoors.

The doorbell had been ringing, and slowly Terry's house was filling up. I was completely beat from the hours of surfing, and my first beer made me drowsy. This wasn't going to be allowed though, and pretty soon Terry noticed I'd gone quiet.

'Shut up mun, Tom! No one else can get a word in!'

The Americans around him laughed. Sarcasm – if anyone could teach it to them then it would be Terry.

'Sorry, man. I'm knackered.'

'You wanna get off the beers, you do – have a JD and Coke instead!'

The doorbell rang again. He was right – I needed to liven up. This was probably one of the last nights I'd spend in the States before heading back towards Canada. I tried to think in the moment – here I was, right now, with someone I hardly ever saw. Marc was being a legend, we'd scored all the waves we wanted and seen a million places from some of the most interesting roads in the world. It deserved a toast.

Energy is a state of mind, I reminded myself, and walked back out to the rear porch to where Terry was sitting.

'So how's Marc doing then, butt?' He nudged me, raising one eyebrow. 'The boy seems in really good spirits, eh! D'you know what; that knobhead hasn't returned an email from me in like three years. And then I see him turn up at my house of all places and he's bloody bouncing. As sound as he's ever been. I said to him earlier, "not good enough for an email then, am I, doctor?" and he just laughed it off. Prob'ly nothing in it. But good to see you both, eh! You've been working on him, I reckon.'

'Yeah. He's a mad one, isn't he.'

'Aye. Off his head. I love him, though. Like a brother.'

'He doesn't, though,' I found myself saying. 'Love him, that is.'

Terry nudged me again, and laughed, gesturing towards me with the hand he was holding his drink in. He spoke to the others sitting with us. 'You have to get used to Tom saying clever things like that,' he said. 'He's my "reasonably intelligent friend".' He turned back to me. 'People would fuckin' love you in America. And him too.' He was pointing back indoors to where I could hear Marc entertaining what was now a small audience. He was telling them about the Hamptons.

'Seriously,' Terry carried on, 'they haven't seen anything like the Welsh way of doing things here. It's great. But then I love the way they live too. When they're not bombing stuff, mind.'

He got up to get another drink. 'You want one?' he asked.

'OK. Same again.'

That was one of the last sensible conversations we had before I succumbed to the whiskey. Terry kept running the show, taking the piss out of people in a way I hadn't seen since leaving home. He seemed to know half the city. People were throwing an American football around in the street out front, and inside a red-haired guy was on his knees playing air guitar to 'Welcome to the Jungle' – much to the ire of two others who were trying to concentrate on a baseball game. I went outside and got roped into the football. An older friend of Terry's asked me to grab hold of some guy I'd never met, while someone behind us threw the ball. Sometimes it would land in other peoples' gardens, and someone would run to fetch it. Marc, who knew all the rules and half the stats, was playing in a wide position for the other team.

After a few goes I started to work the game out a bit – while Marc kept stopping to try and tell people about rugby.

When I finally went back inside Terry had gone to bed and the house was getting quieter. I sat in the kitchen and drank another beer, listening to a ringing sound in my ears, looking forward to sleeping off the waves, thinking about the journey and the decisions it had thrown up.

I walked over to the couch. Laying back, a light feeling whizzed around my head. I breathed deep and even, and closed my eyes. Outside I could still hear the football game, and marvelled at how cool Terry's neighbours must be. A car pulled up, and I heard cheering, before the quarterback started calling people back into position.

Normally voices were the one thing that could keep me awake forever, but these ones were more interesting than usual. The accents, the dedication to what they were doing. I was mesmerised by it. I heard them calling plays to each other, and arguing over what distances the ball had been thrown.

I rolled over and tried to remember my best wave from the day, and then the week, running back through them in my mind. There were too many, and each time I tried to remember one I'd get too drowsy to see it through.

Eventually, I noticed the game outside had stopped, and then thick, insentient sleep started to grip me. I didn't want tomorrow to come quickly, nor did I want to go back to any previous time. It was bliss. If someone had said I could stay in this exact position forever, I'd have taken it, right then. Swell, friendships and the journey. Where else would I want to be?

CHAPTER EIGHTEEN

EXTRA-TROPICAL TRANSITION

Terry woke me up by letting his dog jump on me. 'All right, butt! Have a good one or what? Let's go and get brekkie. Dunkin' Donuts, I reckon. Box of Joe. Coffee. Loads of it. How's your 'ead?'

'Er, OK,' I said. 'Where's Marc?'

'No idea. Not here. I've looked.'

'Really?'

'Yep. No sign. Don't worry about him. I'd kill for a coffee.'

I sat up, and looked around the messy living room. Light was pouring through the half-lowered shutters.

'It's another awesome day out there,' Terry declared. 'Shame I'm good for exactly feck all!'

I asked him again about Marc. Where could he have got to?

'Not very bloody far. His computer's by the front door. He prob'ly went off with some of the others. They sometimes go and play American football in the park over there once they've had a few. Idiots. I'll try his mobile. It's the one you texted me off yesterday, isn't it?' Terry started tapping the keypad of his phone. I walked out onto the back porch to assess another clear morning.

'Can I get online somewhere?' I asked.

'Aye – by there, mun.' He pointed to an Apple Notebook. I opened it up and looked for the wind and wave reports. I ached from head to toe, so much so that I feared the prospect of more surf right now. It was with relief that I learned Maine and New Hampshire both had grey star ratings for the day – meaning the wind wasn't good and that the swell had dropped too. One last day of waves was predicted for tomorrow, very small but with a chance of no wind again. With a headache and an old friend to catch up with, I reckoned it could be given a miss today.

We walked out of the house to the Betty Ford, and drove six blocks up to where Dunkin' Donuts stood on the edge of a big shopping complex. Meanwhile Terry kept trying to phone Marc.

'It's ringing,' he said. 'But no answer.'

'Keep trying. He's probably asleep. Where could he be, though?'

'Ah, he'll be around in a bit.'

'So what is the "Box of Joe"?'

'Oh, it's awesome, man. You'll see, it's like three litres of coffee or something, and then they give you a muffin selection too. I always get 'em in for the Premiership games, coz, you know, they kick off in the morning over here. Love it. That's what I do every Saturday in the winter. You won't believe how cold it gets here. We've got snow chains for the car – can you imagine that!'

We waited for Terry's order, while he carried on telling me about the Maine winter – driving to ski slopes for the day, fishing from holes bored in the frozen lake by Anna's brother's house.

'You ever coming home?' I asked.

He answered without needing to think: 'No.'

'Really?'

'Well, for a holiday, like, but no. I love it. I'm a Yank now, butt. Well, a Welsh one like, but a Yank nonetheless.'

When we got back to the house one of his friends was sitting on the porch waiting. He'd come for breakfast, and I recognised him from last night.

'Hey – how's it goin'?' he asked me.

'All right. How about you?'

'Yeah, great, man. I'm great. I'm Jon.'

'Tom. Pleased to meet you.'

'All mine, dude. How's your buddy this morning – Mike is it?'

'Marc?'

'Yeah, Marc! That's it. He was killin' it, huh?'

'What d'you mean?'

'Man, dude was like making everyone laugh. Funniest English guy I ever met.'

'WELSH!' Terry grimaced.

'Sorry, Welsh. Man, fuckin' funny as hell. And then he goes outside to get another drink and a car pulls up with two super-hot girls in it. One steps out and kisses him, and then they pull him in and drive off!'

I looked at Terry. He shrugged his shoulders – So much for the simple theories.

'What car was it?' I asked.

'Dunno, man. Kinda small.'

Terry mumbled, 'Fuckin' nutter, that boy. I tell you.'

I looked at Jon again. 'Was it a Honda Accord?'

'Coulda been. Why?'

'I might know them. Was it gold coloured?' I asked, hoping to jog his memory.

'Gold? No. It was white.'

'Ah, I see.' I looked at Terry again. 'Any idea?'

'Nope,' he replied, pouring coffees out from the box. 'Why. Have you?'

'Dunno. That girl Lauren had a gold car.'

'Could someone else be driving?'

'Maybe. Any joy with phoning him?'

'None yet. It's still ringing though when I try.'

Jon chuckled. 'Dude – if I ran off with two chicks last night I wouldn't be answering my frickin cell phone either!'

Terry handed the mugs out to us. 'We'll find him,' he said, absently.

I wanted to tell him that I wasn't so sure, but the smell of the coffee rose up to me, relaxing and refreshing.

'Well, he can look after himself,' I said, taking a sip.

The other two nodded.

We didn't find him. Just like I had thought. That night we watched a baseball game with several of Terry's friends, all of whom had been at the party last night. Another guy had seen Marc leave too, but couldn't even come close to describing what the girls looked like. Apparently Marc had looked surprised to see them, but was more than happy to get pulled into the car.

The thing that confused me most was the computer. Normally Marc guarded that thing with his life. That was the only part of the puzzle that didn't make sense to me. Terry had put it in the basement now, where I was starting to think it might remain for a while.

Tomorrow, when I left, Terry would have to hold on to it. He could wait for Marc to reclaim it in his own time.

When we'd still heard nothing the next morning, I took all Marc's stuff out of the Betty Ford, and got directions to Higgins Beach. This time I certainly wasn't going to wait around for him. He knew how to find Terry, like he'd known how to find me earlier in the week.

'Boy's mad, like, isn't he?' Terry kept repeating, as we stacked his bags and boards into a corner. One of them clunked – a metallic sound. 'Got pots and pans with him in America!'

Marc had never even unpacked those, I realised – remembering the start of our trip in Miami and the sight of him stepping out of The Standard looking like a proper feral camper.

'I know,' I said, nudging the bags with my foot. 'I ribbed him for that one as well.'

'Did you use them?'

'What do you think?'

Terry smiled, and tutted: 'Fuckin' tool.'

One more surf, I thought, one last lunch with Dean, and then it was time to leave the Right Coast.

I borrowed Terry's phone and tapped out a message to Marc: 'Hey. No more money so got to go back to TO. Have a good one. Terry's got your stuff. See you again. T.'

I wouldn't get to know if there was a reply. It didn't matter anyway. Marc was wherever he wanted to be. This time I knew it for sure.

The Welsh flag was hanging down, dead still and clear for the whole street to see as I pulled away with Terry's crumpled directions to Higgins beach in my hand. A deep, trembling, involuntary sigh took hold of me as I rounded the next corner and his waving figure dropped out of sight. It was just me again. And Dean – or what was left of him.

★　★　★

I've thought about it plenty of times, trust me. That last rendezvous with Dean was the most intimate of all. That final morning at Higgins Beach, as the swell dropped around me to leave a flat, deep blue ocean, I was able to feel the throes of the hurricane's death.

It didn't matter where anyone else was that day. This was my private moment with the ocean.

I pulled into the parking lot at Higgins to see the most sublimely lined up row of knee-high waves imaginable. They were peeling with a gentle crackling sound over a sandbar with only four other surfers – all of whom got out as I arrived.

Although in the lee of Portland city, the beach town was model quiet. There was hardly anyone around. No clouds in the sky, which spread pastel-blue from horizon to horizon. The New England homes seemed to blend into the pine trees and craggy shoreline, as the cold ocean lapped patiently but persistently away.

The power in the tiny waves was unlike anything from the rest of the swell. It wasn't brutal, angry, violent or confused. It was mature. The waves held up, marching on the shore with dignity. And whenever I chose to ride one it always seemed to work with me. For an hour this was how things were: me, and the remnants of Hurricane Dean.

And then, with a single puff of afternoon breeze the swell stopped, dead. I knew the next wave was my last and took it calmly to the shore, wading in with resignation. There was nothing left. The ride was over.

There are feelings better than pure happiness or satisfaction. The air of sadness that filled me that day brought euphoria much more complex than the simple celebration of a swell, or a life-changing journey.

I was still trying to figure it out hours later, after the edges of Portland had receded into forests reddening with the onset of autumn. Maine began to feel, as with some of the Deep South weeks ago, like a place I'd only visited in my head.

And then, a hundred miles later, so did New Hampshire, and Cape Cod. Then Point Judith and Long Island. The transience of surfing had placed me there on certain days, in a certain swell, which was now gone, never to be replicated.

I began wondering again about what had happened to Marc. Somehow I doubted he was sitting at Terry Perry's right now, drinking tea and enjoying being reunited with his belongings. He had belonging of another kind to worry about. I asked myself what I'd do in his position – a pointless question. And then I thought about whether he was going to turn up in Wales again in the near future. He had people who relied on him, after all. Or did he? Would it matter if Marc never went home?

Mount Washington passed through a gap in the hills, and then Vermont came upon me quickly. With it appeared the magnificent September palette of maple trees. Sometimes a mile of forest would be as green as it had in August, but then as I got higher into the hills leaves began to be lit by cartoon yellows, browning purples and shades of red that normally belonged on strawberries or peppers. The landscape drew my gaze, and slowed my driving as I climbed higher, further from the sea.

I searched for radio channels, and found French voices.

The sound of static drifted in and out of the car, punctuated by the odd piece of music until, approaching Burlington, I was able to get hold of ABC News. It ran for twenty minutes before coming round to a familiar topic – perhaps for the last time.

The storm known as Dean fizzled out today, and might send a bit of cloud into New Mexico. A feisty one all right, we're all glad to see the back of this one. Experts are now looking back to the Atlantic hoping that the worst of it is over for another year. Should they materialise, the next storms of the season will be called Felix, Gabrielle and Ingrid. The names are taken from a list compiled six years ago, which is changed based on the effects of the storms named. Joining me on the line now is...

I turned the dial off. Not in Vermont. It was time to think this through for myself. And I knew it wouldn't be easy.

It could be years before I'd work out exactly what the nature of my relationship with Dean was. And then there was the other question:

Did I really want to know?

Another glade of autumnal maples breezed by, their plump colours surrounding a sign for the Canadian border. As I slowed to check the directions a few of the leaves swirled upwards, and then fell back to the ground. There were no other cars in sight. Over a hill to my right I saw a faint moon, showing its face by daylight. From the coast, the same moon would be pulling the tide, right now, and for the rest of time as we knew it.

I looked up at the rear-view mirror, into my own eyes and then out at the forests beyond, before accelerating away again.

ACKNOWLEDGEMENTS

Chasing Dean was written with the assistance of a Writer's Bursary from Academi, the Welsh National Literature Promotion Agency and Society for Authors. The author would also like to thank the following for their contributions in helping bring this book to completion: Jennifer Barclay, Chelsey Fox, Rob Middlehurst, Trevor Byrne, Barrie Llewellyn, David Pearson, Anna Martin, Dean Chant, Cathy and David Hutcheon, Basia and Anthony Davey, Tim Kevan, Jeremy Hooker, Meic Stephens, Rob Minhinnick, Chris Hollowood, John Howells, Angela Atkinson, Rhyd Lewis, Fiona Carroll, Breige Lawrence, Christian and Sarah Perry.

All maps by Breige Lawrence.

'Dean Advisories' have been used with the permission of NOAA.